Feta
Compli!

Part One of the
"Ramblings from Rhodes"
trilogy

BY
JOHN P. MANUEL

"Feta Compli!"
Copyright © 2008 by John P. Manuel

First published 2008 by Lulu.com
This revision 2011

Typeset in Janson Text 9pt
...with tons of mistakes no doubt!

Further copies of this book may be purchased from:

http://www.lulu.com/
Plus good on-line book stores

...Go on, support a struggling writer!

8th Edition. April 2011

ISBN: 978-1-4092-4626-8

For my wife Yvonne-Maria
and her late mother Lela (1925-1982),
without whom the Feta would never
have become "Compli!"

By the same author:

MOUSSAKA TO MY EARS
ISBN No. 978-1-4092-6732-4

TZATZIKI FOR YOU TO SAY
ISBN No. 978-1-4466-4709-7

The author's website:
http://honorarygreek.blogspot.com

All of John Manuel's books
are available from his website,
the publisher's website (www.lulu.com)
and from Amazon

CONTENTS

1 - Somewhere on the A38

"£800 quid. Can't go less than that. That's if you drive it away as seen." So said the salesman at a small commercial vehicle dealers on the A38 somewhere south of Bristol one May day in 2005. We were discussing a 15 year old Mitsubishi L300 van. "Long wheelbase mind you, more room inside. Got to be good, that."

How came we there? Well, the decision had been made late the previous year to "up sticks" and re-locate to Rhodes after over 30 years of marriage and innumerable visits to Greece, both as tourists and as relatives, since my wife Yvonne-Maria's mother was from Athens and she still has family there and elsewhere in that country. We had sold the house and virtually everything in it. Or at least so we thought, until we started packing up what was actually coming with us and realized that to drive what was left of all our possessions overland all the way (well, apart from the bits where a ferry would do some of the work of course) would require a small commercial vehicle of some description.

Since I am a graphic designer, were I to have applied to be a contestant on Mastermind, "small commercials" wouldn't have been my specialist subject. So we began trying to find dealers by looking on the internet and had been for a ginger look around a couple of forecourts when Yvonne's sister's fiancée, Garry, rang from Portishead to say he'd found this Mitsubishi for £1000 cash if we wanted to nip across the Severn Crossing one day and take a look. So, having arranged to do so, we zipped away from our little (sold) bungalow in the Vale of Glamorgan in our soon-to-also-be-sold BMW Mini (still grieving over that) and duly arrived at Christine and Garry's for the official inspection visit to the dealer who had just taken the Mitsubishi in part-ex.

I hadn't a clue whether a 15 year old van was good bad, ugly or a shed. It certainly looked like a shed, it has to be said. Rust spots were dotted all over it as an evident reminder that the previous owner hadn't ever heard of a touch-up brush. The near-side sliding door was creased toward the bottom where it had obviously been backed into a bollard or something. The rear bumper wasn't just rusty and several crunches away from its original shape, it also sported a couple of nice rust holes that resembled a map of a couple of Greek islands. Perhaps a good sign?

I rather hesitantly took a look inside. Hmm, upholstery not torn or worn too badly, that's good. The seats gave ample testimony to the fact that the previous owner had also owned at least one dog from which they were very obviously inseparable. What's this? No gear-stick!? Upon registering my apprehension the salesman was quick to point out that it was a "column change."

"Take it down the road if you like. It's easy to get used to." He said in a chirpy tone.

"OK." I replied, not sure what a test drive would actually accomplish, but deciding I had to exude the kind of air that would suggest I knew all about such vehicles and their commonly known plus-points and potential problem areas, "...fine."

He whipped the keys out of his pocket, plunged the appropriate one into the ignition slot and merrily turned it, whilst throwing me a smile that said "I hope to God this thing goes or I've lost this punter!"

Deftly stopping before the battery drained to a state of total exhaustion, he (still smiling) said "She usually starts up first kick. Hang on, I'll ask Bob." Bob, we assumed, was another fella who knew all about why old vans didn't "start first kick" as it were. Bob was summoned from across the road (the van was parked in front of a farm gate on the opposite side of the road from the garage) and came trotting over exuding a similar smile to his business associate. "Good van this!" he chirped. "Engine's excellent. Was thinking of having her myself, doing her up a bit and keeping her, but decided against it when we heard you might want her."

Within a minute the air was full of a rather largish black cloud of exhaust and the engine was humming with life. Fortunately, it had truly been a bit of a false scare. Apparently, explained Bob, this model doesn't have automatic plug heating, you have to push in a button for a few seconds to heat the glow-plugs, then turn her over.

"All yours," they both enjoined in unison. "Should be enough diesel to get you down the road and back." Bob's associate now assumed the job of selling us this prize example of an old van and ran through the gear movements with me as if to say (well, in fact he probably did say...): "Piece of cake, you'll soon get the hang of it."

Garry and I hopped into the cab (Yvonne didn't want to risk it, despite the fact that there are three seats) and I attempted to locate reverse gear. Not too difficult, so we swung her round to face the road and then I went for first. Not quite so easy; after a fair bit of shoving and waggling and wear and tear on the muscles in my upper arm I found it and we kangarooed out into the flow of traffic, which, mercifully, wasn't too frenetic as it often can be on the A38. I drove down the road about half a mile, found a lay-by, turned round and drove back, having learned precisely nothing apart from the fact that it "went," as it were.

"£1000" you say," I ventured. In fact Yvonne and I had sort of decided we'd spend up to £3000 on the van, since it had to get us right across Europe, from the far Northwest to as far South East as you can go before falling into the Mediterranean sea somewhere south of Asia Minor. So if we took a bit of a gamble on this one it wouldn't be the end of the world, as we still had several months to go before the "Off" and had time to get it thoroughly serviced and anyway we could always sell it again for a couple of hundred profit and buy a newer one.

"Well, we were going to ask a grand. But that would be after cleaning her up a bit. If you don't mind taking her as she is, we'll say £800 for cash."

To cut a long story short, a week later the 1990 Mitsubishi L300 2.4 diesel (long wheelbase, it's got to be good, that) van was standing proudly on the roadside outside our garden in South Wales. The neighbours, who all knew of our plans, began to opine on our chosen vessel for the voyage. They were especially keen to pass comment each time I started the van up and frequently went into mock coughing fits whilst vigorously waving their hands from left to right in front of their faces. I wasn't worried, honest. I booked it in for a thorough service with the ever trustworthy Terry (recommended by my friend - another John), in Cardiff.

"Oooh, I don't know." He rather un-reassuringly remarked on first sight of our L300, "All sorts of things can go wrong with these you know. Could be a pig in a poke."

Bearing in mind the van's appearance (as partially described earlier, though I hadn't even gone into what the wheels looked like), I suppose this was to be expected.

"All I want is for you to give it a good going over. Check the timing belt and stuff like that. If you think it won't get us there, we have time, we'll sell it and get another." Was all I could think of to say.

"Leave it with me then and I'll ring you when it's ready. But if you ask me you're taking a bit of a risk." He encouragingly chipped in through our Mini's window as we prepared to drive away. Next day he telephoned. I answered the call rather in the manner of an expectant father whose wife was in labour for the first time. To my surprise and relief, he said:

"Your van's ready. S'alright actually. Got to admit appearances can deceive. As long as she doesn't overheat she should get you there. Don't thrash her though, about 60 to 65 tops and you'll be OK."

We collected the van, christened her "Mitsos," which - come to think of it - makes her a "him" and set about fitting it out for the trip. A set of shiny plastic wheel trims from the local accessory shop made the wheels look ten times better. Then, while clearing out our garden shed, Yvonne came across a fairly new tin of smooth white Hammerite paint, which was soon put to use covering all the numerous rust spots that peppered the entire surface of the paintwork. For added security on the journey I had a carpenter friend of ours fit a plywood panel behind the cab area to isolate the rear cargo bay from the cab. We fitted padlocks to the inside of both the rear "up and over" and nearside sliding doors, then bought a high security lock over the internet from a very nice man in Cheshire, which was fitted by our good friend Mark to the remaining off-side sliding door.

The only apprehension I held about the van was the clutch. If I didn't catch it just right when pulling away, it shook you so much your fillings would threaten to fall out. But still and all, it had only cost us £800 and, if it would just get us to our new home in Rhodes, it would be money well spent. Not to mention a fair bit well saved.

So dawned August 19th 2005 and we were on our way. Had we bought a smaller van, or even - God forbid - the short wheelbase model (long wheelbase, it's got to be good, that), we'd never have got all our stuff in. As it was the van was packed tight and low on its springs as we left South Wales on the M4 before dawn's first light and headed for the final time towards Dover. Four days later, at 9.30am on Tuesday August 23rd, we drove off the Pireaus ferry in Rhodes town's old harbour and began the last 50 minute section of our voyage to our house on Rhodes. Trusty Mitsos (less one rear exhaust bracket) had got us all the way. Right down across eastern France and into Switzerland. Across the Alps and through innumerable tunnels on into Italy. Then down past Milan and San Marino to Ancona for the long and relaxing crossing (we had a luxury cabin) to Patras and from there a blood-curdling dash to Piraeus to arrive at the quay 25 minutes before the departure of our overnight ferry to Rhodes. For 6 hours or so a day on the Friday, Saturday and Sunday, then over 3 hours on Monday the 22nd, Mitsos the 15 year old Mitsubishi L300 charged at around 65 mph across Europe. It never faltered, never failed to start and even got us through a deluge in northern Italy the like of which probably hasn't been experienced since Noah. I had even bought a can of diesel oil for the journey as I was quite convinced that as I checked the oil each morning at our hotels before departure, we'd find it had used quite a bit and would need topping up. In actual fact Mitsos only used a plastic cupful of oil in well over 1300 miles of motorway. If they had a Halfords in Rhodes I'd be tempted to try for a refund.

So why had we finally decided to make the move to Greece? My wife Yvonne (Maria) is half-Greek. Her mother was from Athens, having settled, after the birth of her first child (my wife's older sister), in the UK with her British husband Ken around 1950. They had met while Ken, serving in the British Army, was posted in Greece following the end of world war two. My wife was born in Bath (UK), the second of four, her older sister having been produced prior to the happy couple re-locating to the UK and her two younger brothers then being born in Bath. Since I'm also from Bath our paths crossed in a smoky pub one night in 1971 and much of what followed is recounted in this book.

So there you have it. John Steinbeck had Charley. Bill Bryson has his inimitable sense of humour. Peter Mayle moved to rural France and had his quirky French plumbers. I had a Mitsubishi L300, a big fat Greek aunty in Athens and a Greek mother-in-law in Bath. Recipe for "Feta Compli." There follows the tale of how we ended up living on a Greek island. Though not necessarily in any particular order.

2 - Seems Like a Dream

When you sort of think about the idea of moving from rainy, chilly old Britain, with its "beer and curry" mentality, its total impossibility to park on a bank holiday (or any other day when the weather is remotely conducive to going out for a day) in anything resembling a beauty spot (at least without having to fork out sufficient cash to purchase a moderate-to-good meal out for the privilege), its quaint habit of fly-tipping in every other gateway or lay-by down a country lane, its total preoccupation with the pursuit of the next great offer from a certain Scandinavian furniture store (where moustaches on its clientele were initiallly frowned upon) and its unhealthy obsession with low-budget "reality" TV shows to a Greek island, it has to be said that idea has a certain seductiveness about it. Go on, admit it, it does doesn't it?

So when, in 2004, my wife and I began to hatch the plan that would see us up-sticks and drive like lunatics most of the way across Europe with all our worldly possessions in the back of a 15 year old Mitsubishi L300 (long wheelbase – got to be better) van, it all still seemed like a dream.

We set about working out the finances with enthusiasm and eventually decided that, after shedding most of our capital assets, along with most of the furniture as well, we could achieve what we'd often dreamed of on the plane home over the course of many years from numerous foreign holidays (most of them in Greece).

In June 2004 we sat looking up at the milky sunshine from our modest little conservatory somewhere near the South Wales coast and thought about a lifestyle that would include popping out to eat in any one of numerous little tavernas within a stone's throw of home; of sipping our iced coffees through a straw in some bustling Greek pavement or waterfront café whilst "people-watching" (why that's not an Olympic sport I don't know. Be great wouldn't it? Points for guessing which country some bloke with socks in his sandals and a ridiculous straw hat, accompanied by a woman wearing a bra top and shorts when it was obvious that no bum like that should ever be on display without some long loose top hanging well below it came from), of sauntering down to the local beach for a bit of snorkeling before flopping wearily into the nearest taverna for a grilled fish and Greek salad lunch, washed down with ice cool beer. Yes we dreamed of the long hot days when the thought of a cloud interfering with the deep blue of the Mediterranean sky was anathema.

We wouldn't need much. It's all about lifestyle after all, not how much in the way of material splendour you've got around you. We had a couple of good friends whom we'd known for 15 years who were interested in building a holiday home on Rhodes and we were offered the opportunity of "coming into the project" with them. We could live in our half of the house and they could use theirs for holidays. There may have been a few things that would need thrashing out, but the germ of the opportunity we'd long dreamed of was there and ready to become an epidemic in our brains.

In the office where I worked it became more and more difficult to go through the daily grind without letting on what we had in mind. I was working as a graphic designer, and had been for 16 years, in the in-house studio of a small chain of family-owned out-of-town "sheds" based in South Wales. The atmosphere in the office has been steadily deteriorating for a couple of years and it was becoming evident that, as new blood was brought into the board in the shape of the various progeny of the MD, the long knives were being sharpened. Copy dates and deadlines were getting shorter (how do you go from "I want this by yesterday!" to "I want it even sooner?"). I wasn't getting any younger and, since I had some private clients for whom I worked from home, I was working far too many hours. Everyone in the UK knows the familiar scenario by now. Staff leave and they're not replaced. Budgets tighten. You're not allowed to update or upgrade because the budget won't allow for it, but you're expected to do a top-notch job anyway. It's the archetypal "I want out of the rat race before it kills me" situation.

We had two Greek holidays in 2004, during which we prospected for locations for the new house and generally checked out the cost of living, where to go shopping and – more importantly – where were the best beaches? On our return from each I found it more and more difficult to return to the office. So when the day came in February 2005 when I ambled slowly into the Marketing Director's office with my letter of resignation I don't need to describe how I was feeling. What had for ages seemed like a dream was starting to take shape. Whoopee!

Must get to Tesco and stock up on the factor 20.

3 - Smoky Lounge

To really explain how we came to live up a goat track in Rhodes I've got to go back to the late 1970's. There was a time when I hated all things Greek, prior to which I had simply had no interest in the place at all. I knew it was down over there on the map, and that a big one-eyed chap had once terrorized part of it. Oh, and something about a big wooden horse, but exactly what I couldn't remember once my school years were far enough behind me. Then there was the fact that the Olympics had started there, but then they had to have started somewhere and you had to be interested in athletics anyway for that to count. There was no Formula One Grand Prix ...and the language! Well, not so much the language, but the alphabet! How could anyone want to take the country seriously? I remember thinking that a country where most of the populace are called Stavros or Costas and all the surnames ended in "..opolos" was not really worth getting interested in anyway. So I was agreek, in the same way that I'm apolitical!

Then, in October 1971, three weeks after I broke up with a long-time girlfriend, I met this girl in the romantic setting of the Berni Cellar Bar near Bath Spa railway station. She says she only fancied me after I stood up, because at five-eight she had trouble finding boyfriends taller than her. That was the day, as a spotty teenager, I stopped feeling embarrassed about being a beanpole.

We started seeing each other and she'd often raise the subject of Greece. Greek music, Greek dancing, visits she had paid all through her childhood and the long summer she had spent there with her mother's relatives in Athens the year before we met. She would take great delight in telling me how Greek boys would pinch her bum and openly show their approval of her length of skirt when she'd go walking (I would say "parading") around Athens with her cousins. So, as someone whose entire experience of going abroad was a couple of visits to France on a school exchange, I began to seriously hate Greece. "Hate" is perhaps a bit strong. I resented it. Wouldn't you have?

What made things worse for me was what would happen each time I went home with her after a night out at weekends. I'd be hoping for a little intimacy on the settee, but what would greet us as we arrived at the front door would be blaring Bouzouki music from her mother's stereogram (remember those?), the sound of boisterous Greek voices and, when we entered the house, great difficulty in seeing due to the sheer amount of thick blue smoke from the very strong cigarettes that a half a dozen or so Greek sailors, along with her mother Lela and one or two of her female friends, would be smoking.

What would happen was this: My future mother-in-law would frequent a lively Greek taverna in Bristol at weekends. There was always live Bouzouki music and dancing would go on until 4 or 5am. Whenever there was a Greek ship in at Bristol Docks, the crew would inevitably find out about this place and go there whilst their ship was tied up. Sometimes they'd be in for quite a few days and so, once they had met

Lela and friends at the taverna, they would be invited over for drinks and dancing. Often my then-girlfriend's mother would also invite "Auntie Ellen and Barbara (her daughter)" another Greek woman living in the Bath area, who was very close to Lela for many years and so was called "auntie," though not a blood relation. She would also invite "Auntie Tassia" a thin woman who was befriended by the others because she was Greek and for no other reason. She was in fact from a remote country village somewhere on mainland Greece and would be the butt (when not present) of all kind of jokes about yokels, goats, chickens and olive stains. She always wore the most weird knee-length boots with all kinds of odd patterns on them. She would wander through Bath mumbling at people in her colloquial Greek. Most who encountered her regularly must have thought she was on day release from somewhere and become separated from her nurse. In fact she was very nice-natured but simply thick. Like Lela, she also had married an Englishman, who had since decided that the best way to get away from her was to die, so he duly died. She lived on as a lonely widow, never really mastering English and so only able to associate with the few, like my mother-in-law to be, who took pity on her and invited her to their Greek gatherings.

So Yvonne and I would get home around 11.30pm, when on any normal Friday or Saturday night her mother would have already gone to bed. But on abnormal ones, we'd know the Greeks were in by the noises we'd hear while still several yards down the road. Now, bearing in mind I had only just turned eighteen at this point, and was trying in earnest to be a hippy, I wasn't all that well off. So to come home with Yvonne represented a major gamble. My parents lived a good four or five miles across town and the only way someone with my sort of money was going to get home was on foot. Now, on the normal nights it was well worth it. You know, I don't have to spell it out, but after a couple of hours on the settee, with her mother and two younger brothers fast asleep above, I walked home on air. But if we arrived home to the Greek delegation, it was instant misery. Within seconds there'd be an, "Ela Yvonni!" from her mother and she would be mingling with all the smoky company and yours truly would be sat in an armchair, eyes watering profusely both from tears of frustration and the thick blue smoke! I wouldn't understand a word of the conversation and, after a year-long thirty minutes, would make my excuses and walk home in a state of near suicidal depression.

Incidentally, the reason why the White household was able to enjoy so much "Greekness" (White was obviously Yvonne's father's family name) was because Lela had divorced her English husband when Yvonne was thirteen. I never actually met her father until we had decided to get married and I felt it was the "done thing" to ask him to give her away. A big mistake, but that's another story.

I could say a lot more about these improvised Greek nights. How the men would get up and do the Zembehiko (my spelling I'm afraid!), or the Sirtaki and Hasapiko that they'd all do in a line. The way Auntie Ellen would read the Greek coffee cups in the same manner that a British Gypsy might read tea leaves. Then there were the gifts. The sailors were always very generous. They'd always arrive at my mother-in-law-to-be's home carrying packages. Trouble is, they all contained little African carvings of antelopes and the like. Once all your shelves, window sills, tops of items of furniture (all the flat-topped ones anyway), mantle pieces and various wall units were full of these little perishers, you ended up giving them to all your friends. It reached a stage where we could have made a small fortune selling firewood if we'd decided to chop the little beggars up. I thought the first little antelope I received was really nice. Then, after the seventy-first Greek sailor had grinned and unintelligibly told me whatever it was he'd tell me whilst vigorously hugging me and taking the top layer of skin from my face with his unshaven cheek as he kissed me on both cheeks, whilst pressing a little paper package into my palm, I began to feel the novelty wearing off. It became a little too obvious that every Greek sailor, as soon as he went to sea, wanted to get to Africa as soon as he could in order to stock his cabin with these awful little things so that, when he got to places like Bristol, he could unload them onto unsuspecting British Greeks and their friends in an effort to endear them to him.

As I said, I could go on about all sorts of little details like these. I could mention the odd one or two times I was persuaded to go to the Greek taverna in Bristol. It was called the Famagusta, after the town in Cyprus. Pretty soon after the Turks moved in Famagusta was annexed as part of Turkish Cyprus and the club in Bristol went into mourning and subsequently died. Funny really. Mainland Greeks are not too keen on Cypriot Greeks. They can often be heard calling them "Bloody Cypriots" and things even stronger. The cuisine is subtly different, as is the language. Not that you or I would notice, but to a Greek these things are glaringly obvious. It's like the English and the Welsh I suppose. They're neighbours and very close, yet love to get the odd dig in whenever the opportunity presents itself. Yet, in foreign countries the vast majority of Greek restaurants and businesses seem to me to be Cypriot-run. And the Greeks don't mind because it's the nearest thing they'll get to home so they bury the hatchet, at least on the surface. If you know what I mean.

So I went to the Famagusta once or twice. We'd get there about midnight and it would be almost empty. Getting on for 1.00am a bunch of surly Greek sailors would come in and I would expect to get a sound thrashing. Perhaps I should mention at this point that I was about nine and a half stone and over six foot tall at this stage of my life. Not exactly a threat to anyone. If they breathed out I'd fall over. Fortunately my fears were entirely groundless. This may be when I first began to smell a whiff of affection for things Greek. They are simply nothing like the British. They are fun-loving optimistic people who, no matter how much they drink, never seem to get into a drunken stupor, and certainly never get aggressive or confrontational. They dance with a fire and enthusiasm which is so infectious that even a reluctant associate like me would be entranced. I felt myself thinking for the first time, "perhaps it would be nice to go there." Then I'd pull myself together.

But the resolve was weakening.

4 - *Tear Along Dotted Line*

We rolled off the ferry at Rhodes Town's commercial harbour an hour late on Tuesday August 23rd 2005. The trip had gone well. That's if you consider the word "well" to include a mad three and a half hour dash from Patras on the western Pelopponese to the ferry port of Piraeus, during which my wife almost jumped from the van on several occasions as a result of the way the Greeks were driving, coupled with the fact that, what we had been told was "motorway all the way" was in fact mostly two lanes with a sort of "hard shoulder" on each side which Greeks used capriciously as the overtaking lane. I won't even mention the condition of the road surface! Blast, I just did.

Our ferry docked just about on time at Patras after the crossing from Ancona in North East Italy. We'd enjoyed a very relaxing crossing after three hard days of driving with a couple of hotel stops along the way, in a sumptuous luxury cabin right at the front (is that right for ships?) and facing forwards. The bright moonlight had lit our beds as we dozed during the night and we'd enjoyed breakfast in the cabin with newspapers on the Monday morning. We even had TV and could watch the morning news in English, though the Greek morning TV is much funnier. I was very tempted to just stay on the boat and repeat the experience all the way back to Ancona. We were due to disembark at around 3.45pm and our ferry to Rhodes from Piraeus was departing at 7.00pm that same evening. We'd never done the drive from Patras to Piraeus before, but the bloke who built our house on Rhodes had done it loads of times.

"It'll only take you 2 hours from Patras to Piraeus," he'd cheerfully informed us, "but probably an hour more when you get into Piraeus just to get to the ship." Of course, we thought he was exaggerating. We'd be hitting Piraeus at about 6pm, but surely it would be well signposted to the island ferries. In the UK when you approach a ferry port the signs are so big you could pull them down, lay them flat and play football on them. You could be sure you'd be rolling on to your ferry almost without having to think about it. Surely, even if it's not quite as good as that in Piraeus, it's not going to be hard to find a dirty great big ferry that's as high as a 5 story building!

Circumstances, needless to say, conspired to place time at a premium as we found it much more difficult to extricate ourselves from Patras than we'd hoped. Once again, in northern Europe the road signs and road infrastructure are designed to get you off and away from the port in the minimum possible time. You're certainly not taken anywhere near what would be termed "the town." Not so in Greece. After numerous sets of traffic lights and a jam that Piccadilly Circus would have been proud of (caused by some reeeeally helpful road works on the main road out of Patras) we'd lost half an hour already by the time we got up to a respectable 65 mph on the road along the northern coast of the Peloponese to Piraeus, via the Corinth Canal.

Once on the road and finally "moving," we looked for it to turn into the expected "motorway." What fools we were. Now and again a bit of centre reservation appeared and we thought: "here it is, we'll really be able to make up time now," and no sooner having thought such hopeful thoughts, it had disappeared as fast at it had appeared and we were back with the two lanes plus a sort of hard shoulder.

There was a faint painted line that sort of demarcated the "*hard shoulder*." Not that it had evidently been re-painted in recent years. It brought a whole new meaning to the word "faint." But you know on some forms you fill in it says something like: "tear along dotted line." Well, that seems to be what a lot of Greek drivers wanted to do literally. Only the line wasn't always dotted. But they tore along it nevertheless. This meant that you were either right up behind someone looking for a safe opportunity to pass with nothing too close coming the other way, or some other twerp was already passing you on the INSIDE in order to force you back one space so they could try the same. You also had to keep a wary eye in your left-hand door mirror, because even if you were right out and running with your wheels on the centre lines (which were invariably double and unbroken, I suppose meaning: "*don't overtake here buster or you're gonna get pulled over*") there was still some geek with fat wheels and a spoiler who'd come past anyway if he thought he could squeeze back into the flow with more than a millimeter or two to spare before coming into contact with whatever was coming the other way. Add to that the ones who drove as if they thought they had fat wheels and a spoiler and not in fact a 15 year old Opel Ascona with all the metallic paint peeling off and only one brake light glass still intact and you had real road fun.

This road wouldn't have been so bad if it hadn't been so

busy. Let's admit it too, we'd been spoilt by the French, Swiss and Italian motorways, which had all been large, wide and quite civilized by comparison. We'd been warned about Italian drivers. "They're all mad. They'll switch lanes and cut you up in double quick time. Need your wits about you." No we didn't. The motorway around Milan had been quite sedate. Perhaps aided by the fact we'd experienced the greatest deluge since someone's neighbours had been saying, "I used to think old Noah was an OK guy, but that thing he's building is going to play havoc with property values in this neighbourhood."

The fact was the Italians were pussycats in comparison with these Greek drivers. A bit of aquaplaning and they were all scurrying to stop under bridges until the deluge had passed, while we motored sedately on at around 10mph, our wipers hopelessly inadequate to deal with the tons of water that the heavens were dumping on us, but sure that we'd miss our Ancona ferry if we didn't at least move forward rather than becoming stationary.

This Greek road was about as expected as a ham sandwich being passed round at a Jewish banquet (no offence). When we finally arrived at what a civilized Brit would call a motorway we were crossing the Corinth Canal and only 20 minutes (so we thought) from Piraeus. Now (so we thought) we'd see some enormous "THIS WAY TO THE FERRY PORT" signs, wouldn't we? Well, it has to be said there are some signs. If you blink you'd miss them but there were a few which sort of indicated it would be good to go that way if you were looking to catch a ferry from Piraeus.

Before what seemed like no time at all we were in urban sprawl and frantically looking for signs as we approached each set of traffic lights, at most of which someone would beep us impatiently as we moved forward with great doubts as to whether we'd chosen the right direction. We evidently had, although it's a miracle how. Some more stressful minutes elapsed before we found ourselves driving up some narrow Piraeus street with high buildings on all sides, with only room for a vehicle to go one way as every inch of kerb was occupied by a parked vehicle of some description. There were pedestrians going in all directions, a 90° junction every 100 metres or so and all sorts of things hanging off the sides of the buildings; stuff like shop signs, balconies, climbing plants, plus peoples' washing. The one thing there was not much of was signs. Signs telling us whether we were in fact heading toward the ferry port or hopelessly lost. The more intersections we passed, the more we became convinced we'd gone wrong somewhere. How could it be right? In the UK it's virtually motorway all the way to the port gates. Here we'd been driving for 15 minutes or more through tiny narrow urban side streets watching the last 40 minutes before our ferry's departure time ebbing away.

We were driving our 15 year old L300 Mitsubishi van, our friends who were doing the trip with us were driving an MPV towing a small boat!

Just when we decided we must be lost and I'd suggested to Yvonne that she open her window and ask one of the passing pedestrians (who were moving almost quicker than we were) how to get to the ferry port for the Dodekanese ferries, I looked up and, to my amazement and almost hidden by a tree (which the Greeks seem to love placing all along the most narrow of pavements, thus making it virtually impossible to walk for any distance along it before having to resort to jaywalking), not to mention an electricity pole and probably a lamp post too, there was a small sign, fetchingly loose and hanging at a precarious angle, saying 'FERRY PORT." It was the next right turn.

We turned right and some 500 metres ahead saw the blue of the sea. Upon reaching the end of the street we emptied out by means of more traffic lights into a dual carriageway of sorts, which was experiencing a rather alarming gridlock situation. Turning right as directed we now found the port railings to our left and simply had to follow the signs to the 'DODEKANESE FERRIES," which as a total lack of luck would have it, were the furthest away.

Turning finally into the gateway leading us to the quay where our ferry was berthed and already steaming (or is that *dieseling?*) up, we checked our watches to find we were 20 minutes from departure. I had a printed booking reference, sent me by email from the Greek Blue Star rep with whom I had booked our passage, which we simply needed to present at the Blue Star Ferries ticket office to receive our tickets. Yvonne jumped down from the van and ran the 10 metres or so across the paved area to the ticket office window, waving the booking reference earnestly.

Why was she standing at that window for so long? Why, if they were simply processing the booking reference and printing out our tickets, was she making exasperated gestures with her arms and pointing back at me, sitting anxiously in the van with the engine running? I sensed that it would be a good idea to be standing next to her at this moment.

I switched off the engine as our friends with the boat in tow drove happily by waving their tickets and disappeared inside the rear doors of the ferry. I exited the van and ran over to Yvonne and asked; "What's happening? Surely all they need is that reference number. Why aren't they printing out our tickets?"

"They say there's more to pay. How long is the van?"

"How long is the v…?! What do they need to know that for? I gave all the dimensions of the vehicle when I booked by telephone from the UK. I spoke to some woman - in this very office no doubt - who took all the details, gave me a price, took my Mastercard number and e-mailed me the booking reference!! All they need to do is type in that reference and the tickets should pop out of their machine! We're running out of time here!"

The pretty Greek girl sat behind the window in her crisp white shirt and company tie didn't look in a hurry at all. She simply wore an expression that said, "No good getting all aerated mate. I'm a jobsworth and I can keep you waiting here until you can wave at the passengers on board as that boat sails off into the sunset."

"Why do they want to know NOW how long the van is? It's on one of those printouts somewhere, let me have a look." …I ranted whilst snatching the printout from Yvonne's hand and frantically scanning the various e-mail messages as they ran down the page, showing what had gone back and forth between me and the Blue Star rep earlier in the year.

"She says that it's over 3.5 metres and there's a further 75 Euros to pay."

"That's rubbish! When I booked I gave the exact dimensions then! The girl I booked with gave me the price based on the van's dimensions. It must be right."

"Well this girl says it isn't. Unless we give her another 75 Euros we can't have our tickets. Apparently it's in the four metre category and more expensive."

Now, had I been able to speak Greek fluently at the time, I would have gone for the full argument and thrashed it out. But looking round I could see the last few lorries, cars and pedestrians boarding and had visions of the rear doors lifting whilst we argued the point. She had us over the proverbial barrel and she knew it. To this day I'm convinced she drives a BMW and buys expensive makeup and perfume directly as a result of her methods with the foreign mugs like us.

We reluctantly gave her the money. But she received one of my very fiercest scowls. Tickets finally in hand we drove aboard, only to find that the men marshalling the vehicles around hardly gave the tickets a second glance. They'd never have had a problem with the tickets if she'd just printed them out from the reference we brought with us.

The following morning we awoke to a brilliant blue sky and sea and rolled off the ferry at Rhodes Town's commercial harbour an hour late, but totally euphoric that "Mitsos," our 15 year old van, had got us almost "home."

October 2005.

Just before "Mitsos" the van was to depart to become the property of a lucky Greek!

It's now (2010) had a respray and sports a two-tone effect, with the "skirt" area [from bumper level, down] a proud shade of Greek blue. It lives at at a taverna just a couple of miles from us and is still going strong.

5 - First Impressions

There's one more thing that awoke in me a faint desire to visit Greece. I think I mentioned before that I was an aspiring hippie, though not that we ever liked to use that expression. It was too trendy and American. But if you had seen me around 1970, that's how you would probably have described me. Not that I ever had a chance of achieving my goal. For a start I couldn't get on with smoking at all. Never got hooked (for which I am now very grateful) so back then it made me a bit of a misfit when they passed around the roll-ups or the wacky baccy.

But those days it was very cool to hitchhike across Europe as far as Greece, then find a cave on one of the islands to live in until the Americans and Russian went to war. In the early 1970's, there was no doubt that this was going to happen. It was only a matter of time. So, to drop out in the manner described was very appealing. So you can see why I gradually began to think Greece may be cool after all. But, as with many of my daydreams at the time, I never even got near to achieving it.

Yvonne and I got married in the spring of 1974. We still

didn't have much money for foreign travel, so we spent a three-year period just being newlyweds. You know the sort of thing, arguing over every little thing. Deciding we'd made a big mistake but it was too late now, threatening to kill each other, all those normal things people do during the first few years of marriage. I can never understand people who get divorced after a couple of years. Once we'd got through all that we started getting happier and have gone on doing so ever since (sick bags available at reception). In 1976 - soon after Yvonne's mum re-married - she and her new husband, Dave, suggested we go to Greece as a foursome. We said we couldn't afford it. Plus, I was still a bit resentful of the whole Greece thing. It was like it gave Yvonne superiority over me, a parochial English lad, who was not well-travelled, while she had already spent quite a few months of her life in a foreign country. The reality was that it was simply my attitude that was wrong. I couldn't accept the Greek part of her heritage. It bugged me. She never had any intention of thinking herself superior due her Greek connection. It was simply something in her that she had to acknowledge. She genuinely needs to have an infusion of Greek language and culture from time to time to help her with her identity. Not having any such connections, I couldn't understand this for many years.

Anyway, what swung it was when Lela (without telling David) offered to pay one of our fares if we would agree to go. She wanted her family in Athens to meet both David and myself and wanted both of us men to experience what all the fuss was about. Feigning disinterest, I acquiesced. In September of 1977 we planned to go for three weeks. Yvonne started saving with avengeance. The flight itself was a stupendously exciting experience for me. The only time I had flown before was when I was 15 and had gone Bristol to

Bordeaux in a Viscount turbo-prop on a school exchange. Viscounts were not exactly state-of-the-art even in the sixties! So, to get on a real Boeing 737 made me feel like James Bond, or that chap with the box of chocolates. Or, no, perhaps Man in a Suitcase or the Saint.

The first thing I remember about coming out of the aircraft door in Athens was the heat. For someone as inexperienced as me, it was just like walking into a furnace. But the unforgettable smell of the Greek air I have loved ever since. Even the fact that, at an airport, the smell of the Mediterranean vegetation is mixed with aircraft fuel doesn't detract. As soon as I walk out of the plane I know this is Greece. But the heat. My armpits decided they would attempt to empty my body of all fluid wastes and its entire water content before I got into the terminal building. Not having done this before, I had worn a heavy cotton shirt and jeans. I was like one of those jacket potatoes you put in silver foil on the barbecue. All the heat was getting in, but precious little was getting out.

Yvonne's relatives lived at the time in Katopatissia, a bustling suburb of Athens just a couple of miles north of the centre of town. The street was quite small; mainly two and three story buildings and, at either end, one or two with a couple more. In the house where we stayed lived Auntie Effi and uncle Stomati. They lived in the sort of granny flat downstairs, whilst upstairs was a self contained apartment in which dwelt their daughter Christina with her wheeler-dealer husband Taki and their young daughter Effoula, also known as Effi. The floors were what I noticed first. Everywhere was crushed and polished marble chip. Smoothed so well that you could do wicked skids in your stockinged feet.

Christina's life consisted of work, work and - just to ease

the tedium - a little more work. Whenever I have been in her home she has always been working. She's either cooking, cleaning or doing the same for her mum downstairs. Both her parents have since died, but she's always worked 20 hours a day, so nowadays she's also the surrogate parent of her daughter's two children too. Well, perhaps the family thought she had too much spare time on her hands.

But when we arrived at Othos Potli (Potli Street) in September 1977, she was in her thirties and her parents were very much alive and almost kicking. About fifty yards down the road lived more relatives, uncle Theodoraki and auntie Vassau. After an hour or two and a cold drink, we were invited in very persuasive ways to go and visit them too. Yvonne had to present her "new" English hubby to them for their approval. It struck me right away how much Christina resembled Auntie Vassau. Auntie Vassau was a big woman, a bit of a barrel actually. Christina at that time was in pretty good shape, but the resemblance in the face was very evident. I made the mistake of raising the subject with Yvonne's mum. She was oddly reluctant to discuss the matter. Only when we were alone some time much later did she enlighten me. Christina wasn't the daughter of Effi and Stomati after all. She was Vassau's daughter. She had been conceived out of wedlock by Vassau and Theodoraki and, though the details are still not particularly clear to me, the long and the short of it is – she was taken to Auntie Effi and Stomati to be raised as theirs. The fact that Vassau eventually married Theodoraki didn't change things. Christina grew up with Effi as her mum. In those days in heavily Orthodox Grecian society, such things didn't happen, not officially anyway. One thing I was soon to learn about all the men in the family was that they were all philanderers. Old uncle Stomati, who when I first met him was stooped and didn't so much walk as shuffle everywhere, had spent much of his married life being unfaithful to his long-suffering wife Effi. This, apparently, was par for the course. In fact, to this day things are still very much the same. Greek men tend to sow quite a few wild oats. In their late teens they are called up into the military and then when they come out they get various jobs and enjoy the single life until they reach about thirty and then find a young teenage girl to marry and settle down with. Once married the wife begins her career of slowly but surely growing in size, while hubby begins to cast his eye around and, wherever it settles he samples the goods whilst his beloved wife washes, cleans, cooks and generally looks after his every whim and need. Greece isn't such a bad place when you think about it.

It was while staying with Christina that I learned we were to visit my first ever Greek island. I never had a clue what the conversations were about when staying with my wife's relatives. They would all gabble on unintelligibly and occasionally cast a laughing glance in my direction, in response to which I would smile and nod although not having the faintest idea whether they were saying, "look at that stupid English nerd. He's six foot tall and nine and a half stone, we could use him as a mast on one of our caiques!" or, "isn't he nice. John, would you like a beer?" I'm sure I refused many an offer that, had I been able to understand it, I would have certainly accepted without hesitation.

So, whenever a decision had been made which affected my movements, great ceremony was embarked upon whilst Lela carefully explained what was going to happen to the slow English boy. In this instance I was told, "Tomorrow we go to Poros for a week. You like?"

I liked.

6 - Air Conditioning

Forty nine minutes after disembarking the overnight ferry from Piraeus, we found ourselves turning off the road at Kiotari and beginning to negotiate the goat track that led up to our new home, almost exactly one kilometer up a gently sloping valley. We knew what the view would be like from the front terrace of the house, having the previous October (just ten months before) walked on precisely the spot where the house now stood, as we surveyed the site prior to making to final decision that this was where we were going to make our indefinite home.

Driving up the valley and glimpsing the house for the first time we were struck by the inconsistency of the appearance of the roof. The house, which is in fact two dwellings, is U-shaped. Each front (represented by the two top strokes of the right-angled "U") sporting French windows to take full advantage of the view down the valley to the sea, whilst the central terrace was backed by what would be the bottom (horizontal) part of the "U." So it may be more accurate to describe the building as three sides of a square, with the open end facing south and out to sea. The temperature was around the mid-thirties centigrade this August mid-morning and we were at least consoling ourselves with the fact that the house was fully air-conditioned, so at least we'd be able to sleep at night during the torrid heat of a Greek summer.

Yes I've read books by those who, far more intrepid than I, had moved to some Greek island or other and begun life in a tumble-down house with no running water, a leaky roof in winter and gaps big enough to get your hand through around the window frames. No we weren't going to have to endure such material depravity and discomfort. We were moving to a brand new house, built with modern construction methods to withstand any earthquake that this part of the world could sum up with which to rock it, with all the latest insulation technology to keep it as cool as possible in summer, whilst accomplishing precisely the opposite in the cool winter months. The house was designed to look rather more like a Spanish villa than a Greek one, insomuch as, although it was constructed with a watertight flat roof, there was resting above that a pitched roof of those lovely curvy Italian terracotta tiles.

At least, that was the kind of roof that the finished property was going to sport. It was patently clear to us as we drove up the valley that, whilst the wooden frame for the pitched roof was indeed sitting atop the house, replete with clear plastic membrane (ideal for growing tomatoes, if that were what we'd wanted to do up there) and a percentage of the wooden laths required to hold it on, the terracotta tiles were only covering around 40% of the roof area, and that was the side our friends were going to be using as their holiday home. Our side, which of course was to be 100% residential, still sat beneath what one could describe as a plastic hothouse.

Looking at each other with facial expressions that betrayed a tinge of disappointment, we consoled ourselves with the thought that, well, at least the air conditioning would help, since the roof was undoubtedly going to be hot enough to grill your fish on. Imagine living under a horizontal radiator in the heat of a Greek summer.

As we rounded the final steep bend in the lane and approached the entrance to our new "garden," it was also immediately apparent that the house was still standing in what could only be described as a "building site." There was no driveway at all, simply a vast expanse (the house sits in 4000 square metres of its own land) of dusty clay. Sitting on this dust was to be seen a variety of vehicles belonging to the builders (beaten up cars, plus some rather fetching ancient vans in varying stages of disintegration), various pallets loaded with terracotta tiles and bloc paviours for the (eventual) driveway, piles of sand and cement, planks of wood, scaffolding thingies, generators, cement mixers, shovels, picks and piles of debris from the actual construction of the house.

We pulled up as close to the house as we could to be met by the tall figure of Gary, our builder, all smiles and vigorous handshakes. He obviously registered our rather bemused expressions as he at once began to explain the situation.

"It looks bad, but the building is virtually complete on the inside. We've done our best to make it habitable. The bathrooms are finished (save for all the siliconing round the showers and sinks), the kitchens are all in and hobs, hoods and ovens all work. We still have to put silicone around all the worktops though. Oh, and you've no mains water."

"No mains wa…" we began. Gary hurriedly continued, "…but we've installed a huge plastic tank to act as a reservoir and arranged with the pig farmer further down the valley for your supply to be taken off of his and pumped up to the tank, which is set on the cliff above the house to give you a "head" to create some pressure. It's not wonderful, but when you turn on a tap, water comes out. So that'll do won't it?"

He must have assumed that we agreed that it "would do" and continued, hardly stopping for breath...

"And the phone line's in. You'll need to buy telephones, but it's connected." This was something I was well concerned about as I intended to make a lot of use of the internet once I had installed and set up my Apple Macintosh. My sigh of relief at this was undoubtedly audible.

Gary went on to explain about all the hitches he'd encountered during the build, which would help us understand why the house was now three months behind completion date and there was evidently a lot still to be done, all of which would now take place around its two new residents. The front terrace, which was meant to be very nicely tiled, was still a concrete "screed," the roof I've already mentioned, plus there was to be a wood-burning stove in the living room for winter use, though this hadn't arrived yet. Lots of stuff "hadn't arrived yet." Gary explained that this was par for the course when you were building houses on a Greek island.

Slowly the realization dawned on us that there didn't appear to be any electricity poles coming up the valley carrying our mains electricity; something we'd virtually taken for granted would be installed prior to our arrival. We already knew that the electricity company had levied a charge of 21,000 Euros to bring us our supply. They'd already been paid this vast sum and therefore we hadn't really entertained the thought that the supply may not as yet be installed. Gingerly we offered the question to Gary: "But we do have electricity, don't we?"

"No. You're on a generator. But we're hoping it won't be

too much longer. They've been paid the fee to bring the supply up the valley. But, hey - this is Greece. Things get done when someone decides to do them. No one rushes anything here."

"But the completion date was to have been last May! How come the electricity supply still isn't connected now, as it's the third week of August." The date was August 23rd. The temperature in the daytime was around 95°F in the old money, which is 35°C. The one thing you really want in your house when the temperatures are in that region is air conditioning. Walking in through our new front door we were greeted with a sight we had most feared, that of our air conditioning units, not mounted on the walls as hoped, but sitting neatly in their boxes and as yet unopened.

"Welcome to Greece." Offered Gary, cheerfully.

7 - *Sugar Cubes*

We took the electriko to Piraeus. The sheer number of new sensations which bombarded me were both wonderful and slightly frightening. I would have panicked at the thought of being left alone in this place. The electriko is Athens' version of the London underground. There is only one line. At least, there was up until the last time I was in Athens, which was 1982. It ran from the northernmost edge of the metropolis, down through the heart of the city to a terminus a couple of hundred yards up a busy street from the harbour in Piraeus where all the island ferries come in. No doubt, post-Olympic Games, things have changed.

Piraeus is not really much of a place for tourists. The buildings are all fairly modern and slightly dowdy. Around the port area there were giant neon adverts advertising Greek cigarettes and loads of other things with impossibly long names which in 1977 I didn't have a hope of reading, leave alone understanding, because of the fact everything is in that peculiar alphabet of theirs. My pathetic attempts at reading some signs drew loud guffaws of laughter from Yvonne and Lela. I mean, fancy using "P" as an "R". Where's the logic in that? And why is a "B" a "V" for goodness sake? Didn't the Greeks learn anything at school?

Notwithstanding the above, the quay where the island boats and ferries tied up was lovely. Mainly because there was an exciting row of sterns, all brilliant white in the sunshine against an impossibly blue sky and all with great banners stretched over their enticing walkways stating which islands they were stopping off at. Interspersed among the walk-on ferries were the vehicle ferries with their huge metal ramps lowered to swallow up and spew out the ever ebbing and flowing mass of trucks, coaches cars and mopeds which some very smartly dressed men were attempting to shepherd around. These men were all in white. They wore white trousers, sharply pressed, white shirts with short sleeves showing off their perpetually tanned arms and white "captain's" caps with braid on the dark-coloured peaks. A lot of Greek men are terminally scruffy, but not these guys. You see them everywhere where there is a quay for a ferry to tie up. They are in charge. No one seems to be paying them any attention, mind you. But they look so smart and dashing that you can't help being slightly in awe of them.

Fortunately I could spot the ferry we were to board because the banner was in the English alphabet as well as the Greek. You pay on-board so we marched up the walkway and on to the top deck, which was fitted out (as so many of the more substantially sized Greek island boats are) with very uncomfortable bench seats made up of those long wooden or sometimes metal slats screwed to a series of metal supports. Parts of the deck were shaded with large tarpaulins stretched across some metal posts and bars. There was no chance of getting under these. The Greeks had already colonised these areas and sat resolutely with that "No way are you going to get my bit of shade" look on their slightly stern faces. So we sat in the blazing sunlight. "No problem," I thought. There's a nice breeze so it won't get too hot. Yvonne and her mother were immediately seen to be covering their exposed flesh with gallons of suncream. When they both looked like they had dipped their faces in fresh clotted cream they were ready for the voyage. I thought, "I don't need all that stuff. I'm not even too hot. Anyway, it's all a rip-off this suntan lotion nonsense." Someone was getting very rich at peoples' expense, but they weren't fooling me. I was never one to waste what little money I had on such vanity. The exceedingly irritating heat rash and burns from which I suffered for the next week or so seemed to play a not-insubstantial part in changing my thinking on that subject.

The ferry's first stop was Aegina. A not-all-that-interesting-to-look-at-from-a-ferry island, the coast of which we skirted for some twenty minutes or so before entering its harbour. There doesn't appear to be much in the way of hills or mountains on Aegina. This is largely why we never really had much desire to get off a boat there. We have done though. This is because my wife's brother had spent a summer on the nearby island of Agistri, which was only accessible by small ferry from Aegina. We'll come back to Agistri another time.

After Aegina we stopped briefly at Methana, which appears at first to be an island, but is in fact a peninsular jutting out from the Pelopponese northward into the Saronic Gulf. It is made up of a narrow isthmus leading to a larger landmass, quite mountainous-looking from the sea, with a very boring looking small harbour town where the boats stop off. All the buildings there look featureless from a traditional Greek point of view. It looks like the whole place was only built in the last forty years or so. Apart from the fun we had watching the smart men in their white uniforms blowing whistles and generally looking important, we wouldn't write home about Methana.

Poros, however, is a different story. About three hours from Athens on the regular ferryboat (the one that carries vehicles too), you enter from the west the bay at the eastern end of which sits Poros. To the left is the larger, mostly uninhabited part of the island, covered in scrub and trees and yellow soil. To the right is the mainland Peloponnese with, in the distance on the right, the small town of Galatas. Well, it's more of a village actually and it sits just a couple of hundred yards across the narrow strait that separates it from the smaller, heavily inhabited part of Poros island. Poros is almost two islands really. In fact, since a small canal was built across the isthmus connecting the larger part to the smaller, you could say that technically it is. The first sight you get of Poros excites you. At least, it did me, as someone who had never visited a Greek island before. The town sits sprawled like a load of sugar cubes tipped out of some giant dish over the little hill that makes up the western end of the smaller portion of the island. Atop the white hill sits a clock tower, like a candle stuck in the top of a large icing-covered cake. In the brilliant sunshine, set against a sea too blue for its own good, Poros does not disappoint. The boat eventually drew near enough for one to see the front. There is no harbour as such. There is no need. The entire bay forms a naturally protected harbour and so the front at Poros has simply been turned into a quay, the boats just sidle up, chuck their ropes over and park. If you were to look to the right, you felt as though you could almost take a run and jump on to the quay at nearby Galatas. It's certainly close enough to read the shopfront signs. The largest sign on Galatas front at the time read: "ΠΑΣΟΚ", which was the political party of Mr. Papandreou, who ran the country for much of the 1970s and 80s. It's still around as I write this, though now I believe in the hands of his illustrious son.

Looking left over the side of the boat was just wonderful. There were the white-uniformed chappies again ordering things put here, vehicles parked there and pedestrians everywhere. Across the narrow bit of waterfront road were numerous zaheroplastaeons (cafes which sell Greek sweet cakes) with their tables and chairs all sprawling most of the way across the road.

We fought our way along the vehicle deck and down the metal ramp which, when the ship was at sea, formed its bows. Half a dozen or so small Greek women were jostling to attract tourists to their "Rooms for rent, very clean!" but we had our accommodation already sorted. I just went with the flow, because my trusty mother-in-law, Lela, had already made our residential arrangements. Dragging suitcases and wrestling with shoulder bags which seem to be cleverly designed to fall off your shoulder at all the right inconvenient moments, we fought our way across the road and up a small street in the far right corner of the harbour front, between two cafeneions. Almost immediately the noise subsided and the heat intensified as we made our way past the fish market and the almost death-inducing smell of the public loos along a charming little backstreet. We turned left just near a small bakery, closed for siesta at the time, and after a few more yards turned right to face about thirty steep steps. I was almost wrung out like a prune from dehydration, but struggled up the steps, the top of which afforded a breathtaking view all down the bay in the direction of Hydra. A few more yards along a white-painted street, so narrow you could walk up one wall with your back against the other, and we saw a small sign above and to the right, fixed to a small balcony and saying "*enoikiozontai domatia*" – rooms for rent. Just to the left of the building we entered a small courtyard and encountered Kyria Mellou.

Kyria (Mrs.) Mellou was about thirty yet already a widow with a young son not yet ten years of age. Using no small amount of initiative she had decided to convert the upstairs of her house into rented rooms in order to make ends meet. She immediately treated us like family. The four of us, My mother-in-law, her husband David, Yvonne and I all sat with this charming little lady and her son in her small lounge as she fixed us all a cold drink and pleasantries were exchanged.

In 1977 Poros was still essentially "Greek". The visitor would have found the menus all in Greek, save for one or two tavernas and bars right on the front where the boats came in. There were no English bars, no snooker, not even any Italian restaurants. The only disco, if you could call it a disco, was at the end of the waterfront, almost a mile from the main town, set about 50 feet above the road in what looked like a part of the hill that had been blasted out with dynamite. From the dance floor, which was a slab of concrete about thirty feet across and almost circular, laid between three or four large trees, you had a view all across the bay to Galatas opposite and on to the "Sleeping Lady" mountain, over which the sun would set in a blaze of red fire every evening. The "Disco" was called "Sirocco". We walked along to it one afternoon for a "reccy". It was several hundred yards past the last of the houses and up a steep flight of steps, these being just very roughly set in cement with no handrail, just the hillside to one's right and left. The road immediately turned around the end of the hill just past the Sirocco and went winding its way around the largely barren east and north side of the smaller part of the island. The only ones who ever went on round that corner were the rubbish men, because the Poros "Tip" was situated round there. You could see it smouldering away all day from Askeli beach, which was on the larger part of the island, facing south across a small bay from the "Tip". We walked as far as the entrance to the Sirocco and looked up the steps with disdain and dismay.

"We don't come all the way to a remote and beautiful island like this for discos!" We self-righteously exclaimed. After suitably telling anyone who may be listening, whilst no one in particular was about, we set off briskly back to the sugar-cubed town to immerse ourselves in a true "Greek" environment. All along the front, once you re-entered "civilisation" as it were, one could browse the various tavernas and bars, deciding which one to eat in that coming evening. Virtually all the tavernas at this time were what I would call "rough and ready". They all had rickety tables and rickety old chairs with rickety and mangy old cats hanging about. The idea of a printed "bill" being presented to you at the end of your meal would have been foreign to any taverna-owner at the time. It was the done thing for the bill to be reckoned from his head as he jotted reminders down on the paper tablecloth. Then he'd round it up or down to the nearest Drachma, which meant sometimes you won and sometimes you lost, but it all evened itself out in time.

The loos were so awful you had to steel yourself to venture into them, but it didn't matter. This was the real Greece!

8 - Beware of the Goats

I've mentioned that our house is "up a goat track." How true this was to prove we had no idea when we first arrived. Rhodes has an enormous population of these independent creatures. Somebody owns them - they must do - as they are all marked in one way or another. Yet it seems that any piece of land which isn't fenced or walled in is their natural grazing area. In fact, even land that is fenced in or walled isn't immune from incursion by the intrepid Greek goat. They have a habit of finding their way through most defences, but at least with a wall or fence your plants (if and when you're lucky enough to have anywhere to plant them) stand a fighting chance.

Standing on our front terrace there's a very pleasant view down the valley below to the sea. The track is very visible as it winds its way the one kilometer or so up the valley to our house and then beyond. We're reliably informed that it used to be the only access road to the village of Asklipio, which is 4 kilometres further up into the mountains. Though nowadays there is a tar-Macadam road just a few hundred yards down the main road from our track which enables one to reach Asklipio with the springs (not to mention tyres) on the car still intact.

On at least 3 days in any normal week you can stand on our terrace and see upwards of 100 goats grazing or simply standing in the way that goats do, with that slightly blank expression they have, all across the track about half a kilometer below us. "How bucolic," we mused during our first few weeks here.

Our house, by virtue of the fact it was a "new build," had yet to have its perimeter fence constructed, leave alone front gates for what we hoped would eventually be our "drive." And what plans we had for the "garden," which at the time more closely resembled a building site with, not just dust, but dust like you couldn't even imagine! For the first few weeks we ate dust, sat in dust, showered in dust and sunbathed in dust. Dust has a particularly unique way of making the skin feel when you've covered yourself in factor 30 from head to toe and then walked outside to take the air and admire the view. A small gust of wind, someone trying to sweep up somewhere, or a moving vehicle, not to mention the ever-present builders and their dreaded "disc cutter" cutting terracotta tiles for the roof – any or a combination of the foregoing had the effect of making your skin feel like the side of a box of Swan Vestas. Though, as it was August and this was Rhodes, temperature-wise it also felt as if a match were being struck on you perpetually, with no air conditioning!

Anyway, where was I? Oh yes, the goats. Since there was no sign of our promised perimeter fence we made the decision not to even attempt to create a garden until said fence materialized. We weren't to know at the time how long that was going to be. So we set as our priority the fixing up of the interior of our new home which, it has to be said – despite all the work that still had to be done on it – looks impressive and has wonderfully large rooms. We were soon charging around in Mitsos (long wheelbase – got to be better) looking for furniture shops, since we slept on a blow-up mattress on our bedroom floor the first few nights as we didn't as yet even have a bed. Of course, that was after we'd cleaned up the dirty mess on the bedroom floor caused by a water pipe that had burst somewhere above the bedroom ceiling and which had created a rather fetching 18 inch square (not exactly symmetrical though) hole in the plasterboard just as you walked through the bedroom door. The expression "things couldn't get any worse" began to take on a whole new meaning.

Imagine: We'd originally planned to move out to Greece in May 2005, which was when the house was supposed to have been finished and ready. We actually made the move in August of that year and – on arriving - discovered no mains electricity, a half-finished roof, no front gates, drive, walls or perimeter fence, no mains water, no air conditioning, no washing line and a rough concrete (one day it would be tiled) terrace upon which we'd soon be attempting to sit out in the evenings with our gin and tonic in a vain attempt to admire the wonderful sea view it would have afforded if only the piles of terracotta roof tiles weren't plonked squarely in the way whilst still bound to their wooden pallets with that horrible black flat plastic string sort of thing type stuff. Then there was not only the perpetual noise of the "genny," ("we'll replace it with a quieter one for you soon," said Gary, with that chirpy grin on his ever-optimistic countenance) but the constant presence and inevitable noise made by the three builders as they continued (slowly) the work that we had hoped would have been completed well before we wound our weary way up the track on the day we arrived.

I mean, what do you complain about first? Spoilt for

choice we became resigned to accept Gary's explanation that this was what happens in Greece. He had no idea of what previous connection my wife and I had with the country and, since he'd already lived on Rhodes for 6 years or so, he soon acquired the habit of appealing to this "experience" as grounds for telling us that ..."you'll get used to it." Or he'd repeat the expression "welcome to Greece" whenever we ventured to enquire as to why something wasn't yet done.

So anyway, the goats, yes the goats. We were told by all and sundry (Gary included) that it was futile to attempt to plant anything while it would be at the mercy of the goats. But that didn't stop friends we soon began to make, neighbours from down the valley and even Gary himself taking any opportunity they got to hand us cuttings and stuff. In fact we were given geraniums (to be pedantic – pelargoniums, which can grow to enormous sizes in the Greek climate), yuccas and - as the autumn came upon us - onion sets and lettuce seedlings, all of which simply had to "go in" as it were, but what were we going to do? There were goats about on a daily basis and, as the days turned to weeks and the weeks to months – still no perimeter fence.

So we earmarked a half-moon shaped area in front if the French windows (once the last pallet of roof tiles was used and gone) dug it over (well, pick-axed it would be more accurate), went and found some "black soil..."

"What's that?" you cry.

Well, since the "soil" here is pretty much a yellow clay that sets like concrete when trodden on and baked dry by a Greek summer sun, it isn't the greatest stuff in which to attempt to nurture tender little plants. But there is a certain kind of bush (fortunately growing in abundance all through our valley and beyond) which sports lovely (and edible) reddish–orange berries in December through February, not unlike lychees in appearance, save for the colour of course. I still can't pronounce the name of this bush, but it grows from ground level up to a height and diameter of two or three meters and beneath its dense evergreen foliage there forms a rather rich black compost that is ideal for nourishing new plants. Greek friends we've made who have lived here all their lives (well, not yet) put us on to this "black soil" which they all go out salvaging with a will whenever they're working a bed into something resembling an acceptable home for their new plants to take up residence. So we soon got into the swing of things and could be seen (still can in fact) cheerfully trotting off with a wheelbarrow a spade, trowel and loppers (to cut away sufficient of the bush to get at what's beneath) to collect a load of "black soil."

Black soil duly worked into the modest bed we'd prepared, we began planting all the cuttings and other stuff we'd been given. Of course, whenever he was about (which was pretty much always) our British builder Gary wouldn't let an opportunity to dazzle us with his superior knowledge and wisdom gained from his 6 years of already living here pass.

"No good putting those in. The goats'll have the lot." The fact that he'd actually given us about 30 or so pelargonium cuttings seemed not to be a relevant factor.

"Well, they either go in or they get chucked out. We'll just have to keep an eye out won't we."

"Won't do any good. You've only got to be away from here a few minutes and they'll down the lot."

"Well, we haven't shelled out any hard cash for any of this so we'll just have to see what happens won't we." Before long there were pelargoniums, onions, lettuce, yucca and various other stuff all lovingly inserted into this "nursery" and awaiting their fate. Each day we'd be on the lookout constantly and if a goat so much as drew to within 100 metres of our place we'd be out there running and shouting and clapping hands vigorously like some charismatic Pentecostals to frighten them away. At least most herds included several with bells round their necks so we could often hear them coming closer. I could frequently be seen charging over the hillside, arms flailing, with a dozen or so of the enemy "high-tailing" it away from me at a sprint.

I thought I was very clever because I'd been told that the goats won't eat onions. This in mind I planted a row of onions either side of the lettuce seedlings in an attempt to afford them some protection. The pelargoniums would have to fend for themselves.

A couple of weeks passed and the pelargoniums were looking larger with some even sporting flowers. The lettuce were also swelling day on day as were the onions. No sign of any munchers as of yet. Mind you, we were nervous wrecks every time we had to go out. On most days the builders were about (since they'd become so much part of the scenery it was as though they lived with us. Cost us a fortune in milk, tea and biscuits. Maybe that's why they were stringing out the work of finishing the place. Damn, if only we'd realized earlier, we'd have made them Earl Grey. Builders don't like Earl Grey, "Ruddy peculiar-tasting stuff. Only fit for toffs who drink with their pinky sticking out while they chew their cucumber and cress sandwiches while watching the cricket from the boundary on the village green. Give us *Tetley* and make it *strong!*"). At least if the builders were about it would deter the goats from getting too near.

But there were occasions, especially evenings, when we'd

arrive home holding our breath until our tender little green protegés came into view. I'd then water the bed at the end of the evening and we'd retire in the hope that goats slept nights too. Although Gary (ever the cheery one) had told us they'll be up and about any time day or night.

One awful morning after maybe three weeks had passed and we'd started to think we were going to get away with it, I opened the shutters of the French windows to a scene of utter devastation. All the pelargoniums were eaten, there being gaping holes where some gnashers had evidently ripped the whole stalk out of the earth. There were a few inch-long sections of stalk still laying on the surface. All the tops of the onions had been eaten, though the bulbs, small though they yet were, for the most part still remained in the soil. Just about everything else was gone and the bed bore hoof marks all over it.

I just stood there in a daze. I couldn't decide how to react. Yvonne was still in bed. How was she going to take it? She loves gardening with a passion and this had been our very first attempt at it on Rhodes, and even though we had been aware of the risks, we'd begun to think we were going to get away with it.

As I turned to go and make breakfast, trying to act resigned and to console myself with the fact that at least we hadn't spent any money on the plants, I caught sight of a movement at the far end of our plot. We needn't have worried about the damned goats. A load of sows and their dear little offspring had escaped from the pigpen further down the valley and feasted on our babies!

It's true, goats don't like onions! But pigs - well that's another story.

9 - Sirocco

The first night on Poros we ate at Taverna Lucas. The next six nights we also ate at Taverna Lucas. One of the biggest mistakes most Brits make when they go abroad is to assume ownership of the first Taverna they eat in - and its proprietor. I know, it's precisely what we did. You come across them all the time. Often, if you go on a package, (which we never did in those days), one of the worst things you can do is go to the welcome meeting. You know what's going to happen:

"Have any of you been to this island before?" asks the Rep.

"Yeah, ...Yiassou Stavros! We'll have two cold beers please...parakalo I mean!" They've already established for those who are unfortunate enough to be only on their first visit (or even if they're not, it makes no difference), that they're superior and know the taverna's owner where the welcome meeting is being held as if he were their brother. The Rep will explain all the various excursions the company has on offer (at exorbitant prices), whilst the old hands interject with "We loved that place last time, remember old Mihalis and that donkey!" and "Does Yianni still drive the boat on the round-the-island barbecue? We loved Yiannis. He loved us too, gave us lots of extra Metaxa." Before you get a chance to open your mouth they're telling you which bank or exchange office gives the best rates, where to hire and not to hire your car or moped and which tavernas will give you a free Metaxa or some other delight at the end of your meal. The fact that you may be a member of the Greek government is of no consequence to these people. They simply want you to know they've been here loads of times and know everything there is to know about the place. I hate these people with a passion. Sorry, went off on one there didn't I?

I remember once eating a delightful lunch in a little beach taverna on Symi. To be precise, it was on tiny Nymborio beach. Yvonne and I had retreated from our loungers at the hottest part of the day for a Greek salad and some whitebait, a cold beer (for me) and iced coffee for Yvonne. The taverna only had about four tables under olive trees out front. The beach was shingle, punctuated by a couple of dilapidated old concrete jetties where the taxi boats from the harbour would deposit and collect their weary wayfarers. The table we sat at was about six feet from the water on one side, and about the same distance from Maria's Taverna on the other. The table next to us was occupied by a British man and his evidently longsuffering wife and child. He was very large, as was his voice. I remember he had the most peculiar and rather effeminate-looking cord around the back of his neck from which to hang his sunglasses when he wasn't wearing them on his nose. It was quite thick and like a threefold string of pink, pale blue and white. Yvonne and I were quietly chatting about I can't remember what, when the booming voice from the table next to us interjected, "What part of Wales are you from then?"

Now, we are not Welsh. We lived in South Wales (which

we loved) for many years, but we are (as stated in chapter one) from Bath. So it struck me as a clever wise-crack right at the outset. Behind that line there was: "I'm really talented at spotting peoples' accents. I'll impress you with such a knowledgeable deduction right at the outset that you're bound to think I'm clever." In fact we both cast a knowing glance at each other meaning: "Here we go. a right smart Alec. Wouldn't it be nicer if he weren't here to spoil this lovely moment." Problem was, he was. He continued, almost without a pause...

"Marvellous place isn't it? We love Maria's Taverna. Been here a lot. The grilled fish here is probably the best on the island. Maria runs it single-handed you know. Have you been to Symi before? (a question that arose in me the faint hope that he might want a conversation, but ...no) We've been eight times. Love it. Nice that it's off the beaten track. You don't get any riff raff here. I need this sort of place. Back home in Cheshire (we live in Cheshire you know) I'm so busy and stressed out I need complete relaxation when I'm on holiday, don't I love?" At this point his wife attempted a smile and acknowledged the rhetorical question before returning to contemplating the view. Possibly she was also contemplating how nice it would be if there were man-eating sharks in this bay and her husband had just fallen off a caique, who knows? After he'd tried pretty hard to show off his knowledge of all things Greek and the one or two islands he'd visited he continued, "What do you do for a living?" at which point I said, "well..."

"I run my own business you know. Does pretty well, keeps me on my toes. But you need to get exercise when you're stuck behind a desk or in your car a lot. I play squash..." By the size of his gut I presume he meant the type that involves driving a steamroller. He certainly didn't look as though he knew what a racquet looked like. "...and I do a lot of charity work. I'm Chairman of our local Round Table..." He continued on, but somehow I had lost concentration and didn't hear much more. Can't imagine why. I exchanged glances with Yvonne and we both looked out at our sun loungers, exposed to the scorching early afternoon sun, and decided we didn't mind getting fried alive. I looked over to the chair outside the Taverna door, where Maria the Taverna owner was sat fanning herself. I called over to her:

"Signomi Kyrie, o logoriasmo se parakalo?" Which, although my Greek wasn't very good at the time, came out wonderfully confidently. It means: "Excuse me ma'am, but could I have the bill please?" At this point the bluster from the next table stopped in a manner that, had he been a radio, one would have thought it had experienced a power failure. The realisation came over him rather frighteningly that perhaps this couple he'd been talking at actually knew something about Greece. Perhaps even more than he did. Perhaps these handy people to bounce his voice off of actually spoke Greek and could tell him a thing or two (although chance would have been a fine thing). The fact that my wife Yvonne looks very Greek was something he hadn't noticed in his hurry to impress us. If he had noticed it may have tempered his enthusiasm for demonstrating how knowledgeable he was, but his type are never very observant are they? The only thing they observe is that there's someone nearby who'll be handy as an audience. As we rose from our table with what I would have thought were audible sighs of anticipated relief, he muttered, "Oh, you speak Greek then..."

"A little." I said as we walked away.

Now all that chat about him was just to illustrate the types you get at "Welcome Meetings." In fact, prior to this I was talking about those who establish a rapport with their favourite Taverna Owner and then assume ownership of not only him but also his eating place. We made the same mistake on our first visit to Poros. As it happens, it wasn't that much of a mistake because my Mother-in-law had previously met Yiorgo Lucas by chance on an aeroplane and he had told her all about how he was Greek National Sirtaki Dancing Champion and had recently been to Britain on a cultural trip to demonstrate Greek dancing to us pale skinned Brits. He ran his own little Taverna at which his older brother was chef. He would charge in and out of the building with four or five souvlakis up his arm and, when the opportunity arose, would roll out to the door a very, very old American jukebox (the kind that played 45's with those massive holes in the middle), put on a recording of Frangosyriani (an ancient Sirtaki/Hasapiko record) and proceed to entrance all his diners, together with those in the tavernas either side and any who were promenading past at the time, with a meticulous dance sequence that was a sheer joy to behold. Yiorgo Lucas told us how wrong we were to write off the Sirocco Disco.

Now and again, as the evening wore on and all the tourists had eaten and left (you know, after half past nine – ten o'clock), the Greeks would emerge and arrive to eat at Taverna Lucas. Things would slow down nicely and Yiorgo would end up sitting at our table chatting to Yvonne and, if she was there too, Yvonne's mother. Occasionally I would pick up the meaning of what was being discussed. In fact, Yiorgo, to my great and evident relief, spoke a bit of English. I bemoaned the fact that, on this still very Greek island of Poros, with very little evidence of tourism having ravaged it, there was a disco at the end of the bay. The thin end of the wedge and no mistake, I would say. Yiorgo said we should go there. Despite my protestations, he said:

"After the midnight. The Greek island boys they there. You see the boys dance. Iss good. Very good."

"Yeah, but we don't want to see Greek boys dancing to Barry Manilow singing Copa Cabana." I said.

"Yes, but, only half-hour English/American music. Then half-an-hour Greek. Omorphi. You not see anything like in all Greece."

So it was that, after Yiorgo's little bit of encouragement, we decided to stay up until way after midnight and walk along to the Sirocco to see if it was worth it. Yvonne and her mother have always had a habit of seeking out the real Greek dance venues wherever they go. Not the "Greek Nights" you understand. Greek Nights are heaving with people, but none of them Greek. Except perhaps a few waiters and may be a dancer or two. I remember one particular Greek Night where there were three dancers rather fetchingly dressed up in Greek National Costume, not just your white shirt, black trousers and red sash, but the full kit. Even down to bobbly shoes. There were two men and a girl. The girl was more blonde than a Scandinavian. I thought, "There's no way she's Greek." She wasn't. She turned out to be Scandinavian. The other thing wrong with Greek Nights it that they demonstrate all the complex dances and then get the audience to join in with the *Hasaposerpiko*, which is nothing more than what I call a Tiller Girls routine. It goes step, step, kick one way then the other, step, step kick one way then the other and on and on and on...

To be fair, Yvonne knows all the real steps and dancing is in her blood. So to go to a Greek Night is like making Wayne

Sleep watch a London stage musical from the auditorium, then asking him to dance ring-a-ring-a-roses. So we only went to Greek Nights when it was an absolutely last resort. The thing is, if you want to see the Greeks dancing extemporaneously, as it were, you've got to stay out way past midnight and then know where to go. It turned out that on Poros, the Sirocco was the place to go.

We arrived at the foot of the flight of steps leading up the hillside to the dance floor to the sound of the Love Unlimited Orchestra (Don't forget, this was the late 1970's).

I wasn't keen.

Yvonne began the ascent without delay. At earsplitting height we reached the small gate leading into the Disco. You didn't pay to go in, but the drinks would require one to take out a small mortgage. One beer can last a phenomenally long time in such circumstances. We found ourselves a table near the raised concrete circular dance floor and sat down, where disgustingly expensive drinks were served. There was no conversation. It simply wasn't possible. Now and again we would look at each other and attempt to communicate by expression. Mine was usually: "I'm tired, my stomach is vibrating from the bass and I don't think this was a good idea at all." Yvonne's was more often: "Let's give it a little longer. Things are bound to work out soon. Just wait through one more Bee Gees track." Unfortunately, they were playing 12 inch versions.

After well over half an hour I had almost got her to agree to give it up as a bad job when, with no warning whatsoever, a *Sirtaki* record began. Within seconds the floor cleared of disco dancers and immediately filled again with a selection of local boys all aged between seventeen and thirty. They formed into one or two, or even three, long lines and commenced the dance. Pan's People – eat your hearts out. Gillian Lynne, who's she? This was perfection. They were all dressed in jeans and short-sleeved shirts or Levi's T-shirts. There was absolutely no need for costume, the way these boys danced made what they were wearing totally irrelevant. The dance changed to *Sirto* (or something like it). In this dance the leading dancer is attached to the next in line by a white handkerchief. These boys performed in a way that would make circus gymnasts look stilted. They were flipping over, doing triple summersaults, jumping on and off the tables which were close enough to the dance floor to reach with a single leap and generally contorting themselves with great gusto and fury to the passion of the music. And that's the thing I truly came to understand that night. The music arouses a passion in a Greek male that can only be expressed when he dances. And oh, how they dance. That year (1977) we visited Sirocco several times and each time I was totally spellbound. I have never seen anything like those boys from that day to this.

It was, as Yiorgo had said, "Omorphi. You no see anything like in all Greece."

I wonder if our friend from the Taverna at Nymborio beach on Symi knew about this place.

10 - The Bloke in the Box on the Top Right

Living in a foreign country presents no particular difficulty for a lot of British people. After all, we're British and everyone else is foreign aren't they? So, all you have to do when speaking to them, if you want to be understood, is shout at them isn't it? Having lived in parts of the UK where there were sizable communities of immigrants and now having re-located to Greece, we were able to empathise with the locals and their view of this growing invasion of northern Europeans, who are steadily changing the face of many a Greek island community as more and more of them buy places here and move to "live the dream" in the sunshine, as it were.

So I resolved that whatever else I did, I was going to learn Greek.

Of course, the first thing you have to do when embarking on this particular project is learn another alphabet. Why couldn't the Greeks be sensible about it and use the "Roman" alphabet that everyone else uses? Well, everyone except the Orientals that is. Oh, and the Arabs, they have a system of wiggly lines don't they? I couldn't handle that at all.

But the Greek alphabet, now there's a challenge if ever there was one. I mean, the "R" is a "P" for goodness' sake. Then the "n" is a "v!" Need I say more? Yes, I need. They have a little "π" for a "p." plus all sorts of things like trees and backward number threes with little squiggly bits at the bottom. Phew. Then there's the Greek "B," which isn't a "B" at all but a "v!" If you want to write down a "b" you have to put together an "M" and a "P." So, when you see the letters "mp" together (only the "p" of course is that little two legged table - "π") it means "b" as in μπυ'ρα, which is "beer!" So all those people sitting in the House of Commons in the UK are all "B's" to a Greek. Come to think of it, that's what they are to most Brits too, don't you think?

Still, I decided to battle on (still battling actually). See, the secret is, don't be afraid to make a fool of yourself. Don't take yourself too seriously because your audience most certainly won't! And all our new-found friends on Rhodes agreed, "you need a TV." We hadn't planned on buying one, but we were told it was one of best ways to learn the language.

"You should watch the news bulletins regularly, and the soap operas..." (notwithstanding that the acting is still at the level of the UK's "Crossroads" the first time around) "...they're full of every-day speech that you'll pick up without the local accent that many of the locals here speak with." ...they all said to a man. Or should that be to an andras, or – to be PC about this – also a yineka!

So we wandered into Rhodes town one October "afternoon" just in time for the shops to open after the lunch break, 1.00 - 5.00pm that is. They call any time up to 8.00 o'clock in the evening the "afternoon." Maybe it's because the midday break stretches to 5.00pm in order to incorporate the siesta, whatever. One "afternoon" we found ourselves driving home with a bargain from one of the electrical stores with a view (good pun eh?) to watching hours of Greek TV during the winter evenings.

It's fair to say that Greek TV news bulletins are an aid to learning the language. After all, like lots of the satellite channels or cable TV there's loads of scrolling text running across the screen all the time, plus captions you can struggle with to your heart's content. And we became more and more fascinated with the passing of time (as we became expert on which channel had their hour-long bulletin on at which time, and which channel had the best weather forecast) with the number of "nip and tuck" jobs there are on Greek TV. It seems the terrestrial channels here are laden with aging women presenters all bent on outdoing each other in the "how tight a top can I get away with" stakes, but even more so in the "how much have I spent on my plastic surgeon?" stakes! So many of them have unnaturally wide mouths that taper to a sort of slit at each end, while their eyes are gradually acquiring a more and more oriental look as they change angles each time they have another bit cut away and what's left is stretched ever further to cover the gap thus created. It's so macabre you find yourself studying their faces so much you forget all about why you bought the set in the first place.

Then there's the penchant the Greek TV news production teams have for splitting the screen into boxes whilst they have endless discussions with people in various parts of the country by video link. This I find hilarious. The anchorman or "daughter of Frankenstein" (as the case may be) will be slap bang in the middle of the screen trying to keep some semblance of order to the proceedings. On either side of he/she will be two "interviewees" whilst there will be three more across the bottom half of the screen too, all looking bored out of their skulls and dying to pick their noses while waiting for the bloke in the box on the top right to finish ranting about the price of petrol or Government corruption or something. Once one of them gets bored enough they'll try and interject, which results in two people ranting over each other until the anchor tries to get a word in to ask another penetrating question. If I didn't know it wasn't written by the Monty Python team I'd swear it was.

It's always the bloke in the box on the top right that causes the problems. Nothing any of the others says is right and this bloke is going to get his 15 minutes of fame, if only for being downright rude and opinionated and shouting down everyone else involved in the "link."

So much for TV helping me learn Greek. Mind you I wouldn't have missed it for anything.

So I struggle on making all kinds of gaffs. When it rained last March I was talking to Despina, our friend in Kalathos, about how good it was for the garden. She appeared perplexed. "Why would rain here be good for Cyprus?" She quizzically queried. I'd said "*Kyprou*" which means "Cyprus," when I should have said "*kypou*" meaning "garden."

Then I was listening to a wedding speech in April when the speaker commented that "marriage wasn't a bed for thirty friends." Well, that's what I thought he'd said and consequently caused no end of mirth when I asked why he'd say such a thing. Hmm, I thought, the Greeks are much more open-minded than they used to be. Must be all those American movies! Turns out that what I thought was "thirty friends" was actually *triandafila* (sounds suspiciously like "thirty friends" mind you) and actually means, yes, you're ahead of me, "roses."

One expression Yvonne has been careful to ensure I don't use in public is the word for "drink" as used when you're telling someone to do just that. As it's so hot here in summer that we each keep a perpetual glass of water handy as we work in the "garden" pick-axing the loamy (not!) soil or carrying boulders around in a wheelbarrow. I frequently have to remind her to "drink!" as she tends to forget and gets dehydrated in the sweaty heat. Feeling very proud of myself, having learned the verb for "to drink" (*Pino*) I duly conjugated it (as you do) and shouted over to her the Greek for "Drink!"

She collapsed in fits of laughter and warned me against using the word in English speaking company. Why? You ask. Well, as she explained, sounds like you're shouting - penis!

11 - An Apology

It was on one particular night at the Sirocco that I was to learn something else about the Greek nature. This time it was 1978 and the Poros boys were still putting on their staggering exhibitions at night in the Sirocco "disco." Some faces had gone, others had returned from their time in the military, but at that time Poros still hadn't changed much from the year before. We were sitting at a table grieving over the price of the drinks we were now very slowly imbibing when a very large Greek lad, who must have been in his early twenties, as indeed were we at the time, came up behind us.

Yvonne and I were both positioned on the same side of our table so as to enjoy the view of the dancing. It was, needless to say, quite dark except for the lights around the dance floor and the first I was aware that this young man was present was when I looked sideways to Yvonne, but couldn't see her. Instead there was the back of this great surly head, with a mass of thick dark hair. He was evidently a little the worse for drink and was attempting to woo my wife with a series of vigorous kisses on her neck.

Without a thought as to how big he was in comparison to how big I am, I grabbed him with both hands and, attempting to stand up in the process, drawing on some inner strength I can't normally summon, threw him bodily across the ground behind us into someone else's table. My chair followed him, but didn't quite cover the same distance. Now, imagine the scene, there's me, six foot and not quite ten stone, standing with fury in my eyes (reckless, I know!) and staring down at this Greek bloke, just dusting himself off and getting up from the floor and proving to be some fifteen or sixteen stone and shaped, from the waist up, like an upside-down wedge. "Dusting himself off" is a good description of what he was doing because the ground was nothing but dry Greek earth and pine needles!

Time stood still. My whole life flashed before me as the full realisation of what I had just done struck me like a thunderbolt. I didn't know enough Greek to try and defuse the situation and, even if I had I doubt if it would have made any difference. I heard my feeble little voice (or so it sounded to me) squealing, *"Gineka Mou!!!"* ("My wife!!!"). My mind was saying a lot more like: "who do you think you are you drunken foreigner!! Get your lips off my wife's neck this instant before I..." Well, that was the point at which I realised that there was no way I would have any better chance than an ice cube in a hot cauldron of tar against this fellow. So my mood swiftly changed from outrage that this chap had apparently molested my wife to sheer horror at the thought of what Greek hospital food was going to taste like.

At this point we shall leave this scene with the two rivals in a state of suspended animation while I make some observations about Greek boys. I don't think I've ever seen a weedy Greek boy. When I say "Boy" I include those from the late teens into the late twenties. One time we were chatting to a couple of Poros boys about what they did to earn a living in a place like Poros. I mean, apart from tourism in summer, which basically involves waiting tables for seven days a week from April to October, what was there for them to do? Short of going away from the island for good and trying to earn a living at sea or in Athens, there was virtually no way a Greek boy could forge a career on a little Greek island like Poros. The result of this is that you'd see (and still do) lots of very bright and intelligent young men carrying trays in cafenions and tavernas all morning and every evening until after midnight for a very small wage. We got chatting to a couple of young men around a beer or two and asked them what they did in winter to avoid having to leave their island home. The two we spoke to were the lucky ones. They had managed to get construction jobs. Now don't have visions here of JCB's and power hammer drills or dumper trucks. Don't imagine cement mixers and compressors and all that. On Poros in the late 1970's (and most probably now to a large extent) construction was hard labour. It was largely manual and the only hi-tech equipment these boys were fortunate enough to handle was a shovel. The tractor was a donkey. So, they had managed to stay around the previous winter by working in "construction" and they showed us their shoulders to prove it.

Showed us their shoulders? Yes, they dropped their shirts off their shoulders to reveal calluses the size of golf balls on each side, the result of carrying bricks and concrete blocks and hods all day long from October to April. I asked:

"Will you be doing that again this coming winter?" (For the sake of brevity, you'll have to imagine that I'm having this conversation through my spouse as interpreter).

"No." Was the reply, "The job is finished and we don't have any idea what we're going to do at the end of this season." At this point the young man talking had to wipe his eyes because they had begun to fill up.

I counted my not inconsiderable blessings for living where I did and being able to enjoy this island in my leisure time.

So, as I said, I don't ever recall seeing a weedy Greek lad and the one I was currently having a face-off with was a good example of the other sort, i.e.: big and strong. Some would have called him strapping. I wondered what the headlines would read next day. "British Man pummelled to death at Greek island disco. Wife runs off with young Greek Romeo." The amazing thing is, this didn't happen. After what seemed like several years looking each other straight in the eyes among the flashing lights from the dance floor, but was in fact probably only about thirty seconds, a couple of his mates crowded between us and ushered him away and soon they were lost among the bubbling crowd. I don't remember how much longer we stayed that night. I don't remember hardly anything except how wonderful it felt to still have all my teeth and to be able to see out of both eyes. Life was sweet.

The odd thing is, I can't remember ever seeing a young Greek the worse for drink either before this incident or ever since. They simply don't have the "yob" or "lager lout" mentality that we seem to breed with such abundance in the UK. So this incident was all the more puzzling. It didn't remain a puzzle for long though. The next night we dined, just for a change, at Taverna Lucas.

We'd been sitting there a while and were well past our stuffed tomatoes and into the souvlaki, which we inevitably ate for main course. It wasn't simply lack of imagination on our part. At many tavernas like Lucas in those days everything, and I mean everything, was grilled and came with chips. You couldn't find all the traditional Greek vegetables like *Fassolia*, *Gigandes* and the like. *Fassolia* are like runner beans done in the oven or boiled and marinated in olive oil. *Gigandes* are what I would call giant baked beans. I suppose they're butter beans done in tomato (and various other stuff) sauce. In the 1970's you would never see lettuce in Greece. You would never see a banana either. It really is only since Greece has been in the E.U. that some of these exotic fruits and vegetables have arrived in the fruit markets on Greek islands.

So, anyway, we were sipping our retsinas when - who should walk into the taverna but none other than my adversary from the night before. He looked even taller and broader to me, since it was still almost daylight. Taverna Lucas is not very big. All the tables are quite cosily placed out front as they spill out onto the edge of the small road, the other side of which was the sea. This young man walked straight past our table and up to Yiorgo, who was having a quick cigarette on his doorstep before resuming his frantic routine of running in and out. They conversed for a few moments and cast furtive glances over to our table. For some odd reason I lost my appetite. I began to feel quite strange. I fully expected this bloke to demand that I step out into the road and take what was coming. The fact that HE had insulted MY wife would be of no account. He must be wanting satisfaction because I had thrown him (goodness only knows how) into some other tables in front of all his friends and damaged his pride accordingly. It would have to be an airlift to hospital. Probably a helicopter, because there were certainly very limited, if any, medical facilities on this island in 1978. I swallowed hard as both Yiorgo and the young man approached our table. Should I make a run for it? No chance, the tables were too close together. I'd have been totally tangled up in flying *Taramasalata* and *stifado*, not to mention tables, chairs, other customers and mangy Greek cats, before I made it as far as the open road. And anyway, it would have meant leaving Yvonne to his lecherous advances. The best I could do was draw myself up to my full height and hope to brazen it out. What chance I had of doing that, when at over six foot tall and under ten stone, I don't know.

Yiorgo spoke on the young man's behalf:

"Stavros want to hask, pleess can he dance one dance with your beautiful wife here tonight? Iss very sorry lass night. Was just home from navy and drank too much. Very dishonourable. Very bad behaviour. Donn know what come over him. Please to apologise and shake hanss."

I watched as Yvonne graciously accepted the offer of the dance. Yiorgo hurriedly rearranged several tables to make a postage stamp-sized dance area and Stavros and she danced one *Tsiftateli* to one of Yiorgo's prized old 45's in his old jukebox, which was duly rolled out for the occasion.

Now the *Tsiftateli* can be a very erotic dance. It's more Turkish than Greek and involves quite a lot of gyrating of the hips, with the male partner sidling up very close with one arm either side of his female counterpart. But Stavros kept a respectable distance the whole time, occasionally glancing over to me for approval at the way he was comporting himself. When the dance was done, he again shook my hand and summarily left the Taverna.

Yiorgo explained subsequently that his mates had all castigated him roundly for his behaviour at the Sirocco. They had insisted that he make amends in the fashion he had duly and obediently done.

I felt my admiration for this warm, sunny and wonderful country swelling by the second.

12 - Missing the Boat

In 1980 we again stayed on Poros, but this time a couple of friends who had not long been married had asked us to take them to Greece with us. They very much wanted to experience a Greek island and felt that to do so with someone with a bit of knowledge, not to mention language, would be a good idea. But they asked us anyway.

We stayed once again at Mrs. Mellou's. She welcomed us as she had done before and, after a drink and the usual exchange of pleasantries, which always included the inevitable enquiry you always get from a Greek – *"yiati then ekiteh pediah?"* (Why haven't you got children?) – we were shown to our rooms. Every Greek we met for the first fifteen years of our visiting the country as a married couple would enquire (usually within the first minute of conversation) why we had no children. We would explain that we didn't want them, but a Greek couldn't understand that at all. In Greek society to not want children means there must be an immediate need for commitment to a sanatorium for treatment. 'NOT WANT

CHILDREN?" That didn't compute. Everyone gets married to issue forth offspring, devote your next twenty years or so to serving them and launching them into the world, before passing your dotage quietly and dying, leaving your children presumably to do something similar. The idea of a couple being quite content with each other and gaining fulfilment through their pursuits and relationships was not simply daft to a Greek, they just couldn't get their heads round it at all. Once we got into our forties the question, mercifully, didn't come up as much. The Greeks we meet nowadays probably assume we've already launched our kids into their adult lives and are enjoying our new-found freedom to worry about them until we die. We don't bother to confuse them by raising the subject. But whenever in the past the question was raised and we would take great delight in explaining that we didn't particularly want children, there would often be an exchange of glances between those in our audience as if to mutually agree: "Sad. They obviously can't have children and are putting a brave face on it."

The rooms at Mrs Mellou's were very basic, although spotlessly clean, with the usual rough white walls and a little cheap picture forlornly hanging smack in the middle of one or two of them. In Mrs Mellou's you'd get a wardrobe that consisted of a metal frame with some plasticky material stretched over it, looking somewhat like a frame tent with a flat roof. It was fine. You don't take too many clothes because you tend to spend most of the time in shorts and a light top anyway. The rooms at the front were wonderful, not because of the rooms themselves, which barely had space for a double bed or two singles, the plasticky wardrobe, a small table, one chair and a bedside table, but on account of the view. You would enter the room from the landing, which simply had a communal fridge at the end where you came up from downstairs and a shower room/WC at the other. To the left were four doors and to the right three. The three to the right overlooked the street. If you leant over the railing on the balcony of any of these, you could easily shake hands with your neighbour across the street. This outlook itself still had charm. The balcony ran the length of the building both front and back, so you could walk right past the room next door. If you went out on to the rear balcony, look to the left and, in the narrow space between the walls on each side, you could see the "Harbour" area and Galatas across the water. Look to the right and you would see up the street a hundred yards to a small church in a paved area surrounded by more sugar-cube houses.

The only thing we didn't like about staying there was the fact that every morning that wretched church bell would chime almost loud enough to be felt through your bed springs, leave alone heard in the normal way – with your ears! Mind you, you wouldn't have felt it through your bedsprings. The beds were, and nowadays frequently are, simple wooden frames with the mattress resting on a load of laterally nailed (if you're lucky) laths. I have never yet slept in a Greek bed (in rented accommodation that is) that had springs or didn't creak so loudly that it woke you up each time you turned in the night. Plays havoc with your sex life when staying in small rooms with thin walls I can tell you.

If you were staying in one of the front rooms the view was simply superb. Open your full-length shutters, which served as both doors out onto the small balcony and as the only light source for the room, and a simply stunning vista gave your eyes a banquet of beauty and a panorama of essentially Greek landscape. In the morning the sun would be to your left, in the direction of Hydra and the beach at Aliki. Just above Aliki were the lemon groves, which were clearly visible on the hillside as an oasis of darker green among the paler green and ochre of the hills. Right opposite you could see all of Galatas, the village across the two hundred yards or so of Saronic Gulf which separates Poros from the mainland Pelopponese. Panning round further to the right, as Galatas thinned out, the hills became mountains, over which lay Epidavros, en route to Corinth, Argos and Nafplion. The mountains here were shaped very much like a nicely contoured woman asleep on her back with her legs up and knees bent. It was over the "Sleeping Lady" that you could watch the sun setting each night if you were there in September. Right below you were the terracotta and flat white roofs of Poros town. Here and there were gaps through which you'd catch a glimpse of the front. Always busy with traders, tavernas, mopeds and people going to and fro. Except, that is, during siesta time, when you would almost have had the town to yourself had you chosen to go out for a walk instead of sleeping. Sadly, owing to the development of tourism, this has changed a lot over recent years. "Supermarkets" are now open all afternoon, as are many of the bars and tavernas, which at one time would have all been closed from 2pm until 5.

It was during the early evening that I most preferred to sit out on this balcony. We would have risen from our siesta at around five, had a cup of tea and a biscuit and then we would sit and read our books. Inevitably my attention would wander from the book to the scene below. Only some twenty to thirty yards to the left of our balcony was the Mitropoleos. A steep thoroughfare, which led from Mrs Mellou's street straight down to the front, getting less steep and wider as it descended. At the top it was mainly residential, but with one small taverna. Further down it became a busy street of tourist shops selling leather goods and all those phallic Greek statues that everyone who's ever been to Greece has had a little giggle at. Right below us was someone's courtyard from where would rise the sound of a Greek family's voices and the wonderful smell of Greek home cooking. Also the smell of the charcoal smouldering at the taverna in Mitropoleos would greet my nostrils and tantalise them with promise of what I would be doing a little later. Then the sound of Greek music would gently begin as the locals set about their evening with gusto. In those days all the tavernas would play genuine Greek popular music. You'd never hear Nana Mouskouri. You'd hear Zambetas, or the new singers like Dalaras, who has since become one of Greece's biggest singing stars. Any of the tourist shops would sell you a Greek cassette (remember, CD's weren't around in the late 1970's – early 80's) or vinyl album. But these would contain all the stuff every British tourist would think was "Greek" music. But you'd never catch a Greek buying or listening to one of those.

So I would sit for an hour, or even two, whilst Yvonne went about staring into a mirror preparing herself for our nightly promenade along the front. We'd amble along looking into all the tavernas. Every one had its "get them in" waiter who would call out to us in as many languages as he could in the hope that we'd speak one of them. If you caught his eye, he would extend one arm towards their fine establishment and try as hard as he could to persuade you that theirs was the only taverna in the whole of Greece worth eating in. It was sheer delight. Because we knew that, once we sat down, the almost ecstasy-inducing smell of charcoal cooking was going to be converted into food on our plates. In those days we weren't vegetarians. Had we been it would have been very difficult to eat. It was all grilled meats and chips. Nowadays one can get a plethora of vegetable dishes in Greek tavernas, making it no problem for vegetarians to enjoy eating out. Not so in 1980. In those times the bill was still roughly calculated in ballpoint pen on the paper "tablecloth". Not so today. They've all got pads and little computer printouts now, even in the islands where tourism is much less developed. Isn't the European Union wonderful?

So we took Mark and Sarah, our two young friends, with us to Poros. They were enchanted as much as we were by Mrs. Mellou's place. And so we come to the reason this chapter is called, "Missing the Boat".

We decided to do a day-trip to Spetsai. This involved either catching the "Flying Dolphin" hydrofoil, or one of the ferries, around to Hydra, then Porto Heli (across from Hydra on the Pelopponese), after which they'd go on to Spetsai. We decided that, in order to get a good long day in, we'd go by "Flying Dolphin". These were the yellow and blue hydrofoils that somewhat resemble a squat aircraft fuselage with two pairs of truncated wings, the front pair of which serve as walkways to go aboard when they tie up alongside the quay. Once they are under way when clear of the jetty and harbour area, great steel "stilts" attached to the underside of these "Wings" become visible as their ailerons under the water rise up almost to the surface when the "Dolphin" gets up speed. I think they do about thirty-two knots. We purchased our tickets from the harbour-front ticket office and were told that the 8.30am hydrofoil was the one going to Spetsai. With great anticipation, we rose early and were down on the quay in good time.

We joined an unruly queue of mainly Greeks going inter-island in the course of their usual routines. There were one or two back-packers there too. How they can enjoy a holiday carrying half of their home country around on their backs in those rucksacks that seem to go from just behind their boots to several feet above their heads I'll never know. But you always see one or two getting on or off some vessel or other at a Greek port. Then there were the women looking for clients for their rooms. They would hover from very early on and set about accosting anyone who looked remotely like a potential island-hopper as they came off whatever vessel had just tied up.

Also in evidence were the chappies in the white uniforms who seemed to be in charge. Smart as ever. Trousers pressed to knife-blade sharpness.

Pretty soon after we got there we could see the Dolphin approaching from the west having just come through the gap at that end of the bay from Methana. Coming across the bay and viewed head-on they look like some giant preying insect skidding along the water's surface. We looked forward to an enjoyable voyage to Spetsai.

The Dolphin was soon alongside and began tying up. We all moved forward in the queue and were just about to step on to the "wing" to the waiting stewardess (that was another aircraft-like aspect of these wonderful Russian-built machines, aging examples of which still ply the Greek waters today), when one of the white-suited chappies, who was examining every ticket very diligently, told us we couldn't get on this one.

"But it's the 8.30 to Spetsai!" We wailed.

"No. *Ochi!* Ziss not to Spetses, this only Hydra! Next one in twenty minutes go to Spetsai!"

"But the ticket office chappie said definitely we were to get the 8.30!"

"*Ochi, Ochi.* Ziss go to Hydra only. No Spetses." No matter how emotional our protestations, this white-suited jobsworth was enjoying this little bit of drama. They wait all week for a chance like this and our man was going to milk it for all it was worth.

"But," I interjected (among the interjections of the other three), "It says SPETSAI" on the front!"

"NO SPETSES! HYDRA. YOU MUST WAIT!"

So we "must wait." We stood back in anger and watched the rest of the lucky passengers going aboard. It was rather amazing that no one else appeared to want to go the Spetsai that morning, so we finally decided that the sign on the front of this Flying Dolphin must indeed have been wrong and that the ticket office chappie was mistaken too. Why we didn't see this as an indication of what other disasters might come our way that day I don't know. Most others would have decided that "fate" was trying to tell them something. We don't believe in all that twaddle so we settled back into the small metal "bus shelter" thingie, that was woefully inadequate to shelter all the waiting passengers from the baking sun, to wait in the baking sun. Although it was now just after 8.35am and our Flying Dolphin was now casting off, it was already so hot I could have shut my eyes and thought I'd got into an oven pre-heated to do some roast potatoes.

We didn't have long to wait. In fact, before our Flying Dolphin had disappeared at the eastern end of the bay, the next one was fast approaching from the west. It was soon alongside and, as if by magic, what appeared to be thousands of other passengers emerged from absolutely nowhere to crowd around us and board the hydrofoil. They were also dead keen on beating us aboard. We soon discovered that they did this for two reasons. One, because they were regulars and knew that the "bus shelter thingie" wasn't big enough so they would wait in a cafenion or zaheroplasteon rather than fry; and two, because at this time of the morning a Flying Dolphin plying its way from island to island was the equivalent of the 8.35 from Dorking to the city and would be jam-packed. In other words, if you didn't barge your way on PDQ you would be standing all the way.

We finally got to the man in white, for the second time that morning. He waved us aboard. So we went aboard. Inside they resemble an aircraft even more, but with one exception. There was standing room only by the time we got into the cabin. Half way down the vessel there was a bit of an observation deck. A sort of standing area with a small roof to keep the sun off, but open along each side. Also, at the rear there was another standing area at which you could watch the vessel's not inconsiderable wake when it was in motion. This was where we chose to install ourselves. It was actually a lovely experience to look back from the tail of this intriguing machine as it charged across the surface of the blue ocean from one island to another. By straining your head around the side, you could get a glimpse of what was ahead too. After an enjoyable quarter of an hour or so, the ticket inspector arrived.

After what seemed like a year looking at our tickets, he looked up and said, in fairly good English for a change: "You on wrong Flying Dolphin. You miss Spetses sailing. Should haf been on one before, 8.30 from Poros. Thiss only go to Hydra. You have problem."

I saw red. Looking at Yvonne I could tell she could see the same colour. Mark & Sarah looked equally convinced they had crimson before their eyes. Who was going to shout at this guy first? The lot fell to me.

"We were not allowed to board that one. The ticket man

said we had to wait for this one. I told him that one had Spetsai on the front but it made no difference. It's not our fault. It's your problem, kyrios."

"Well. I see what can be done. But don't know what."

Anyway, the long and the short of it is: they decided that, after we had called in at Hydra, before going wherever this one was going, it would see the other one across the bay coming out from Porto Heli, a little port on the Pelopponese mainland, and heading around to Spetsai. The crews decided that both Dolphins would meet in the middle of the bay and we would be transferred. So it was that, after we had delighted at the beauty of Hydra harbour, we headed out into the deep water between Hydra and Porto Heli and the two vessels came alongside each other.

Terror strikes you at the most unexpected times doesn't it? The full realisation of what we were about to be expected to do dawned as quickly as the blackboard rubber finding its place when the schoolmaster realised you were shooting bits of chewing gum at your class mate instead of doing your logarithms. There was a swell of about a foot to eighteen inches, although it was a perfectly blue and beautifully hot day. So the two hydrofoils could not afford to get closer than about three feet from each other. The stewardesses gleefully opened the half-doors out on to the "wings" in preparation for the four of us to make our "leaps". I suddenly realised I was not a great "leaper" when it came to jumping from one hydrofoil to another in the middle of the Mediterranean Sea. Well, I hadn't been getting in as much practise as I ought in the run-up to this trip. It seemed the eminently sensible thing to say at this point was: "ladies first!" So I did. Strangely, Mark uttered those very same words at almost the exact same moment. I previously had no idea he was so chivalrous.

The stewardesses seemed to think this was quite the best way forward so they ushered both Yvonne and Sarah, their fairly large bags and all (after all, you don't go on a day-trip like this without your beach mat, towel, bottle of water, book, personal Hi-fi, suntan cream and all those other little accoutrements women, oh alright then – and men, must have about their person), out on to the "wing" of the craft. The "wings," by the way, were about six feet wide at the point where they protruded from the fuselage, tapering to about two feet six about eight feet out, where their edges were straight and parallel to the fuselage itself. The girls seemed slow about walking to the outside edge. Can't imagine why; then, one after the other, they took the leap and were - rather over-enthusiastically in my view - caught bodily by a male crewmember on the other craft. Now it was unavoidable. Mark and I had to do the same. Just at this point it seemed to me that the sea decided to remind us that we were about to jump from one hydrofoil to another. Mark went across and then I approached the deep abyss. Looking down it seemed about a mile to the surface of the deep turquoise waters. It was probably about eight feet. Was that a dorsal fin heading up the gap right between the two vessels? Why did I always feel dizzy when jumping hydrofoils in the middle of the ocean? Anyway, with an amazing boost of the imagination (I told myself I had a box of Milk Tray and a small calling card in my sweaty palm) I successfully made the leap.

It soon became apparent that this little event had turned us into minor celebrities on the vessel to which we had been transferred. People were looking at us the whole time until we disembarked at Spetsai with that unmistakable: "They must be famous or very rich to get treatment like that. To think, they have enough influence to get two Flying Dolphins to detour and rendezvous in mid-ocean, just so they can change boats. Wonder who they are." ...looks on their faces. I rather fancied that one girl thought I was the actor playing James Bond. My mum always said I looked a bit like Roger Moore when he was younger. Mind you, mums are very biased I suppose. Most of my other acquaintances say I could pass for Bruce Forsyth or Russ Abbot. I rather think I'll go with mum in this instance though. John Cleese has even entered the frame on occasion, do you think he was good-looking as a young man?

So we eventually berthed in the small harbour at Spetsai. It felt as if we'd had a full day's adventure already and it was only mid-morning. The harbour is quite pretty at Spetsai. In fact the island is quite pretty. The only thing it doesn't have is a mountain. I always get a bit disappointed at an island without a mountain or two. Spetsai was famous for having those horses and carriages which charged a small fortune to take the tourists who could afford it (or who couldn't afford it but wanted to do it so others would look at them and think they could afford it) along the front and back. There are other islands that have them nowadays, but at this time Spetsai was of particular note for their presence.

We hadn't been there more than a few minutes when a Greek voice wailed out about a particular beach that its owner was departing for directly in his taxi-boat. Looking around we saw one of those boats that induced Shirley Valentine to go on a round-the-island trip and eventually succumb to adultery. You know, the nice curvy ones with a cabin in the middle and painted in bright colours. Not the powerboat type things that zoom all over the place these days. You get into a dirty great big speedboat as often as not today and before you've begun to take in the view you're soaked in spray and getting off the other end at your selected beach before you can say: "These things aren't as cheap as the old caique-type taxi-boats used to be!" And the fact is they're not. Twenty years ago you'd enjoy the whole experience of getting a taxi-boat to the beach. They were all manned by wizened old Greeks with silver teeth and great big grins as they helped the scantily clad ladies on and off with a gently helping hand on the rear. They were all the old "rowing boat" shape and had ancient diesel engines amidships to power them sedately on their way. They all had flimsy tube-type frames covered in a bit of canvas to keep the sun off the passengers who would lazily drag one hand in the water, which was invariably almost up to the top of the side because the boats were also usually full to capacity at the end of another skin-shrivelling day. These old boats had character. They made each trip to the beach a really Greek adventure. You felt as though if you didn't get to the beach on one of these, you'd missed a greatly enjoyable part of the day. In fact, an almost essential element would be missing from the days when we didn't hop into and out of one of these. Very frequently they would have an old plastic pair of "Binatone" car speakers dangling from under the canvas too. Only one of which would ever be working. From this would emanate an almost impossibly tinny and rough-sounding tape of some old Greek singer with the ubiquitous bouzouki accompaniment.

These old caiques were always laughably cheap. Well, when you consider that all their owners were only minutes from becoming their wives' reason for wearing black for another ten years, what would they want to make a fortune at their time of life for? They almost used to do the job for the sheer enjoyment of it. If they weren't doing this, they'd already have died of inactivity, probably whilst sitting in the local cafenion over a backgammon game, Greek coffee still half-consumed. I sorely miss these beach-taxis I can tell you. Today there are still beach-taxis. But they're all run by Miami-Vice type younger Greeks sporting designer polo shirts and gold jewellery. They all bomb along at a frantic pace adding significantly to the noise levels too. They charge several pounds a trip and so, to use them every day for a fortnight adds a considerable sum to the amount of money one would need for a holiday. Sometimes I wish desperately that time could go backwards. Still, there we are. My wife calls me Victor by the way.

Where were we? Oh, yes, just arrived at Spetsai. So, we responded to this old Greek's call and, after enquiring about what time we could get back so as to get our ferry back to Poros, we boarded and enjoyed a leisurely chug down the coast to a very pleasant beach, backed by olive trees and with two rickety tavernas, one at each end.

After a glorious day of snorkelling, playing with crabs, examining flora in the undergrowth behind the beach, reading and sleeping, we obeyed the summons of the klaxon from the taxi-boat and trod wearily up the boardwalk and on to the boat for our return to the harbour. Now, we had decided that our return to Poros would be by more sedate means, meaning the inter-island ferry. It left Spetsai at 5pm and the taxi-boat man assured us that he would have us back in the harbour in plenty of time. It was a good twenty-minute chug up the coast back to the harbour, but we (rather foolishly) had absolute faith in our Captain. As we turned the last small headland and saw the harbour coming into view, we saw a large ferry steaming up and beginning to cast off. It sounded its horn a couple of times and we thought, "hope that's not our boat!"

It was.

As we tied up, and our little party of four frantically

enquired of our taxi-boat man whether we had missed the boat to Poros, we were assured that, no we had not missed it. That wasn't it. Or maybe it was, but if so, there would almost certainly be another before the evening was out, so no need to worry. We clambered off the boat whilst the ferry was just leaving the confines of the harbour and we all waved at those on the stern who were vigorously doing the same in the hope of a little response from our end. Little did they know that we were all unconsciously experiencing that sinking feeling that comes from knowing instinctively that things weren't exactly going to plan.

We very soon established that we had indeed missed the boat, thanks to our very laid-back beach taxi man who, by now, was nowhere to be found and anyway, what would we do about it had we found him? We had, though, ascertained that the next boat was due in about 9pm and would tie up for the night, before making the return trip at 7.00am next morning. We soon began to cheer up with the thought that we would no doubt be able to get aboard and sleep the night on the deck under the stars to be ready for the early sailing in the morning.

What fools we were.

13 - Move Along Now

So we'd missed the boat from Spetsai back to Poros. Things could be worse. We were, after all, on a little Greek island with cash in our pockets and a harbour full of tavernas and bars to explore. Having cheerfully seen the next morning's Poros sailing tie up for the night against the Spetsai harbour wall, we set about finding a taverna in which to spend the best part of the evening. After a last minute dip just a little way along from the harbour area as the sun was going down, we repaired to the taverna which was perched just above the little beach from which we'd swum. The small beach was backed by a small road, the other side of which was lined with mainly small houses painted in various pastel colours and nestled in among these was this taverna. All the tables were on the beach side of the road on a rickety wooden platform built precariously on wooden stilts over the beach. The water literally lapped about a metre below our feet. The waiters crossed the road with all manner of plates and drinks lined up their arms and frequently dodged mopeds, those little three-wheeled trucks and the regularly passing horses and carriages.

The meal was washed down with liberal quantities of retsina. If you've never had retsina (it's virtually the national table wine of Greece) you've missed a truly memorable experience. The first time I tried it I thought they'd brought me petrol by mistake. Not having ever tasted petrol I imagined that this was what it would taste like. It looks very suspiciously like urine too. What's worse, twenty years ago you'd always have it plonked on your table in these little red aluminium half-litre jugs with straight sides and a little curved aluminium handle welded on near the top. They didn't have spouts for pouring, just a bent-over rim all the way round. Go into any Greek supermarket or hardware store today and you'll still see these jugs on sale. Virtually everyone on the Greek islands made their own retsina in those days. What makes it unique is that it contains resin as well as the juice from the grapes.

To be fair, once I had acquired a taste for it (largely because I thought you weren't "like the Greeks" unless you drank retsina) I ordered it regularly for many years, before I finally reached the state of maturity where I realised that, if you don't like the stuff, what's the point of drinking it just to try and look like you were a true Greek-ophile? Yet, for many years I drank it with my meals from those little aluminium jugs and thought I looked cool at the taverna table. The fact that it was the cheapest drink you could have with your meal, with the exception (just) of bottled water, I swear had nothing to do with it!

Yvonne's cousin Christina and her husband Taki (the Greek version of Del-boy from "Only Fools and Horses" only slightly more upmarket!), who lived in Athens, used to make their own retsina at Kalamos, where they had a summer villa half a mile up the hillside from a small shingly beach. Once when we were staying at the villa, after a particularly enjoyable and well-washed-down evening meal on the veranda, with a stunning view of the Kalamos coastline and of the large island of Evia across the water, the grape-gathering project was embarked upon. It was September and we were spending a week at the villa because it was still too hot in Athens. The workmen were fixing new tongue-and-groove pine to the ceiling of the veranda. At least, that's what I was led to understand, although I don't actually recall seeing them do any work of any sort whenever I was around the villa. About mid-evening, at the climax of a day which had seen cousin Christina spend every waking hour in the kitchen, which, come to think of it, was what she did most every day, we were all called to the veranda for the evening meal. Around the table were myself, Yvonne, her mum Lela and husband Dave, Auntie Vassau and uncle Theodoraki (their villa was right opposite), Cousin Christina and husband Taki, Christina and Taki's teenage daughter Efi, then there was auntie Efi too and three or four of these so-called workmen who were reputed to be doing some carpentry on the place. It was quite a gathering.

The last few plastic bottles of Taki's previous brew of retsina had been consumed, along with taramasalata, Greek salad by the cauldron-full, *dolmades*, octopus, *kalamaraki* (squid), stuffed tomatoes and peppers, *souvlaki*, various vegetable concoctions whose names escape me now, copious quantities of that gorgeous Greek bread with the sesame seeds on top and finishing up with plate-loads of *karpouzi* (water melon) and *pepponi* (sugar or honeydew melon). The table was evidently a candidate for the world "how many bottles of beer can you get on to an already overcrowded table without it collapsing?" contest. We had also downed a few bottles of shop-bought retsina and that other wine of international note (not!) at the time - Demestica. The name's resemblance to a famous product in Britain, which you use to cleanse your drains, is not a coincidence I'm sure!

So, as darkness gathered and the last hint of redness was fading in the sky to the west, and the women were all in the kitchen clearing up, the men sat out on the veranda enjoying the sensation of getting consumed by mosquitoes and knocking back Metaxa brandy. The workmen being still very much in evidence made me wonder two things. First: whatever they were getting paid was only half of what it was costing Taki to employ them, when one considered how much food and drink they had consumed and, second: Didn't they have any homes to go to?

It was during this sublime time that the need for grapes for this year's retsina came up in the conversation. Taki had two enormous barrels in which he kept his home-made retsina. These were in the basement area below the villa, in the room behind the one in which Yvonne and I were sleeping. They clearly gave evidence of the quantity of grapes that would be needed to fill the two of them with wine. Yet Taki didn't have a vineyard.

"Neh. Neh! I haf vineyard, ...next-door!" He announced with a devilish grin for the benefit of those present who hadn't been involved in the project the previous year.

Soon it became apparent to me that the reason why everyone had now begun to don stout shoes and amass plastic bags, plus a pair of secateurs or scissors each, was that they were going "over the fence" to the vineyard at the top of the hill to gather this year's raw material for Taki's retsina. I decided, with a proud air of cowardice that I didn't want to be flying home early with my passport stamped "undesirable alien" and so I was excused with some disdain and the other men were soon lost on the gloom of the night.

For days after that Taki was busy making his new batch of retsina.

So, our evening meal in Spetsai was over and we wandered along to the harbour-front cafe to sip a beer and watch the bobbing boats. It is these moments during a Greek evening which are simply magic. The air is warm enough for one not to require anything more than a light shirt or T-shirt. The stars are vividly contrasted against an ink-black sky, in which the Milky Way is clearly visible, cutting its way from horizon to horizon and often inducing me to look up and become so engrossed that my head nearly falls off as I get lost in the sheer magnificence of it all. These are the times when, if you keep looking up for just a little while, you're almost certain to see shooting stars. I often find that, once my spine problem "clicks" in - I see plenty!!

We sat around a lazy table with a liberal sprinkling of Metaxa, iced coffee, beers a couple of little plates of peanuts and put all the world's problems right. It's always amazing how a little bit of alcohol and a relaxing time with friends can give one a wisdom unsurpassed by any of the great thinkers that ever lived isn't it? You begin to see all the political mistakes that the current politicians are making and, were you to get elected there and then, you could solve the world's economic problems at a stroke and set about getting all the world's starving fed to boot. Shame we don't get on the blower to the U.N. at these times, but then, why not have another beer first and get chatting to the waiter as business begins to slow and he finds the time to sit at the table and have a drink with you. Before you know it, the opportunity has passed and you've entered "too silly" time. You know, when everything becomes so funny that you all fall about crying with laughter and quite unable to control yourselves. Any poor soul that happens to walk within a few yards of the cafe at this time is dead certain to be described in derogatory terms and become a complete buffoon in the eyes of all those around the table. Whether it's the style of dress, hairdo, bodily shape, height or the fact that they've got socks on with those awful leather sandals that only the British seem to wear on holiday, it doesn't matter. They're handy targets and we shoot away with gleeful abandon. I know, I'm usually the one walking by.

So, at some time that must have been around eleven p.m., we decided to get up and walk the few yards out along the crumbling concrete quay to the door in the side of the ferry and ask the crew as politely and pathetically as we could if it would be alright for us to board and sleep upstairs on deck. We got up and bade farewell to the two or three other Brits we'd asked to join us and had shared the past hour or two with and confidently approached the ship.

The door in the ship's side was right up to the quay and so level with it that there was no need for a walkway. You could simply step over the metal rim of the open door and you were aboard. Before we attempted this little move though, we noticed that in the centre of the lounge, into which the door gave access, the crew were sat lazily round a black and white TV watching some Greek-subtitled episode of Rawhide or something. They had a few beers on the table, which we interpreted as the signal that they'd be feeling mellow and so we pushed Yvonne to the front and gently, but firmly, encouraged her to attract their attention and make our most-reasonable request.

A bit of unintelligible banter was exchanged and Yvonne didn't look too happy. Without understanding a word, it was fairly evident that the Captain (or whoever the one in charge actually was. We thought it was the Captain so that'll do) had said rather dismissively:

"Go away. We're off duty and it's not our problem that you were dull enough to get stranded. No one boards this boat until a quarter of an hour before we sail tomorrow morning, so goodnight."

We were shell-shocked. These guys were Greeks. Greeks were supposed to be lovely friendly people. They're always obliging. Not. These guys were so unobliging that they completely ignored all further attempts to communicate with them. Even during the brief conversation that Yvonne had had with them, they had never once turned their heads toward the portal at which we forlornly stood. We were so stunned that we decided that it was probably because they were too engrossed in the programme to be bothered and, if we hung around long enough, the programme would end and they'd become normal jovial Greeks again and invite us in to share a few beers and then usher us up on deck with great kindness and cordiality.

We were wrong again. In a vain attempt to elicit some sympathy, all four of us curled up on the concrete to pretend to go to sleep right outside the boat's portal, so that, should they deem to turn their heads, they would spot us and be overcome with pity and mercy. No such luck. After some twenty minutes on the hard concrete with not so much as a "You'll catch your death! Don't lay down there!" in Greek from within the boat's lounge, it began to dawn on us that it was now getting on for midnight and we had nowhere to retire to.

It was at about this time (i.e. the 1979-81 period) that the Greek government began a major clampdown on back-packer types who would arrive in Greece for a holiday without pre-booked accommodation. Camping on Greek beaches had become a major problem and was causing a build-up of rubbish and hippie-type bodies everywhere one went. The image of Greece as a pleasant holiday venue for people who liked peace and quiet was getting tarnished because it was not uncommon to search out a remote beach only to find a clutch of shabby tents already there and a fair bit of debris surrounding them. Hygiene was obviously a problem in these conditions too. All of this meant that, if you were still sat in the cafenion when it finally closed, which could be as late a 1.00am, you needed to walk off purposefully in the direction of your accommodation to avoid the *Astinomia* (Police) arresting you.

We rather dejectedly made our way back to the bar where our former company still sat, finishing their drinks. By now it had also begun to get cold and we were all too aware that we had nothing appropriate to put on to cover our Goosebumps. In fact, the girls were beginning to shake uncontrollably. What had seemed a great adventure a few hours earlier was turning into a potential disaster. The thought of Greek prison food wasn't all that encouraging. That was always assuming there'd be food! Perhaps there wasn't a gaol in the island, only an old deep dark dungeon! I cursed my vivid imagination. The guys at the cafenion asked us where we were staying, in response to which we all began at once to pour out our woeful experience, hoping to get some sympathy. This was the only bar still open. The rest of the harbour was now looking decidedly settled for the night, with just the few street lamps burning in the darkness. To top it all, a Greek police car approached and the two guys in it got out and began a chat with the bar owner, casting furtive and almost hopeful glances in our direction with regularity. They were sure they had a major transgression on their hands. Greek island policemen have the easiest job in the world. There's virtually no crime, so these two obviously had visions of almost unbearable pleasure at the anticipated apprehension of these four villains who had managed to get past all the mainland police and those on several other islands in the hope of dossing somewhere here on Spetsai, but these guys were going to be the ones to apprehend these heinous foreign individuals.

One of the Brits we'd been talking to suddenly hatched an idea. "Where I'm staying is just a simple block of rooms," he began, "and I'm pretty sure that the one below me is empty this week. I've had a gander inside out of curiosity to see how it compared to mine. There's no bed linen and the key is in the door because no one's staying in it. Why don't you come back with us and you can sleep there. You'll be gone so early in the morning no one will be any the wiser." This sounded wonderful in the first instant. Then Mark said:

"But how far from the harbour is it? I don't want to sound ungrateful, but if it's miles how will we get back in time for our boat. Not only that, but even if it's in the town, I'm not convinced we'll be able to get ourselves up in time." The ferry was leaving at 7.00am, which meant we'd have to rouse ourselves somehow by 6.30 to have a realistic chance of catching it.

"It's only ten minutes walk back from the harbour." Replied our willing benefactor. "It's up to you, but we're going back now so make up your minds."

Circumstances had already done that for us. We put several old Greek streets between us and the Policemen with some relief, until, after the umpteenth twisty turny little corner, we began to wonder whether we were either being led into an ambush, or even supposing these people to be genuine, whether we'd ever find our way back to the harbour next morning. But, just as we were all thinking these things, although no one voiced any concern for fear the others may not yet have thought it, we entered a wrought iron gate into a small courtyard overhung with an enormous vine and there we were, staring into a room with twin single beds. Had it been the honeymoon suite at the Hilton it wouldn't have looked any lovelier. Think of the alternative! Saved by a whisker from having our necks felt (our T-shirts didn't have collars, remember!) by a couple of surly Greek policemen who were evidently anticipating their first bit of excitement for years.

We had to sleep two to each single bed. The problem now was going to be how to get up in time for the boat back.

"I've got it." I said, feeling almost dizzy with such a brainwave, "One of us can stay awake for half an hour and then rouse the next when he or she can keep watch and so on until 6.30am!" We all decided that, in the absence of an alarm clock, that was the only workable solution.

Thank heaven for Greek cockerels. Within minutes we were all sound asleep two-to-a-single bed. A cock crowing at the crack of dawn woke us all at the same time. Blind panic forced me to look at my watch and it told me it was 6.45am. Fifteen minutes to sailing! Everyone was running everywhere and queuing up for the lone loo, and all trying not to make a sound. Fortunately we hadn't undressed the previous night or it would have been a nightmare trying to put things on as well. Within minutes we were all flying down through the narrow streets as the sun was pushing its way over the distant horizon for another attempt at roasting us all alive. We tore along the quay and jumped aboard. How we found the harbour was sheer luck and a vague idea that if you kept going downhill you had to turn up in the right spot. We all clambered up onto the top deck, sat down for a few minutes, looked around and saw absolutely no one, not a soul, up there, came to the realisation that, even in Greece in summer, at 7.00am at sea it was Eskimo weather if all you had on was shorts and T-shirt, and as one all tore back down the stairs and into the ship's lounge, the very one in which the crew had been sat the previous night watching their black and white TV.

I decided that, whilst in general Greeks were indeed lovely people, Greek sailors must have had some other gene source. Even to this day I find the majority of Greek ferry crews to be quite unlike all their compatriots. You rarely see a smile and constantly expect them to whip out a cutlass and have your throat cut within milliseconds.

We made it back to Poros, though. They must have had their fill of pillaging and raping for that week. Funny how it never occurred to us that there may have been some issues with insurance had the crew allowed us to spend the night on board.

14 - A Bit of Sport

We have visited Spetsai a number of times. I remember the first occasion particularly. It was a brilliant blue and scorching day in early September. Walking around the sea front from the harbour you pass along a very pleasant, if somewhat sweltering, mettled road, with rocks and the sea immediately to your left just below a very low concrete parapet, and high walls topped with bougainvillaea to your right. The sea and sky are always so vividly blue in Greece in summer. It's almost impossible to take a bad photograph in such conditions. The front at Spetsai showed the country's assets in this department to very good effect.

We had only walked a few hundred yards around from the main harbour when we decided we needed to eat, bathe and rest, although not necessarily in that order. We came across a small concrete slipway that sloped gently into the blue sea and around it a small area of pebbles. It was just beside the "road." I put "road" in parentheses because it was more of a pedestrian promenade, although the occasional small vehicle would pass along it. There were no other people either sitting or laying in this place, but it looked ideal to us. We always wore our cozzies under our T-shirts and shorts for any eventuality, so within seconds our towels were stretched out and laid on the slipway, our bags duly dropped onto them along with our clothes and we were jumping into the cooling waters. After a sufficient time to reduce our body temperatures from "boil-dry-in-minutes" level to "well, a bit warm, but you'll survive" level, we came up from the sea and flopped out on our towels. At the time I had a very nice Accurist watch with a stainless steel case and strap, which I wore everywhere, except in the sea. It wasn't waterproof. I have always had this one concession to my normal stressful life when on holiday for any length of time. I find it impossible not to wear a watch. Nowadays I'm sensible enough to wear a cheap plastic waterproof one all the time when I'm in a "very likely to want to cool off by getting pretty wet" situation, but in those days I only had the one watch, so I would take it off and position it very carefully near the "head" position on my towel, beach mat or whatever I would be lying on. It's not that I don't de-stress you understand. It's just that, well, I always like to know what time it is. I don't even spend much time working out what would be going on back home at whatever time I looked at my watch. I simply like to know what time it is. You have a problem with that?

Now Yvonne is quite different. She never wears a watch the whole time we're away. She'll say, "I'm governed by the clock the whole time in my day-to-day existence. So when I'm away I'm just going to do what I want and do it when I want and pay no regard to what time it is. I'll get up naturally and go to sleep when I'm tired. That's the way we were supposed to live after all." Fine - in principle. But it's odd the way she regularly asks me what time it is. The ironic thing is, she doesn't really need to bother. She doesn't just ask me, "What time is it?" Rather, she'll say: "Is it ten past one?" In response to which I'll look at my watch and find she's invariably within five minutes either way of the correct time. There we are. Some people have an inbuilt time clock that's running on quartz crystal I suppose. Yvonne is one of them.

So we settled down on our nice little concrete slipway, inches from the lapping edge of the blue Mediterranean. A gorgeous view across the waters showed the mainland Pelopponese several miles to our North, shimmering in the haze of the early afternoon sun. Before long a few more tourists began to see us and, recognising the ideal location of the place for a quick hour or two sunbathing, whilst within easy reach of the harbour for some refreshment in the shape of an ice-cool beer, they joined us in stretching out their beach mats and towels. Eventually our little area was as full as it could comfortably be with maybe ten or twelve sun-worshippers. Some of the girls had removed their bikini tops as they lay on their fronts browning their backs all over, minus strap-marks. Yvonne and I got out our scrumptious bread rolls, fresh from the little bakery just down from Mrs Mellou's that morning as we walked down to catch the ferry, along with our "beef" tomatoes, which we would eat just as one would eat an apple. A bite of the delicious sesame seed-topped bread, then a bite from the juicy tomato which rather resembled a grapefruit in size rather than the weedy little tommies we get in the UK. That was the way we would eat lunch. Then a swig from our bottle of water. We were very comfortable. Soon we found ourselves waving at the passengers on the deck of a large white ferry as it glided gracefully past just a few hundred yards offshore on its way round the corner into the harbour. The boat was close enough to enable us to make out their expressions clearly as those on deck waved at anyone whose attention they could catch on-shore.

It hadn't occurred to us to wonder why there had been no one already splayed out on our convenient little place of refuge. We only had about six feet between the parapet of the road above, just three feet or so high, and the sea below, into which the little slipway along with its small pebbly area dissolved. To have found such a convenient place to pitch oneself for a little bit of sunbathing and to rest one's weary legs from all the walking in the heat of the day, without there already being enough bodies there to make finding a place a bit like using up your last piece at scrabble, was totally out of the ordinary. But that hadn't occurred to us. Of course, once we were settled, others were bound to think, "What a bit of luck! There's a nice little place to spend a few minutes enhancing the tan."

The ferry had disappeared around the small headland covered in bits of Spetsai town and into the harbour. In fact probably about ten minutes had gone by when it happened. Yvonne and I had finished our lunch and begun to doze on our towels. All was right with the world. We were in Greece, it was hot, and we were well fed and watered.

Then we were very wet.

Anyone living by the sea or any seafarer knows that boats have a habit of making waves, they leave wakes. Suddenly it became very evident why this little area was deserted when we had arrived and claimed it rather foolishly for ourselves, to be followed by a bunch of others who must have thought we knew what we were doing! A two foot high wave swept over us all without prior warning, causing every man-jack (and woman-jack) of us to leap upright in milliseconds, whilst all our bags, towels, personal stereos, clothes and my Accurist watch were engulfed in the Mediterranean sea! Within ten seconds there was this little group of ten or twelve virtually naked people all standing up on the road on the edge of Spetsai town and all dripping wet. The girls who'd undone their tops took a couple of seconds to gather their wits before jumping back down to our sodden sundeck and reclaiming their modesty. Even back then (circa 1978-80) women were usually topless on beaches. But, remember, this was not a beach. There was a road immediately above our heads on which Greeks were "to-ing and fro-ing" prior to their siesta time on foot, mopeds, donkeys and in the odd small car or three-wheeled truck.

It was now all too apparent why not only had the area been devoid of other sunbathers, but also why the passing Greeks had been grinning at us in that funny way. Every time a ferry passed close by on its way into the harbour, the wake would hit this bit of coast about ten minutes later.

The Greeks of Spetsai enjoyed their little bit of sport.

15 - Naturally

Askeli was our favourite beach on Poros back in the period 1978-80. We've never particularly liked sand when it comes to relaxing near the sea and Askeli was a gently sloping strand of pebbles, about a few hundred yards long and probably twenty yards from road to water's edge at its widest. It was the only beach on Poros, as far as I can remember, that one had to pay a few drachmas to get onto. There were a couple of sandy beaches elsewhere on the island and one popular one called Aliki on the mainland, just across the narrow straight in front of Poros town and slightly further south from Galatas village. To get to most of these one would stroll down to the busy front at Poros town and listen to the old men standing on the quayside, one hand steadying the makeshift metal, tarpaulin covered frame that sprang up from their caiques, the other cupped to their mouths as they called out the name of whichever beach they were going.

All you had to do was stand there for a few moments to make your choice.

"Aliki Beats!!!" "Ella Galatas!!" "Yia Monastiri!!!" Were among the spindly, yet powerful cries one would hear

emanating from the row of wizened old bodies each stationed
by their particular floating pride and joy. I didn't spell "Beach"
wrongly, by the way. That's the way an old Greek would
pronounce it ...*Beats!!*

More often than not, If we were going to Askeli, we would
walk. It would take about twenty minutes and was a pleasant
route round the north west end of Poros town front, slightly
ascending for a few feet as one would pass the Naval Academy
full of young conscripts who would take great delight in calling
every foreigner who passed nearby a *"Malakas!"* which is not
very nice. Most, of course, would smile and nod back, thinking
that these lads were very nice, but not realising that what they
had just been called rhymes with "banker" in English. Then
we'd cross the narrow isthmus connecting the smaller
inhabited part of the island with the larger, more hilly, sparsely
populated part. Shortly after crossing the isthmus the road
would fork and if you were to go to the left it would wind along
the coast to one or two tourist settlements which included what
was then the only hotel on the island, plus quite a number of
small self-catering apartment blocks. The hotel had a small
sandy beach across the road immediately in front of it. The
sand had been brought there by the truckload to encourage
holidaymakers to come and stay at the hotel. It served to ensure
that we always passed quickly by whenever we went along that
road; which was well worth going along because, after finally
becoming a dust track, it would end up a kilometre or so later
at what was called Russian Bay, a beautiful deserted bay with a
small damp arc of sandy beach, lapped by almost mirror
smooth water and backed by an old Russian military fort. The
fort now lay in ruins and was covered in all sorts of interesting
flora and fauna and one could scramble over the crumbling
walls in nothing but a pair of swimming trunks and jellies for

hours, trying to catch lizards, or studying butterflies, spiders and strange flowering plants.

Yvonne, Mark, Sarah and I spent an idyllic afternoon there once, just foraging around in nothing but our cozzies, catching crabs and putting them into our very own "crab-arium", a crude circle of rocks and pebbles we had constructed especially so we could study the little blighters to our hearts' content. I can recall vividly the stillness and warmth of the place. Out across the water, probably a mile or so from the shore, there was a little islet with a little white church on it. It seems as though all little islets off Greek islands have little white churches on them. It gives the locals an excuse for a special day some time during their year when the papas (local priest) can rally everyone round and be king for a day as they all make a little pilgrimage out to the little white church and usually carry some icon or other around in the process. Although these occasions look very pretty, and on all the holiday shows on the telly the correspondent usually gets involved and raves about how quaint it all is, I'm afraid I am very cynical about it all. Religion in Greece has been a great burden on the people for centuries (as with many other parts of the world) and I cannot say I have any love for either the Church or its priests. Still, when all said and done, at least the little white churches look very nice.

My very good friend Rob Kay, who lived on the Algarve for many years (as the perils of the British climate finally became too much for him and his lovely wife Shirley a few years back), put me on to jellies. The first time I proudly wore mine on a visit to my sister-in-law's house near Bristol I drew some very disapproving comments from her daughters, my wife's nieces. The eldest was about twelve at the time and, as we sat out on their lawn in the warm evening sunshine, she said, "Those shoes are seriously sad, uncle John!" I distinctly remember replying: "You'll *all* be wearing these tomorrow!" Rather more by luck than judgement I was proved right. Not long after that the jellies with a bit of a heel and loads of glitter set into the coloured plastic became the flavour of the month (or three) among kids just entering their teenage years. Mind you, mine were just flat and see-through. No colour at all. But they really are the very best thing to wear when your chosen venue for entering the sea in Greece is a rocky coast or shingle beach where the urchins have formed a sizeable colony. I enjoy snorkelling a great deal and always wear my jellies when indulging. Why not flippers you ask? Well you might. The truth is, I never really acquired the knack of using them. My stepfather-in-law Dave taught me to snorkel back in 1977 on Aliki beach. I have always been grateful. The first time I ever got the hang of it he showed me an octopus (one of which we chased along the sea bed just a few yards off the shore), starfish, all kinds of things living on the sea-bottom and loads of fish and how to find them. Once I had got used to the mask and snorkel, he handed me a pair of flippers and I cack-handedly got them on. It took me some time to get into the water, but once in I confidently launched myself forward and began vigorously flapping my legs in the full expectation that I would be propelled along, jet-like, at breathtaking speed. I certainly moved allright – but not in a forward direction. I must be the only person on the planet for whom donning a pair of flippers means I can swim feetwards! However I hard I tried I could only go in the opposite direction to forwards. Hence – the jellies. I am nowadays a fairly strong swimmer, so I admitted defeat when it comes to flippers and resorted to the trusty jellies.

Walking to Askeli meant not taking the left-hand fork once one had passed the isthmus. We went to the right. The narrow road twisted and turned, the sea never being all that far from one's right hand side. We'd pass houses and holiday flats and, now and again a few yards of undergrowth and olive trees until, after a couple of bends and gentle ups and downs, the road levelled out right behind Askeli beach. The walk was always made more fascinating by the din made by the cicadas. I have loved that sound ever since I first heard it for myself instead of on some TV show. It is so synonymous with baking sunshine, melting road-surfaces and sleepy tavernas and sounds like a quintet of gentleman's barbers all sharpening their razors simultaneously.

A few small trees lined the back of the beach and also gave the road the benefit of some of their shade. The back of the beach was cordoned off with a chain-link fence, so you would have to enter through the small gate at one end. We'd pay our few drachmas and unroll our trusty beach mats for a few hours relaxation. There was a small refreshment kiosk near the entrance to the beach where you could pick up a *portokalatha* (orangeade), *pagoto* (ice cream) or beer. What more could one ask? There were never more than a couple of dozen bodies on Askeli at any one time and, mercifully, no plastic sunloungers and parasols, the curse of every modern beach. Very often, either before noon or after 4.30pm these bodies would include a number of Greeks too. Only mad dogs and Englishmen... well, you know the saying, and it's all too true.

I loved Askeli because it was composed of beautifully formed pebbles which you could arrange by wiggling yourself on your beachmat into a really comfy "sunlounger" with very little effort. There was none of that awful sand to get into everything. And we all know that sand does get into everything, including your lunch! Not to mention your personal hi-fi and its earphones. Then there's your camera or binoculars. Sand is curtains for any expensive appliance so I hate the stuff. The pebbles do have a habit of shortening the life of your beachmat it's true, but then how much does a beachmat cost?

It was during one of our many chilling-out sessions on Askeli when I got into J.J. Cale. I'd never heard any of his albums. My personal hi fi would have Van Morrison, Dire Straits, Chris Rea or a bit of Led Zeppelin on. John Martyn is a must. But one day when I was in a pleasant state of torpor, eyes half open under my baseball cap, shades almost off the end of my nose, just contemplating whether to make the effort to get up and go in the sea again, some music wafted over from the small kiosk. The young lad who was manning the kiosk had a beaten up old "ghetto-blaster" on a shelf behind him and, now and again, he would play a tape. This particular year, when Yvonne and I were there without company and went to Askeli more often than anywhere else, the tape was always the same. You never heard anything else.

"...They call me the breeze, ...I keep rolling down the road..." were the first words I made out. My first reaction was to remark to Yvonne that it was a pain not to be hearing Greek music. I could get this stuff at home! But, after a few more tracks I began to think, "No we can't. We can't get this at home. I've never heard this on my radio in the UK. Who is it?" I decided I needed a beer. I found the drachmas in amongst our considerable amount of "stuff" and, with great difficulty and some vertigo, got to my feet to shuffle up to the little kiosk. Ordering a Fix Hellas (beer) for me and an iced lolly for Yvonne I cast my eyes about in the search for the cassette cover. No luck. It's at times like these when I yearn to be fluent in Greek. Nowadays I could manage such an enquiry with a fair chance of understanding the reply. In the late 70's I had no chance. You know the sort of panic that comes over you. Firstly you dread another customer coming over whilst you're summoning up the courage to attempt communication. Secondly you become very conscious that your cheeks are turning red enough for it to show clearly thru your sunburn. That's like, red on red! That's really red.

My shopping for anything in those days was usually by pointing at what I wanted and handing over sufficient sized notes to cover the expense and hoping they'd give me the right change, which I'd stick back in my little money pouch with an air of "I'm cool. I know precisely what's going on. I'm in control." Of course, I was anything but.

I visited the kiosk on several occasions before, sheer embarrassment at Yvonne asking, "Well, who is it?" forced me to make the enquiry, after a number of excuses like, "He doesn't know. It's someone else's tape," or, "He can't remember, he hasn't got the sleeve," had begun to "not wash" with her.

"*Afti musiki. Kali inneh. Pios inneh?*" I muttered. I'd rehearsed this bit for ages. Yvonne had given me beach Greek lessons on how to ask in the simplest way: "This music, it's good. Who is it?"

"It's J.J. Cale. It's his first album, it's called 'Naturally,' cool innit?" Came the response in virtually Queen's English. This happens to me all the time. I verbally fumble my way through a well-rehearsed Greek expression or two, after hours of building up my confidence and struggling to suppress the blind panic that I know I'll experience when the Greek object of my enquiry replies, only to discover that he's spent two summers in Australia or something and speaks better English than me. The trouble is, I've got this fear of being a tourist. I suppose it comes from having a wife with Greek blood in her. I strive desperately to appear to be cool and "like the locals" so as not to be despised as a mere tourist, then I forget that one look in a mirror would dispel any aspirations I may have. I look Arian and that's all there is to it. No matter how tanned I become, I'm too tall and my hair is too fair and thin to ever enable me to pass as anything other than a visitor. And I hate it! The only good thing about this slight paranoia is that it has impelled me over the years to learn some Greek. The fact that I have learned it from my wife's family and Greeks I've met in Greece has enabled me to learn spoken Greek instead of textbook Greek too. I'm grateful for that. Mind you, it didn't help when I tried to read things. I mastered an understanding of the Greek alphabet a long time ago and can read virtually anything now. But for years I would read words or phrases I could pronounce like a local without recognising them on the printed page!

Anyway, with a palpable wave of relief I thanked the young man for the information and went back to my beach mat. J.J. Cale. Naturally. Must get it when I get home.

In recent years I have flipped through holiday brochures and looked at pictures of Poros. We haven't been back since 1982, when we were fairly horrified at the subtle changes under way even then, particularly the appearance just off the beautiful seafront in some of the backstreets of discos and bars. There was even a snooker hall with a British name. The architectural beauty I suppose will always remain, but the incursion of facilities to satisfy the younger foreign tourist dismays us wherever we go. The culture of drink, dance and sex later is so ubiquitous today. It has already swallowed up the character of so many European "resorts." What really brought on a wave of dismay was the last photograph I saw of Askeli beach. When we used to go there, it was an oasis of calm, where one could spend a few hours. Alright, so the Kiosk did exude J.J. Cale now and again, but even that was strangely OK. It was not very loud and it was a Greek lad playing it who had really no idea who J.J. Cale was. He'd simply been given this tape by someone he'd met when abroad and so he played it and played it because it made his peers look up to him as someone who'd been places. So it added a certain authenticity to the place. There was never a problem finding a spot to crash out on Askeli. It was never crowded. Twenty five years ago beaches on Poros never were. The sea was gorgeously roomy when you went for a dip. No bodies splashing all around you. Back then very few British knew it was there.

But, sadly, things change. Life goes on ...naturally. They have covered Askeli in sand.

16 - Black Jake

I remember one time in Poros, when we were staying at a room to the rear of Mrs. Mellou's, being awakened at some unearthly hour on more than one occasion by the sound of a bell. This was not the church bell along the way, it was rather the sort of bell you would associate with the neck of a cow or some other bovine beast and certainly not what you would expect to hear right in the middle of the maze of little higgledy-piggledy streets that make up Poros town.

After this had happened on several occasions I decided to check out what it was. I remember that it seemed to happen only on certain days and so I made my plan to be up at 4.45am one particular morning, camera in hand, to find out about this strange phenomenon. I set the alarm on my wrist watch to for 4.45am the night before and we went to sleep, shutters ajar, with the gently sound of bobbing boats and a few Greek voices (of those clearing up at the tavernas and women still working in their kitchens along the street) wafting into our ears.

I was woken up in a grey twilight, feeling very much like not bothering. It was totally unheard of for us to go to bed in Greece before between midnight and 1.00am and so I hadn't had much sleep. I lay there for a few seconds debating whether to leave it as an unknown, unexplained occurrence before the will to solve the puzzle became strong enough to catapult me up and onto the side of the bed, feet on the cold marble floor, head still trying desperately to convince itself I was awake and ready for action.

I am not very quick when I first get up. I can always get up at any hour when the necessity arises, but although up and about in body, I am still going through my re-surfacing period for about half an hour. Yvonne is quite the opposite. She hates getting up before it is absolutely necessary, but once up she flies around like that kid from the Incredibles. I can rise at about seven in the morning and have the breakfast made by eight. She can rise at 7.45am and have the breakfast ready well before that. I stand in the middle of the kitchen for a full five minutes trying to decide what I'm doing. I'll successfully get the kettle on and then look around for another five minutes trying to remember where we keep the cereal dishes. I'll open the blind on the kitchen window and spend another five minutes trying to grasp what's happening in the garden. So here I was sitting on the edge of my little Greek bed in Poros at 4.50am trying to get some movement into my body. Trying to motivate my still-sleeping brain into finding the camera and throwing on some clothes in order for my mission to be a success.

I managed somehow to get out into the street in the early morning greyness. Probably because I had heard the mysterious bell clanging a few streets away and as a result had given myself a motivation boost. I shuffled out into the street, wiping sleep from the corners of my eyes and walked in the direction of the church "square" a hundred yards or so along the way. The streets all around this area were no wider than maybe ten feet or so. There were other, smaller "streets" every few yards, most of which tantalisingly twisted and turned within a few yards of the end from which you peered into them, so they all demanded that you walk along them to see where they would lead. The trouble was, once you had gone down or up one (as the case may be), they would turn again. The word "Maze" is a very fair description of this intriguing place.

I arrived at the "square" in front of the Church and stopped. The bell was now so close that I knew it would make its appearance without my having to move any further. Across the square to my left as I entered it, was a small flight of rough, white-painted steps that ran the length of the far side of the open area. The church stood at an angle, which meant that the far side of the square was much shorter than the side at which I stood. The gap between the far corner of the Church and the left hand corner of the square was probably only twenty feet. The path above the steps ran up at a gentle angle. It gave the effect almost of looking across your school assembly hall at the platform at the far end, although the platform sloped downward from left to right as you looked at it.

In a few more instants my riddle was solved. From behind the Church wall emerged a little stocky man dressed quite dowdily in long grey trousers, dark long-sleeved shirt and brown pullover. His obligatory dark cap had seen better days. Two donkeys followed close behind, the first being led by the man and the second attached by a rope to the first. Each had large baskets on either side of its back. The bell was hanging from the neck of the first donkey. I quickly raised my camera and took a shot. This slide I still have today and it is a bit murky due to the poor light. Why would someone drive their donkeys at regular intervals around these impossible streets, when one usually came across such a scene out in the fields or lanes of the countryside? Then I noticed what the man was doing.

In Britain, the equivalent of this chap was a large truck which made a lot of noise as several dust-coated men threw bin-bags into it or attached wheelie bins to its rear for them to be emptied. Yes, he was the dustman. Only at this point did I notice that there were loads of blue plastic bags laying in doorways, which he was duly collecting and ramming into the donkeys' panniers. The reason he had to come so regularly was because the capacity of his beasts was a just bit less than the trucks we have in the UK. There was, apparently a truck moving around the quayside, to and from which he would go with his donkeys gathering up all the household refuse around all the tiny streets of Poros town. I watched him for only a minute or two. There wasn't a lot of point in following him once I had realised what he was doing and, anyway, I would soon have been lost in the maze.

As I walked back to our room having been enlightened, I was at first a little disappointed. The exotic theories I had entertained were blown. The unknown, almost other-worldly bell was the flipping dustman! How much more down-to-earth could it be? But, by the time I'd got upstairs to the landing from which all the rooms were accessed and grabbed a peach and some yogurt from the communal fridge to mix with our muesli for breakfast, I had begun to realise that even this was part of why Greece held such a fascination for me. Everything here was so different. Everything ran at such a different pace. I felt as if I had been given a great privilege. I had witnessed something that would even make looking at our dustmen back home remind me of this enchanting place. When you're in a place like Poros town, especially staying

right among the local residents, you don't usually think: "How
do they dispose of their rubbish? How does the dustman get a
big truck with a flashing yellow light up here?" It never really
crosses your mind unless you get woken up just before dawn
by a strange unearthly bell.

Taking the water taxi across to Aliki beach was a bit nerve-
wrenching for novices like us twenty years ago. Leaving the
quayside and chugging along parallel to the bustling
waterfront for the first five minutes or so was pleasant enough.
But then the boat would distance itself from the Poros front
and head across the small stretch of water to the mainland
coast and a little further south-east it would negotiate the
"reef". This was an area of about 500 metres where there were
rocks just inches below the water, which, if you were going to
make it to Aliki, the boatman would have to negotiate
successfully every time. These old boatmen obviously had
done this so many times they could do it in their sleep. Yet
they always managed to instill in me a fear that we were going
to be holed and sink without trace. We were only a few tens of
yards from the coast on one side, a coast which we would
move along in parallel with until reaching the small wooden
jetty at one end of Aliki beach. The beach was a smallish
strand of sand stretching in an arc further east from the jetty
for a few hundred yards.

But reaching the jetty when you were in the middle of the
"reef" seemed an almost unattainable goal. Frequently the
boatman would gesticulate for one of his passengers to be
lookout at the bow, one to port and another to starboard. He
would probably quite deliberately move a little too close on
one side or the other and, without warning, shout "Wooaa!!!"
or *"Ohpah!!"* as he deftly manoeuvred the little craft away to

relative safety. If he had been playing some bouzouki music on his battered old eight-track as we approached this area of treacherous waters he would turn it off as we came close to increase the dramatic effect. It always worked on me. It was because of the perils of this fifteen-minute "Titanic" run that we didn't go to Aliki by boat too often. I would have visions of standing in this little rowing boat with an engine (because that's really what these taxi-boats amounted to) and panicking as we sank beneath the surface, all hands lost. Even on the occasions when I had visions of surviving, I'd think about the loss of my personal stereo, my book, snorkel, mask, towel, cash and whatever else we had crammed into our shoulder bags and the inconvenience it would cause. But of course, these boats always made it through, often to a resounding cheer from the dozen or so passengers aboard and much to the delight of the helmsman, whose gold toothed grin would reveal his pleasure at having put the wind up these landlubbers so effectively.

If you preferred you could get to Aliki by crossing directly from Poros to Galatas and walking the three quaters of a mile or so along the seafront. This was what we would quite often do. As we walked along the front at Galatas it never seemed to have the charm of Poros, with which it always had a kind of face-off across the little stretch of water that separated the two seafronts. Galatas was always a bit "dead." Part way along the front was a football pitch of pure dust which apparently had been reclaimed from the sea. It was on a football pitch-shaped bit of flat land jutting out from the waterfront in a very charmless fashion. There were one or two tavernas, often with half a dozen or so octopi hanging on bits of wire across their tired awnings, but even this didn't make the place attractive.

We very rarely went over to Galatas for our evening meal. The most exciting thing about Galatas was that one day, when we were sitting on our balcony at Mrs. Mellou's, enjoying the impossibly delicious view, a helicopter landed on the football pitch when a bunch of lads were having a cup final. It was one of those with a bubble for a cockpit. You know, the kind that used to feature in TV's "Whirlybirds" decades ago. I've no idea why it landed, but it became the major event of that particular day.

We finally ran the gauntlet of the "reef" successfully and disembarked on the rickety old jetty at one end of Aliki beach. Walking to the other end and around a bit of dust track, through coarse undergrowth and myriad rabbit or goat droppings, brought you to another small shingly beach which was a sandbar of only about fifty yards wide with sea on both sides of it. At the far end was another small bit of headland, immediately beyond which was what appeared to be a mast. It looked like a small boat was tied up just the other side of the hillock. Yet there was no motion. The "Mast" was not moving.

Once we had dropped our bags and the others were busy getting settled I trotted up over the small hillock to the other side to investigate. The other side was indeed rocky, with a substantial boulder set just a few feet away from the shore. It must have been about twenty feet high and something similar across, with a hole right through it about eight feet above the water. Built into the hole, which was more like a very compact open-ended cave, was a wooden platform that evidently had been home for someone at sometime in the not-too-distant past. The "mast" was fixed to one end of this platform and rose well above the height of the rock, which was why it was visible from the small shingle beach on the other side. Had I

been twelve years younger, I would instantly have become
"Black Jake" the pirate and played here for hours. Instead I
tried to be all grown up (in case anyone saw me) and played
"Black Jake" in a very cerebral manner. I walked across a very
narrow couple of planks that led from the rocks on which I was
standing to the platform in the "cave" and walked through it
to the open side facing the sea. In conditions like this it was
easy to imagine setting up a hippie home here.

My mind was cast back to my late teens when, since the
Russians were sure to go to war with the Americans (it was the
early seventies then remember), many youths had decided the
best thing to do was hitch-hike to Greece and live in a place
very much like this. Now that I was standing here the reality
of such a foolish dream became very tangible. How would one
eat? How would one keep warm in winter time, when the
waves would doubtless break so high that they would power
right through this hole? In one's teenage imagination these
things are easily answered. "Oh, we'd catch fish and make our
own clothes." ...was what my friends and I would theorise as
we all sat round in a ring listening to Ummagumma (an early
Pink Floyd album. Very ahead of its time. Or was it just crap?
I don't know, but I still like it now). We'd sit in Steve and Ian's
flat in Belvedere, Bath and eat a dried up old rice dish that
they'd attempted to make in the Macro way. Steve would roll
up a joint and we'd pool our meagre resources to see if we had
enough to pop down the pub for a can or two. On would go
the Pink Floyd and we'd all sit round deciding what *"Several
Species of Small Furry Animals, Gathered Together in a Cave and
Grooving With a Pict"* really meant, man. The conversation
would inevitably lead to the volatile political tennis match
between East and West and we would talk about the need to
begin planning the trip to Greece. At that time I'd never been

there, but it was where all the "Hippies" decided would be coolest to wait for the big one.

Standing here on this bit of rock, on a very hot early September day, brought all this back. I scanned the coastline to my right and something caught my eye.

Just a little way down the rocky coastline to my right I made out some more bits of wood. Not just any old bits of wood. No, these were evidently the protruding bits of another platform by the look of them. They were only about fifty to a hundred yards along the rocks. I made my way back to the small beach where the others were and, since they had all crashed out pretty well completely, I decided not to bother them and started the horizontal climb along the rocks.

In the previous chapter I sang the praises of my trusty Jellies. Now they were invaluable. These rocks were smooth in places, but mercilessly rough in others. My feet would have been ribbons had I not worn my jellies. As I clambered along I started thinking, "I'm sure no one could seriously have tried living along here, it's not quite your rose-bordered garden path approaching one's front door."

I reached the wooden planks and, as I turned the corner of the last large rock face, was greeted by a much larger cave than I had expected. Here was a complete wooden structure, much like a very substantial garden shed, built on a platform some eight to ten feet above the water level. It had a three-feet wide walkway all around it and went back some ten to twelve feet into the mouth of the cave. There was evidently a solid roof on it too. I could see the overhang of the timbers. How anyone could have brought all this wood here was one thing, how they could have then gone on to build this was quite amazing. I quietly crept round the walls, fearing someone might leap out and cut my throat any moment. I had visions of dying whilst looking up at my black-bandana-clad assailant, replete with obligatory striped jersey and eye-patch, large dagger between teeth and cutlass soaked in my blood in his hand.

All was quite silent. All I could hear was the sound of water lapping around the rocks below and a couple of seagulls. Somewhere out in the bay a Flying Dolphin was making its way towards Hydra. The shed had no windows, but I found the door.

It was a very good fit and appeared to have a simple wooden latch. By now I had become bold enough to expect that this place was quite devoid of any human presence. Whoever had built it had probably long since returned from whence they came and become an estate agent or something. They'd probably describe this place now as, "pleasant location, very private, sea view."

I decided, heart in mouth from anticipation, although telling myself silently that I shouldn't be so daft as there was no one here, to open the door. It opened with ease and I peered inside to see a little domestic scene that frightened me rigid purely from being so unexpected.

There were three bunks around the walls. In each was a human form, apparently sleeping. I saw a large blond haired man, a woman who was too difficult to make out very well due to poor light, and a child of about ten. The man instantly woke up and said: "Hello. How are you?" He was evidently Scandinavian, and quite polite. He sounded almost pleased to see me. Like I was the vicar come to afternoon tea or something. To be quite honest, I can't remember the actual course of the conversation any more, only the impression I got from the whole experience. Evidently they were a "family" who had decided to do what my friends and I had often discussed when we were practicing to be hippies in earnest.

They had come here to drop out and try to enjoy an alternative lifestyle whilst "waiting for the big one." They had all kinds of crawlywigs in their self-made home, it was damp and smelt of sea (and other things too nasty to mention). They had no sanitation. They fished and worked in tavernas for a living.

After I took my leave and clambered back along to the little beach where my party were gradually becoming lobsters in the sun, I decided it was probably better to "wait for the big one" in the manner in which I was already doing.

Besides, they didn't have a hi-fi so how could they listen to Pink Floyd?

The riddle solved -
at the crack of dawn one Poros morning

17 - *Football Crazy*

Taking the water taxi from Poros town to Monastiri beach was one of the longer beach trips. It took you around the headland at the far end of the strait and across a large bay to the beach, which lay on the far right of the larger part of the island, as viewed from the point where it came into view. As the little boat precariously crossed the bay I was always conscious of how deep the water must be at the point furthest from either bit of land. In those days I was a swimmer, but not a very strong one. I always entertained morbid fears of sinking at sea and flapping my arms and legs wildly as I drank down large gulps of seawater, my whole life flashing before me.

These little water taxis and their owners were intrepid alright. Sometimes out in this bay it would get rather choppy; the water would often be only inches from the side at the mid-point of the boat and would quite often crash over the bows. You would always get a bit wet. Often you'd get very wet. But they never floundered and so I suppose it gave one a kind of confidence. I felt as though I was gaining a victory both over my fears and the sea when we crossed to Monastiri beach. You could get to Monastiri by road if you didn't have the bottle to make the crossing. The only road along that part of the island terminated just above the beach at the inevitable monastery, which was situated some way above the beach, nestled in the trees and glistening like a wedding cake when viewed from the little caique half-way across the bay.

The first time we made this crossing it soon became apparent that there was a taverna at the point where the boat was going to land. Looking towards the beach, which lay to the left of the taverna, and casting one's eyes along to the left one could see the road, here and there, between trees and the occasional small house. Further to the left Askeli beach would be clearly visible.

The beach at Monastiri had another taverna at its other end, which was perhaps fifty yards from the jetty at which we were going to land. It all looked like the ideal place to me. Cold beers, Greek-style omelette and salad all came into mind when I thought of what I might be doing in another hour or two. Mind you, we had our bread and tomatoes already packed in our bags, plus the obligatory large bottle of water. Finance and desire always had a battle on.

Looking almost full astern as we chugged across to Monastiri we could clearly make out the Lemon Groves, shimmering in the hazy heat some way above Aliki beach on the mainland. They were easily discernible as a darker patch of green on the otherwise paler hillside, strewn with olive trees and a few pines, with a lot of parched earth in between. But the Lemon Groves looked like a large oasis of lushness. They could be reached by a narrow dusty track leading up from somewhere near Aliki Beach. You could either walk up, which took, if I remember correctly, about twenty minutes to half an hour, or you could go by donkey, a few of which were led up and down all day by a couple of dusty men.

The nearer you got to the Lemon Groves, the steeper became the path until, a hundred yards or so from the taverna situated in the midst of the lemon trees, the path would level out as it turned sharply to the left and led along into the taverna's large terrace.

One of the wonderful things about Greece is that no matter where you go, no matter how remote the spot, there always seems to be a taverna nestled into the landscape quite symbiotically, to slake your thirst or satisfy your hunger. In Britain, if you're lucky there'll be a pub, which is usually closed at the time when most people would like, nay need, a drink. If not, the cafe you may be fortunate enough to find will be an eyesore spoiling the otherwise lovely environment of the location. All red formica table tops and the smell of burgers, chips and egg with cardboard cups with "Coke" emblazoned all over them strewn across the car park outside. But in Greece, these remote tavernas seem to sink into their environments so that they appear to have always been there, always a part of the scene one surveyed. They probably have been there for many years anyway, judging from the age of some of the buildings, not to mention the tables and chairs.

The taverna at the lemon groves was rough and ready, but wonderful all the same. You'd sit at a table under an enormous vine, which covered the pretty substantial terrace, and the owner or one of his family would bring you a glass of freshly squeezed lemon juice and water. I don't take sugar in virtually anything, but you have to have sugar in this! The drink slides down like nectar and you soon find yourself asking for another and running your finger over the condensation on the outside of your empty glass and thinking, "I could die here and life would have been just right." But then you look out at the view across the water to see virtually all of Poros Island glistening in the hot sunshine and you think, "I don't think I ever want to die. I think I'll apply for a job here instead."

For the more energetic there's a walk deeper into the grove and up to a waterfall well hidden in the trees and rocky hillside. This natural spring is why this area is such an oasis in an otherwise arid landscape. But I was content to sit and look out over the tops of a thousand lemon trees, which, in September are laden with lemons all turning yellow in the sunlight. Magic. Pure magic.

One time Yvonne and I hired pushbikes at Galatas and cycled past the Lemon Groves along the dusty road leading south round the coast. It was probably only the second time I had ever been to Greece and we were still overawed by all the enormous fruits you could buy in the market during September. We would eat giant peaches like there was no tomorrow and then, inevitably, pay the price at the most inconvenient moments. The day we hired the bikes was one of these moments. Anyone observing our progress along the road would have, at regular intervals, observed one or other of us standing alone holding both bikes at the roadside. The other would be scrambling madly into the undergrowth just far enough not to be seen too easily from passing vehicles (Which, remember, would usually be battered old three-wheeled trucks trundling along at nil miles an hour!) to relieve the pressure on the anal sphincter. We had foreseen this likelihood and had visited a "Supermarket" and bought a loo roll for the journey.

"Supermarket," of course, is another misnomer, for these shops were often no bigger than your lounge and stocked with a bit of just about everything. They were somewhat like

Arkwright's in "Open All Hours" but with a Greek accent. We each had a little spring-loaded rack behind our saddle on the bikes and mine was occupied by the loo roll in all its glory, wrapped in a blue see-through plastic carrier bag, the kind you get in just about any Greek island shop anywhere and everywhere, even today.

The loo roll was pretty well totally depleted by the time we had cycled up into a small village on the hillside. I think that by then our large intestines had no more fluid slush to expel, so we were fairly safe in the decision not to find the local "Supermarket" and buy another. We just had to hope there would be no parties of nature ramblers rummaging in the undergrowth along the road we had just cycled. If there were, I didn't envy them.

So we approached Monastiri beach in the little caique. Long before you could make out too much detail of the taverna at the beach end of the jetty, it began to puzzle us. I didn't possess a pair of binoculars in those days and there was evidently a need for them now. We could see the fairly large canopy attached to the front of the taverna building, but underneath it and above the door and windows was a huge flash of red and white. From half a mile or so out it was impossible to make out what it was, except that it evidently dominated the frontage of the building above the motley collection of tables and chairs awaiting some of the passengers on this little vessel.

As we drew nearer the details began to emerge. There was a large photograph taking centre stage of three rows of men in shorts and red and white tops, all sat arms folded and smiling at the camera. This was surrounded by woollen scarves, rosettes, pennants and various homemade painted objects all

in red and white. Above and across the full length of all this
and inscribed in very large letters which could be read as one
disembarked at the end of the jetty were the words-
MANCHESTER UNITED.

This was one Greek family who knew where their loyalties
lay. It came as a bit of a shock to me. Here we were on this
idyllic Greek Island and as far as you like from anything
British. Yet there was an altar to Manchester United on
Monastiri beach. We sat at a table, just inches above the clear
waters and waited for the waiter to approach. Yvonne's mum,
Lela, was soon in deep conversation with this genial chap and,
after he'd gone to get our cool beers, salad and omelette, she
explained that Greece was football crazy and when the Greek
season wasn't on (and even when it was) Greek fans always
tuned in to the British league and followed it avidly.
Apparently Greek TV and radio carried quite a lot of info
about British football and it was not unusual at all for Greeks
to follow diverse British teams.

Needless to say, from that day on Monastiri beach was
"Manchester United." What was all that about tavernas
looking symbiotic (go on, look it up!)?

18 - The Road to Argos

From Galatas, the road to Argos crosses some rugged and spectacular mountains. It twists and turns up through remote villages, where tourists are things the locals only read about. That's always assuming they can read. In fact many an old Yia-Yia (Greek grandmother) can't, owing to the fact that when they lived under the Italians many decades ago, the girls weren't allowed to go to school. After taking you through a pass it gently descends to the plains around Argos, from whence come Greek tomato puree and much of Greece's output of oranges. En route you pass the road to Epidavros, one of Greece's best preserved archaeological sites. Here you find a superb example of an ancient amphitheatre where even today during the summer they stage productions of Greek tragedies and other cultural events under the warm night sky.

Aristedes, (pronounced "Aristee-these" with the "ee" emphasised and the "th" soft) was a carpenter whose workshop could be found just a little way up the street from the front at Galatas. His father, Costas, who had retired, still helped out in the workshop and with deliveries now and then. We became quite friendly with these excellent men and their families. Ari

(as he was more often called) became very protective of
Yvonne and I when we were staying on Poros in 1978. It was
our first ever trip abroad as a young married couple
unaccompanied by family and we were still very
inexperienced. I was a fresh-faced twenty-four-year old and
Yvonne a ravishing twenty-three. Ari was thirty-three and
considered us his "children" He would often refer to us as *"Ta
Pedya"* - the children, which we later discovered to be a
common expression of friendly familiarity. We passed many a
happy evening at their house. They lived above the carpentry
shop with their wives and children/grandchildren and were
very busy. In fact it was the Goritsas' (their family name) who
had done all the joinery when Mrs Mellou, our "landlady," had
converted the first floor of her modest house into village
rooms for holidaymakers.

Yvonne has relatives at Argos. This was a couple of hours'
drive west over the mountains from Galatas. She had not seen
these relatives since she was a teenager and I had never met
them. There were an older aunt and uncle, whose names
escape me today. In fact they even escape Yvonne, because she
had never had a great deal of contact with them. Their son
(Yvonne's cousin) was called Costas. She remembered him
quite well and knew that he had recently married. He and his
wife were a few years older than Yvonne and myself. She
remembered really liking Costas and had quite a desire to visit
him and meet his new wife.

We decided to get a bus to Argos and look them up. We
really had no idea what this would entail, but thought it would
be a doddle. A day or two later we remember quite clearly
deciding that "doddle" wouldn't have been a fair description of
the expedition. "Well-near impossibility" would have been
closer to the mark. But find them we did, though not in the

way we would have expected or planned.

We thought it best to ask Ari and Costas where to get a bus and what times they ran and all that stuff. Of course, with hindsight we should never even have thought of such a thing. In those days most Greek buses were about as reliable as the British weather! Ari asked why we wanted to visit Argos. Yvonne explained about the relatives and he listened with a twinkle in his eye. He explained where the bus could be boarded and then told us it would take five hours or something like that and may even involve changing buses. Arriving at Argos, we would be disembarking in the middle of the town. Did we know where to go from there?

"We'll get a taxi" I replied. Yvonne then translated.

"And where will you ask the taxi driver to take you?" came back the translation, courtesy of my lovely wife.

"Yvonne knows the address, don't you my love?" I replied, confidently expecting the next phrase out of her mouth to be, "Yes, I have it in my pocketbook. No problem." End of story. Not.

What she actually came out with was: "Well, I know they have a large plantation of orange trees. They also have a flat in the town, but I'm not sure of its whereabouts."

"Yes," I replied, growing anxiety becoming evident in my manner, "but surely you have a note of their actual address. Or perhaps their telephone number."

"I know their surname, it's Blatsos. I'm sure that if we get to the orange tree plantation, I'll recognise where we are and be able to find it."

Now, would you have embarked on a long distance bus ride under these circumstances? Evidently Yvonne felt we had sufficient information. Ari obviously knew *"ta pedya"* were a little optimistic. He told us he'd be back in a minute and left us with a couple of cold drinks.

He returned about five minutes later and announced that we were in luck. He had some business in Nafplion and Argos (Nafplion is to Argos what Piraeus is to Athens, well, sort of) and would be driving there in his trusty Toyota pickup the next day. What a coincidence! He told us to be outside the workshop at 8.00am prompt and we would be on our way. If we were successful in finding our relatives we could return from Nafplion by Flying Dolphin when we were ready. If we failed to find them, then Aristedes would do his business and bring us back with him the same evening. So, at 8.00am next morning Ari came round the side of the building in his white pickup truck, we clambered in beside him and were off up the road to the mountains, full of optimism and expectation at what the day would bring.

Before too long we were snaking up through villages which were waking up to another hot dusty day. We passed through many which didn't have all that much character, yet they were possessed of a charm born of the fact that they were evidently totally removed from the tourist trail. You would hardly see any signs reading *"enoikiazontai domatia"* – "rooms to let", but you would see *"Artopoleion"*, *"Kreatopoleion"* or SEIMENS.

Aristedes would slow up on occasion to exchange a few words when someone whom he evidently knew was crossing the road. Sometimes he would just come to a halt, mid-carriageway as it were, and have a hearty laugh with some middle-aged Greek bloke with a map of lines all over his smiling face, gold teeth shining in the morning sunshine.

Eventually we began to enjoy spectacular views on the right northward to Methana and, looking slightly back over our right shoulders, Poros Island. We stopped at one particularly breathtaking view-point for the obligatory photo showing Ari, Yvonne and loads of landscape stretching miles northward down to the Saronic Gulf behind them. Oh, and the pickup was in the picture too, of course. In those days I would take pictures by the dozen and every one I took I would imagine having the pleasure of explaining to my audience back home when we had our slide show.

I can imagine now how our friends at the time would dread us coming back from a trip abroad. They would be saying, "How are we going to make our excuses this time? They're sure to invite us round to show us three hundred slides." We would no doubt soften the pain of the experience by plying our reluctant guests with Metaxa. But even that would be tempered by the fact that we would also assume that they were bound to love the bottled retsina we also brought back for their delectation and delight. It never occurred to me that in a little lounge in Bath, sitting indoors in a carpeted room and eating from a finger buffet, people may not quite develop a taste for retsina. The only reason I had developed such a taste was because of the very nature of an evening in a Greek taverna. The temperature, the smells in the air, the food, the bobbing boats a few feet away and the music coming over the crackly house sound system (if you could call it that) all added to the occasion which demanded retsina to complete the picture. The fact that the house retsina served in those little aluminium jugs was the cheapest drink you could order (second only to water) may also have been a factor.

But in England, in your own lounge during a torturous slide show of someone else's holiday, you weren't very likely to prefer retsina to a nice Rioja for example.

But this never occurred to me. My guests had to be

compelled to adopt a passion for all things Greek because I had.

I would also get really annoyed during these showings because, whilst I was meticulously explaining every last background detail about each slide, someone would insist on talking! I'd be bursting to get all this information out to impress these poor mortals who hadn't had the benefit of all these lovely experiences and they would have the nerve to talk over me! I'd get all frustrated and have to bottle up my feelings as I waited for them to enjoy someone else's experience about something that had happened to them, probably prompted to mind by something they had seen on one of our slides. It was amazing we still had any friends, really.

So we took a photo or two of the view and pressed on over the mountains. Soon Ari took a side turn and we realised he had something unscheduled in mind.

"*Pou Pas?*" (Where are you going) Yvonne asked. Ari explained that Epidavros was only a kilometre or ten off our route and we simply couldn't come this way without seeing it. "What about the time? Don't you have work to do?" we asked, "Don't worry, 'then menyasi', " came the reply, "I have plenty time. No problem."

We arrived at Epidavros. It was the site of some ancient games and the arts too. The setting is simply idyllic (Do you think I use that word enough?). The Greek countryside stretches away to gentle hills and mountains, inducing a feeling of real tranquillity as a sense of history develops under your feet as you walk. There are the ruins of an ancient stadium, running track still visible. The cicadas chirp in the trees and you can go and clamber all over the superb amphitheatre which has survived the millennia virtually intact.

I ran up the tiers of this semi-circle of marble and stone and sat on the very top row. Was it really true what I had heard? That someone could speak in the centre of such a place and yet still be heard by someone at the very back? It seemed hundreds of feet below me. Ari and Yvonne stood chatting right in the middle of the half-moon shaped stage area, seeming almost small enough to hold them in my hands, and, had I been able to understand the Greek, I would have been able to follow the conversation easily. These ancient bods certainly knew a thing or two about acoustics.

After a short while spent strolling through a couple of thousand years' worth of history, we clambered back into the cab of Ari's Toyota pickup and set off for Argos. We were nearing the city when, still some few miles out in the countryside, we turned onto a small gravelly drive and pulled up in front of a lone farmhouse near the roadside.

We all seem to have magical moments just now and again, do you find that? You know, things that happen which just stay in the mind forever and tug at the heartstrings. Sometimes they are so small in the great scheme of things, yet because they are a bit special, they mean more than a whole week of normality. The next fifteen minutes were to become one of these moments. Aristedes jumped out of the cab and beckoned us to follow. We obediently did so.

He walked straight into the small house's front door and we gingerly followed. Inside it was less of a home, more of an outhouse. There were large churns, somewhat like milk churns back in the UK, if anyone remembers what they were like! I don't remember a great deal more about what we saw around the room, but it was what these "churns" contained that made it such a magic moment.

An elderly couple came into the room from a door in the

opposite wall and greeted Ari warmly. He evidently explained our presence and we were accorded the same welcome. It appeared that these were relatives of his. Maybe his wife's parents, or an aunt and uncle, I can't remember now, but they were quite obviously very close. They made their living from making honey. They led us out into their "back garden" if it could be called that. There were the ubiquitous olive trees, chickens and cats, loads of Greek farm debri-type things and, further from the house, a mass of small wooden structures that were evidently beehives. We enjoyed a fairly unintelligible explanation of what they do to gather their substantial harvest of honey and then returned to the house, where we were going to have an opportunity to sample the produce.

We went into a room where there were more of these "churns" and our host lifted the lid of one of them. Raw honey, virtually straight from the combs, filled the vessel to its brim. You could tell it was fresh, there were little bits on the surface, like bees' legs, that sort of thing. The old man gestured for us to shove in a finger and have a taste. We did so and then shoved our fingers straight into our mouths and were transported! It was the most smooth, full tasting honey I have ever devoured. I could easily have done a Winnie-the-Pooh and drank the stuff straight from the "Pot." You could taste the flowers in it. Not that I could have told you which blossoms the busy manufacturers of this superb fluid had visited in the making, but I can still taste that honey when I write this many years on. I have already mentioned my penchant for taking zillions of pictures when on vacation. To my eternal chagrin, I had left the camera in the pickup and took no photographs during this wonderful interlude. Why I didn't rush out and get it I'll never know, but I have no photographs of this magic moment. I've got loads of slides of bits of Greek road, coastline, boats, tavernas, trees and donkeys. I could bore you silly with a slide show of Yvonne dancing, tables laden with souvlaki, horiatiki, tsatsiki, skordalia and the like, us standing by various beauty spots like small bits of ancient pillar laying in the prickly undergrowth, but, alas, I couldn't show you what this place looked like. I couldn't show you one of these "honey-churns."

Still, it's there in my mind's eye. I'll always be grateful for this wonderful Greek gentleman, Aristedes, whom I've not seen since 1980, for giving us this moment to savour.

We were soon back in the pickup, waiting a few moments whilst Ari did what ever he had come to this house to do. I think he was engaged in a little errand for his wife or father or mother-in-law or something. Within a few more minutes he was back alongside us and we charged down the road and entered the town of Argos.

19 - Bats & Oranges

Argos was all streets, shops and cars. Ari looked across at us with a knowing grin and asked rhetorically-

"*Pou, pammeh torah?*" (Where do we go now?). It was obvious that we weren't exactly what you'd describe as "certain." Inside I was panicking. Yvonne said-

"Well, I know I'd recognise their house out at the orange plantation." Aristedes evidently already knew the best road out of town towards the orange groves so he headed in that direction. Soon we were turning off the small mettled road down dusty tracks, fringed on either side by acres and acres of orange trees as far as the eye could see, which - for most of the time - was about as far as the first row of trees on the other side of the fence.

These lanes twisted and turned so much, that, were it not for the sun we wouldn't have had the faintest idea where we were. The fact was we didn't have the faintest idea where we were! There were myriads of turnings and junctions, all leading to still more trees. Now and again we would pass a residence quite near the track and Yvonne would take a long hard stare at it (whilst Ari let the truck tick over) before pronouncing that it didn't "look right" to her and we would create another dust storm as we pulled away. That man had the patience of Job and no mistake. Had I been in Ari's shoes I'd have dumped us both among the green oranges and sped away heaving a huge sigh of relief and putting all the time I had wasted down to experience with mad British tourists.

The problem was further exacerbated by the fact that it was now well into siesta time. There was absolutely no one to be seen. Now and again we would see ladders propped up against a tree, various tools laying around in the vicinity, but not a soul nearby. It was like the *Marios Celestos* on land. Occasionally we'd come across a concrete silo, not much bigger than a British coalbunker, which would contain an electric pump irrigating various ditches around someone's vast tract of tree-covered land. We would hear the hum of the motor as we passed.

"It's really too good and kind of you to do all this for us Ari," I sighed, "but enough is enough. We can't ask you to carry on doing this all day. The chances of us finding Costas now are too remote." In fact, we had been driving around for three hours since leaving the honey house. How Ari was going to get any of his "Argos business" done goodness only knew. Of course, we'd realised that he had no intention of doing any "business" in Argos. He had simply been too worried about us making this trip alone to let us do it and had created a pretext to take us himself.

Ari said he'd give it another fifteen minutes and then would have to start back. The drive back to Galatas from here would be at least three hours anyway. We approached another fork in the dusty lane and, right ahead of us, in the groin of the fork as it were, Yvonne spotted a man up a ladder evidently performing a bit of tree surgery.

"That's Costas!" She shouted. My ears still ringing from the sheer volume of the statement, I replied: "How can you tell? You haven't seen him since you were fifteen!"

"I'm SURE it's him! I'm sure!" Ari screeched to a halt in another cloud of dust as Yvonne threw open the door and virtually fell out of the side of the truck and ran towards the man up the ladder. Ari jumped out to be sure to "look after" her and I was left sitting over the gearbox thinking: "I'm too hot, too thirsty, too tired and it's too late to care. Just give me a beer and a shower and a two-hour sleep, pleeeeease!" Very soon I was watching as the man came down the ladder and through a gap in the chain link fence, of which there were many to choose from, and began a conversation with my two travelling companions. Within thirty seconds there was much embracing going on. You know, all that kissing on one cheek, then the other and back to the first cheek for good measure. There followed some vigorous handshaking between the man and Ari and Yvonne getting hugged in a manner that meant we had either well and truly found Costas, or my wife was about to run off with a Greek. The former proved to be the case.

They all walked back to the truck, from which I had now decided it would be wise to emerge. Yvonne, full of beaming smiles and excitement, introduced me to Cousin Costas, who himself was in a mild case of shock over having just met up with his cousin from England, her having leapt from a still moving pickup truck with Greek plates and presenting herself to him after they had not met for almost nine years. And this not outside some railway station or airport terminal, not at some seaport or taxi rank, but in the middle of his orange plantation on a hot September afternoon whilst he was doing some pruning. Why he wasn't asleep like virtually every other Greek within miles was a mystery never explained.

It was agreed that we would stay with Costas for a few days and Ari, satisfied that we were in safe hands, took his leave after profusely refusing any contribution to his petrol costs and lost revenue from having sacrificed a day at work for these rash English *"pedyah."* We grabbed our overnight bags from the back of the pickup before it created yet another cloud of dust and Ari was gone among the thousands of orange trees.

Costas was a tall, well-built man, with dark good looks and a broad smile, which instantly made you like him. He was gentle in his ways and, like most Greeks who spend their lives out under the sun, looked older than his thirty-two years. Not that this was a disadvantage. He nonetheless looked the picture of health and vitality. His hair was still generally thick and black, but with a curious grey patch just above one of his temples. The patch was about an inch and a half in diameter and almost circular. It turned out that he had had this for many years and this had proved to be the way Yvonne had recognised him when he was up a ladder some thirty yards from us.

A short walk brought us along a lane and into the garden of his house. I'm afraid all the clichés like "idyllic" and such like (sorry) instantly spring to mind when I think of that villa among the orange groves. It was a single storey house, with a pitched terracotta-tiled roof. This was the exception rather than the rule, because most of the houses have flat roofs with long rusting, twirly steel rods sticking out from them. Apparently this was a bit of a tax dodge. As we understood it then, Greek families are only taxed on their newly built homes once they are finished. So, what they do is demonstrate that the house is still unfinished, even though they may have lived in it for years, because... "As you can see Mr. Inspector, there's still another floor to be added yet." I think it's also true that many Greek families build another storey as and when it becomes necessary. Often there are relatives working abroad, more out of necessity than desire, and when they have earned sufficient to return to their homeland they do so and their home is duly constructed upstairs over mum and dad's.

Costas' villa was truly beautiful. Surrounded as it was by miles of orange trees, it also had a garden around it made up of enormous geraniums, roses, grapevines draped over pergolas attached to the house itself, grapefruit and lemon trees, and various different varieties of orange that evidently fruited a month or two before the main crop as they were sporting fruit of the colour one expects to find on one's supermarket shelves. The vast majority of trees were laden at this time (September) with millions of green spheres, yet to ripen sufficiently to be harvested. We spent a thoroughly laid-back few days here, during which time Costas and his wife Sophia treated us like royalty. They took us to see the archaeological site at Mycenae, where we got to see the famous Lion Gate. Standing atop the Acropolis there we were afforded a breathtaking view all across the orange tree covered plains of the Pelopponese. We talked a great deal and I came to really like these people. I had never met them before, yet they treated me like long lost family. What added a bit of icing to the cake was the fact that, whilst Costas could speak with Yvonne in Greek, Sophia could speak a fair bit of French, as could I. The net result was that we were all able to converse quite fluently in a mixture of the two, only resorting to English when things got difficult, which invariably made things more so!

We were given a very comfortable and cool room to sleep in, with large wooden shutters rather like you'd find on many older French houses. The first morning that I awoke in this room brought on another one of those moments that give you the "tingle" factor. I must have woken up just before the sun came over the horizon, as it was still a kind of twilight; but I had no need to turn on the light by the bedside. I slipped out of bed and my feet enjoyed making contact with the cool marble floor. Yvonne slept on soundly under the single sheet that had covered us as I quietly eased open the shutters. With the window and shutters wide open, I sat on the large windowsill, half-in and half-out of the house. I had one leg on the outside sill and one on the sill in the room, with my back against the window frame. The air was a wonderful temperature and I was totally comfortable in nothing but a pair of underpants.

Across the narrow dust track that ran beneath the window began the first of innumerable rows of thirty thousand orange trees, all laden with their still ripening fruit. The smell was delicious. I looked up at the lightening sky and was immediately enraptured by the sight I saw. Above my head there must have been a hundred small bats. Maybe more. They were all circling directly above me, only a few feet up from the window. They flew with great grace and speed and seemed to take turns at alighting on the edge of the terracotta roof tiles above me, then lifting off again. As the light grew stronger and the sky took on a deeper daylight blue, they began entering the spaces beneath the tiles. Gradually, over ten to fifteen minutes or so, they all slipped under the outer-most tiles until the last one seemed to disappear from view the very moment that the sun crested the horizon and wound up the temperature almost instantly to about 25 degrees. I had sat motionless through the whole performance and felt privileged to have witnessed such a scene. It didn't bother me in the least that, just feet above our heads as we slept, there dwelt a sizeable colony of bats causing no problem to us, as we caused none to them. They slept as we played and visa versa.

As I slipped back on to the floor of the room Yvonne began to stir and asked why I had been sat there. When I explained the wonder I had watched, she reacted in quite the way I had expected:

"Ueallgh! Bats! How horrible!"

Ah well. Vincent Price, you have a lot to answer for.

For breakfast Costas picked me a fresh grapefruit straight from the tree. It tasted like no grapefruit I had ever eaten before. We ate under the grape-laden pergola as the chickens clucked around our feet and the cockerels strutted in the yard and several lazy cats draped themselves off of various ledges. I could have stayed there until I died. But then, since that was hopefully not on the agenda, we let the day take us whatever way it would.

The night before we were due to return to Poros by hydrofoil, Costas & Sophia took us out for a meal in a taverna in Nafplion. The town was buzzing with hordes of strolling people. The atmosphere was beautiful. The bars, cafenions and tavernas were alive with bronzed bodies and lively conversation. It was a delight just to walk around trying to select a taverna at which to eat. And the smells that greeted your nostrils as you walked were unbelievable. I don't know about you, but I've always found the actual act of eating a bit of a letdown after the smells!

We selected a taverna just across the road from a large concrete and tarmac jetty, on the far side of which were berthed some lazy boats. Out in the bay the fortress on the island that used to be a prison (not unlike a mini-Alcatraz) was all lit up and created a wonderfully romantic backdrop for a meal to be taken in good company. The water was dead calm and gave us a wonderfully intact reflection of the illuminated fortress to gaze at. It was during this meal that I discovered why it was that Greek couples were so desperate to have children once they were married.

Costas and Sophia were amazed that having children was not on our agenda.

"That would be impossible for us. We are very worried about the time that has passed." Said Costas. They had evidently been married for eighteen months or so and had not yet produced offspring. Sophia had suffered a miscarriage and this had made them worry that there would be problems for them in having any children at all.

"But why don't you leave it a while? Many couples in Britain choose not to have any at all. What's the problem?"

"You don't understand. I'll explain," continued Costas, "...In Greece, if a couple who are childless both die through some unexpected cause, all their property goes to the Greek Orthodox Church. That is why the Church is a) so wealthy and b) so despised by many Greeks."

Now this was in 1978. Things may be different nowadays. Perhaps too, Costas didn't mean all their property, but a substantial amount of it. But the fact remains that this is what he said and it very quickly became evident to us why Greek couples felt they had to produce kids. We felt very sorry for them and, at the same time, glad that in Britain the Church no longer had such a hold on the populace. Religion can be a nasty thing sometimes. I think if I were God I'd not be too happy with a good many of my self-styled reps.

We finished the evening at a cafe-*zaheroplasteion* where I enjoyed a Metaxa after a huge chocolate ice cream. After a woozy drive back to the villa we slept under the bats for the last time.

Next day we were saying goodbye, all kisses on both cheeks and cuddles and expressions of newfound affection, and then we were aboard the Flying Dolphin and away. I've never seen Costas or Sophia from that day to this. A fact which pains me and one which I still hope to remedy one day.

Anyway, I'd love to meet all their kids.

20 - *Auntie Effi's Cuisine*

Yvonne and I were planning a trip to several islands and flew first into Athens to spend a few days with Yvonne's relatives. Late one morning early in September a taxi dropped us outside the house in Katopatissia. It must have been circa 1978-80. I don't know if I've mentioned this before (probably have) but Yvonne's cousin Christina lived upstairs from her "Mother," Yvonne's Auntie Effi.

The house was large and divided into two apartments. Downstairs lived Auntie Effi and Uncle Stamati; upstairs were Christina, her husband Taki and their daughter Effoula (Effi junior). The door was at the right hand end of the house as you looked at it from the pavement. After entering the large front door you were faced with a choice of a curving marble staircase to the right, which led up to Christina's apartment, or to the left of the small lobby you would see Auntie Effi and uncle Stamati's front door.

Since Auntie Effi and her hubby were somewhat quirky, we would often creep in and up to Christina's apartment so as not to be heard by the two downstairs residents. On this occasion, we were out of luck. Laden with suitcases and all the other paraphernalia of travelling by air, we couldn't get upstairs all in one go.

I bounded up to Christina's front door and rang the bell. They knew we were coming, but not exactly what time. I hoped desperately that Christina would be in and that we wouldn't have to "enjoy" the weird hospitality of Auntie Effi below. Right now, after a tiring flight and still in travelling clothes, we didn't need that. Plus we were still adjusting to the heat.

Christina was not in. I stared at her door for a few moments, willing it to open. It's at times like these you wish you were David Copperfield. You know, that American bloke who used to be terminally engaged to Claudia Shiftit or whatever. I saw him walk through the Great Wall of China once. Cousin Christina's front door would present him no problems at all. Sadly, I wasn't him and the door was solid, thick, hardwood.

I was alarmed by noises below. "Oh no." I thought, "let Auntie Effi please not be aware of our arrival ...pleeeeease!"

She was.

As I descended the stairs with a sense of dread I was greeted by the sight of Yvonne trying desperately to be pleasant and look pleased to see her odd aunt, whilst half-falling over the suitcases and duty free (ah, those were the days, eh?) carrier bags in an attempt to look delighted at the prospect of kissing her old relative on both cheeks.

Don't get me wrong. Auntie Effi was really very nice. She was kind and loving, but just, well, Greek and old and odd. She always wore a chiffon scarf draped over one of her hands. She was never to be seen without it. Every photograph I have ever seen of her shows the bright scarf neatly wrapped around one hand whenever she was outside her own front door. I eventually discovered the reason for this. Apparently, when she was still very young she had a major accident in the kitchen and lost a couple of fingers from that particular hand. I can't remember now which it was, probably the right one. To disguise this disfigurement and prevent embarrassment she had always wrapped the hand in a scarf ever since.

Uncle Stamati, Effi's husband, was having his siesta. He would have his siesta any time of day and usually several times each day by this time in his life. On learning the way he'd spent that life I wasn't surprised. He had a lot of sleep to catch up on. He had been a merchant seaman and it was apparently well known that he had often found substitutes to stand in (or should that be- "lay in") for Effi whenever and wherever he could. Now, though, he was a sad old codger who spent all his days shuffling about the apartment. He never did anything else other than eat or sleep from the time I first met him (you could, I suppose, add "go to the toilet" too, but it wouldn't be in very good taste). My only memories of uncle Stamati are of briefly saying hello whilst he shuffled between bed and dining table, no doubt with frequent excursions to the bathroom now and then to relieve the tedium.

Auntie Effi now manifested undisguised delight at her stroke of luck at having been the first to greet the new arrivals from *"Angleea"* (England). There was no alternative, no escape, hearts desperately desiring to run for it, our feet led us into Effi's dining room. Effi's dining room, like many Greek houses in Athens, was stark, and kitted out with very heavy dark-stained wooden furniture. The shutters were permanently closed, creating a kind of twilight that seemed to go perfectly with one's mood when spending any time there. The sunlight outside was brilliant and it took your eyes a few minutes to adjust to this "instant evening" you were entering.

Living here now I have finally come to understand why many Greeks maintain this daytime darkness. It's the only way to keep the temperature down indoors during a very hot Greek summer (especially in the pre air-conditioning era). Contrary to what we'd do in the UK - you know, throw all the windows open and let the chintz flap in the breeze – the best way to keep a house cool is close the shutters and windows and keep the rooms dark. It works, we do it now too!

Effi spoke no English, so there was much gesticulating, with she and Yvonne communicating through many decibels of what seemed to me like shouting at the top of their voices, the essence of the conversation went like this:

"I cook you some food. You very hungry."

"NO! No. We're fine really. No need to bother. We ate on the plane."

"I insist. You need a good meal inside you after your journey. Sit at the table, I won't be long."

"But really, Auntie Effi, there's no need. A cold drink will do just fine."

"No one come to Effi's place and leave hungry! You sit and I cook!"

Now the look of horror on Yvonne's face told me something. But I could only guess at precisely what. The one correct conclusion I did draw was that Effi's cooking probably didn't measure up all that well against Ainsley Harriot's or Anthony Worrel Thingamijig. When Effi had disappeared into the kitchen, leaving us sitting at the table in the twilight, Yvonne risked a whispered explanation.

"It'll be spaghetti bolognese, a penny to a pound!"

"That's alright. I may not be all that hungry, but I'm partial to spag bol. I'll manage it."

"You won't manage Auntie Effi's spaghetti bolognese. It's

not like any other you've ever tasted. She cooks it every day for Stamati."

"Well, if she cooks it so often, she can't be that bad at it."

"She can. It's probably fifty years since she checked whether her method is the same as the Italians."

"Surely she doesn't cook it every day..."

"She does. It's all Uncle Stamati will eat. Take my word for it, I know. When I spent the summer here when I was fifteen I had to suffer it on several occasions. I only just got out alive!"

The whispered undertones had to stop while Effi entered with two glasses of *Lemonatha*. These, at least, looked welcome. I can always drink in Greece, any time, any place. The prospect of a nice cold lemonade was enough to soothe my anxiety for a second or two. Greek lemonade is cloudy and really tastes of lemons, mmmm! Effi disappeared back into the kitchen and I put the glass to my mouth. Lukewarm lemonade. Brain to mouth: "You're sending me the wrong signals here! What are you playing at? Eyes sent me cold lemonade! But your signal doesn't compute!"

Mouth to brain, "Sorry brain, but I haven't got it wrong. Contrary to all expectations, this liquid really is almost warm. I know it doesn't compute, but I can only tell it like it is."

"Oh well," says brain, " no feeling of ecstatic relief for this body then..."

Yvonne and I continued muted conversation whilst the room began to fill with the nauseous smell of Spaghetti Bolognese à la Effi. I was willing Christina to come home as every second passed, but my will wasn't strong enough, evidently. I began to pacify myself with the thought that it wouldn't turn out to be all that bad. Surely it would be edible. Even though I wasn't very hungry, it probably wouldn't be all that much anyway. The amount of sweat on my face must have made it look as if I had just emerged from the shower, when, finally, the silhouette of Effi in the doorway, carrying two plates, manifested itself. There was to be no escape.

The plates were loaded to spilling-over-the-edge capacity with huge splodges of cream-coloured gunge, topped with a light basting of "Sauce". Mercifully, Auntie Effi decided not to stand and watch us suffer ...sorry, eat. She disappeared into the kitchen mumbling *"Kali orexi,"* the Greek for "Bon apetit," which is French for ...oh, you get the picture.

I stared at this substance before me for a while, then decided to shove my fork in and try a twist or two. This stuff was almost as good as Uri Geller at bending cutlery, I can tell you. It looked a bit like spaghetti on the surface, but was in fact a solid mass of gunge not dissimilar in consistency to half-set cement, or perhaps a human brain. It wouldn't have been so bad had there been any amount of sauce to speak of, but what little there was hadn't penetrated the quivering mass beneath it at all. Fighting back my nausea, I carved a chunk of it and raised the fork to my reluctant lips. I chewed this mass for a while and, after deciding that it bore no resemblance to any spaghetti bolognese I had ever eaten, decided that we had to devise a plan of action. This plan had to include anything but actually eating the awful stuff.

In hushed tones we debated what to do. I cast my eyes around the room and spotted a carrier bag sporting a large 'DUTY FREE" on its side. Our cases were still out in the hallway, but we had walked into Effi's carrying the hand luggage and duty free bags. Just as well as it turned out. Boy were we grateful these bags were built of the kind of tough plastic required for supporting several bottles of spirits! And NO HOLES!!

"I'll scrape it into that bag, then we can dump it when we

get out of here," said Yvonne.

"Fine by me," I replied, "but make it fast! We can't have Auntie Effi coming back while we're half-way through disposing of her marvellous cuisine in not quite the manner she would expect!"

Sweat pouring out of every pore we possessed, and some more I shouldn't wonder, we emptied the after shave and perfume from the said carrier bag and, as quietly as we could, began the scraping of cement from plates. It didn't want to go quietly. It made a fairly good impersonation of superglue and took bare fingers in the end to get it off the surface of the plates. Then we had to wipe round the plate edges to ensure that it didn't look like we had scraped it off. Now and again the sweat changed from oozing to gushing as we thought we heard our dear aunt returning to see how we were enjoying the fruits of her culinary labours. Fortunately, these were false alarms. Feeling like I was sitting in a sauna, I finally tied up the bag and quickly exited to the hallway to shove the squidgy bag into my rucksack, hoping that it wouldn't leak. Mind you, there was so little actual fluid in the stuff that leakage was not likely to be a problem.

I got back to the table milliseconds before Auntie Effi came in and, much to her satisfaction and our almost evident relief; she smiled at the empty plates and cleared the table. At this precise moment we heard movement in the hall, made our excuses and fled to the usual welcoming hugs and alternate cheek-kisses of Christina and young Effoula, who were all apologetic for not having been home when we arrived. If only they'd realised what we'd been through!

We all trouped upstairs and I made a couple of trips with the suitcases and accompanying paraphernalia and we were shown to our room. It was mid afternoon in Athens and, since it was still one of my earlier visits to the city, we decided to make use of the remains of the day. We showered and went to the lounge to share a cool drink with Christina. I did the usual "sitting-in-the armchair-and-feigning-interest-in-the-totally-unintelligible-conversation" thing, a skill I became a past master at over the years. It was made a little more bearable by the fact that I had been handed a cold beer. Soon, after Yvonne decided we'd shown sufficient interest in their news and sufficient gratitude for their hospitality, we left the house and walked the ten minutes or so to the Katopatissia station on the Athens Metro.

The walk takes one through a number of streets of modern three and four storey buildings, all sporting metal shutters and wrought iron gates in front of their heavy wooden front doors. Large potted geraniums were liberally sprinkled over front steps and in small front courtyards and the narrow streets were cluttered with dusty cars of all description, some displaying sunshades in their windows, others with a large white sign with red lettering saying *"POLEITAI"* (For Sale). On several corners were small shops, some bakeries, some cake & sweet shops (*zaheroplasteion*) which exerted a strong pull on one to go in and sample some baklava. As we drew near to the station the roads were a little wider and the pavements were dotted with kiosks selling chewing gum, cigarettes, newspapers and various other stuff. Since this was before the era of cellphones these also each had a telephone hanging off an outside corner to which a young Greek would be attached by the right hand and ear whilst carrying on a furiously animated conversation with the invisible person at the other end, who couldn't see the gestures being made wildly with the left hand, but which the speaker needed to make nevertheless. Near the Metro station there was a main artery into the city, on which cars, buses, trucks and thousands of mopeds were haring up and down with apparent total lack of concern for any Highway Code. Here we descended some steps to the kiosk on the platform, where we paid our few drachmas with a *"Theo (soft "th") sti Monastiraki"* as we came to a stop to await the train.

We alighted at Monastiraki station. When you exit here you're greeted by the start of the old part of Athens. On the wide pavement immediately outside the station there's someone selling hot corn-on-the-cob from a small mobile oven/chargrill. There were old men carrying long posts with loads of small bits of paper attached, evidently the Greek National Lottery. Turning right you could pick up a take-away souvlaki at one corner, and start wending your way up the flea market on another.

Athens flea market is a wonderful cornucopia of trashy Greek souvenirs and really good leather bargains. You can buy a Greek record. No CD's in those days, it was all twelve-inch vinyl. We bought the first album by Georgio Dalaras, now one of Greece's biggest recording stars. We still get the same reaction in Greek record shops that we had then. Because I so evidently do not look Greek, they always point us to the "Memories of Greece" section, where you can pick up "Zorba the Greek, Never on a Sunday" and anything by Nana Mouskouri. Then Yvonne has to explain that she knows the real Greek stuff and, after some persuading, they'll play us a bit of the latest by a current Greek recording artist.

Further up the flea market I took an interest in one small booth, not much more than seven feet square, completely open on the side that empties into the narrow street and lined with narrow shelves laden with all sorts of small vases, plates and those little statues of the god with an enormous phallus. Every stallholder up the flea market stands out in the thoroughfare and talks to you in every language he can think of. As you approach he says: "Bonjour, Hello, how are you? Gooden Haffen, Sprachenzee Deutch?" ...in response to which I usually keep totally shtum. That way they keep guessing and don't know quite how to proceed. This guy obviously smelt my cash when I entered the establishment, virtually filling it to capacity. In those days we used to pack our smalls and socks in the suitcase with all manner of small earthenware coasters, vases and plates as souvenirs for family and friends alike. We mistakenly thought they'd all like something Greek hanging on their chimney-breast or their sideboard to remind them that John and Yvonne had been to Greece.

So I was a genuine punter, but was not going to be fleeced. I began to study one small 5-inch high blue and gold vase and picked it up to see how much it was. 900 Drachma. To be honest, I can't remember now what the price was, but for the sake of relating what happened, we'll say it was 900.

"Very cheap. Good quality. Best prices in Athens. I wrap it up?" I continued my silence, annoyed (needlessly) by the fact that he'd decided I was English (since I so obviously was!). At this time I probably only knew ten Greek words, but two of those were- *"Eftinoh"* and *"Acriva"* – meaning "cheap" and "expensive."

I smiled a little and reddened, but remained determined not to say a word. He stood right at my shoulder and repeated his kind offer to wrap it up. Just then Yvonne came in (making the place extremely crowded) and we began to experience a crush due to three bodies in such a confined space. She muttered, *"En taxi?"* (All right?)

This most brief of utterances had a magical affect on our genial host. He immediately decided we were Greeks after all and in a flash opened a section of the rear of the shop, shelves and all, to reveal, through this hidden door, a further showroom of equal size with all the same goods lining the shelves but at prices about 40% cheaper!

We availed ourselves of this bit of good fortune and left with several generously wrapped vases and plates. We felt good. We were enjoying ourselves. We were an hour from Christina's house when Yvonne froze with a yelp of dismay.

"What's the matter?" I cried, thinking she'd dropped her purse or something.

"The spaghetti!" Oh no! The spaghetti! In our haste to get out and enjoy the rest of our very first day in Athens, we'd taken it out of my rucksack and temporarily placed it under our bed until we left, when we were going to take it with us to drop in the first public waste bin we encountered. But it had totally gone out of our minds and here we were walking in downtown Athens with the spaghetti sitting on the marble floor under our bed in Katopatissia. Christina only had to go in to turn over the bedclothes and she'd certainly notice it. What if she told Auntie Effi?

We headed back to the Metro post-haste to discover our fate. Fortunately, when we got back it was still there under the bed in all its horrific glory.

But we'll never know whether Christina had found it and simply let it lie.

21 - Dogs

As previously mentioned in the account about Taki's wine-making exploits, Yvonne's cousin Christina and her husband Taki had a villa at Kalamos, a quiet coastal village north of Athens, facing across the sea to the large island of Evia. The village of Kalamos was really very small, comprising mainly residential buildings with bougainvillaea much in evidence and large hedges of geraniums bordering the road as it twisted down the hillside into the village.

As it levelled out at the bottom of the hill, the road turned left and followed the pebbly coast through Kalamos itself and along a rural patch of a few hundred yards, the hill sloping steeply up to the left and beach a few yards to the right. Then you would reach the area where all the villas had been built, scattering up the hillside for several hundred yards and reachable by ridiculously steep gravel and dust lanes. There were new properties being added all the time. I would imagine that now, some twenty years on, there is a quite large community of Athenians spending summer there to escape the oppressive heat of the city during July and August. This was, of course, why Takis and Christina, as well as Auntie Vassau and Uncle Theodoraki, had built theirs.

Not far from where the road levelled out in Kalamos village, there was a small taverna, with just three of four tables out front bordering the roadside, just a few feet above the level of the road. Yvonne and I were staying at Kalamos with Yvonne's mum (Lela) and her husband Dave, together with Christina, Takis and Effi, Vassau and Theodoraki also in residence at their villa, just across the dusty track from Takis & Christina's, and of very similar design. Both villas were situated quite a way up the side of the hill, making the view from their balconies rather stunning, but the trip up from the beach one of two experiences. If you were walking up it was so steep you'd wilt in the sun and perspire sufficiently to enter the World Perspiring Championships without having to qualify as a wild card. If you were driving up, and Christina had one of those tiny Suzuki four-wheel-drive jeeps that seem to have a very high centre of balance, you took your life in your hands as the little vehicle jumped and skidded all over the place as it negotiated an incline just a hair's-breadth from too steep for it to manage without falling over and rolling all the way back to the bottom with substantial loss of life.

In the daylight hours the climb via the jeep was hair-raising enough. At night, after you'd all spent a long and pleasant soirée at the taverna in the village, you just shut your eyes and hoped you had sufficient retsina in your blood to render you sufficiently dopey so as not to notice what was happening.

One night we walked to the taverna. I would guess now that it was about a mile from where the dusty lane down from the villa emptied out onto the road to the village. As I mentioned above, part of this distance involved open countryside on the hills to one's right (heading toward the village), which consisted of scrubby shrubs, all kinds of herbs, thorny bushes and a few trees. There were a lot of boulders too, many of which had rolled down and parked themselves right alongside the road. Four of us made the walk, Yvonne, Lela, Dave and myself, partly because we were ready to go before everyone else and partly because it was a beautiful evening for a walk before dinner.

After we had been sat enjoying a beer for a short while, Auntie Vassau and Uncle Theodoraki arrived in their little car, together with the jeep containing Christina, Taki and Effi.

There followed a "tingle-factor" evening. The air was warm enough all evening not to have to don anything more over one's T-shirt. The food was superb and included *kalamaraki*, octopus, *horiatiki*, *tsatsiki*, *horta*, *gigandes*, *fassolia*, *souvlaki*, quite a few fish of varying descriptions and all washed down with locally made retsina. After the table had been sufficiently made to resemble the after-effects of an air raid, out came the Metaxa and uncle Theodoraki's accordion. As usual, I had understood very little of the evening's banter. It didn't matter. Dave and I had had each other to bounce off in English whilst the others prattled away ceaselessly in Greek. But the atmosphere was Epicurean. Who cared whether the main conversation was intelligible when you were sitting in a village taverna with the sea (across which were visible the lights of various villages on the island of Evia, all twinkling in the starlight) lapping at the pebbles just a few feet away? Above, the stars were so vivid you could clearly make out the Milky Way. Various insects chirped in the bushes around the village. Occasionally someone would come past either on foot or in their car, but they would all stop and exchange pleasantries with the occupants of our table. Some would ascend the couple of steps to our terrace and there would follow a bit of back-slapping and cheek-kissing and introducing of the relatives from "Angleeah;" whereupon I would find myself standing and nodding and projecting my widest smile at various examples of local Greeks who were fascinated to see a "tourist" in such a place as Kalamos. It was all rather wonderful. I felt so laid back I was the laid-back king of planet earth for the night. Nothing else matters when you achieve that feeling does it?

Britain may as well be another planet away. Work? What was that? This was all there was. Do we ever really appreciate moments like that whilst we are living through them? I don't know whether it's possible. That's why I finally stopped taking shed-loads of photographs. What's the point of being somewhere when you should be savouring the experience, yet whipping out the camera and clicking frantically away and saying: "This will make a wonderful photograph, won't it. Can't wait to get home and get them developed." What!? Surely the best thing to do is savour the moment. Pinch yourself if you must, but make yourself take it in and enjoy it. It's lunacy to spend all the time looking forward to being able to look back on it (if you catch my drift)! When you're back home and immersed in your normal routine you enjoy reveries of these moments and dream of experiencing them over again, but to spend the actual moment looking forward to doing that is a bit daft isn't it. "Oh I'm sooo looking forward to sitting in my little home and thumbing through photo's of this holiday so I can wish I were still here." Wait a minute there! You ARE still here, for goodness sake enjoy it NOW!

The worse thing of all is, you can't re-create such times. It's never quite the same when you go back, A magical moment is just that ...a magical moment - and moments aren't repeatable; they are unique and gone in a flash. Best to savour the memories rather than try to re-live them. I think that's why I eventually wrote this book. Yvonne and I have been down that road of returning to the same place in the vain hope that we will live moments again. It never happens. Perhaps the secret is to let whatever new experiences you enjoy have their own worth. In other words, if you visit the same place on subsequent occasions, don't try and find what you had before, just enjoy what you have at the time. There are places that have changed so much that they don't have the same attraction any more. So, if you can't hack it, don't go there. Let the memories be sufficient. That's what we do now. There are places in Greece we have visited several times, sometimes with a degree of success, but other times with an overwhelming sense of deflation at what had gone forever about that place. So, we haven't gone back there again.

This night in Kalamos, probably in September of 1977 if my memory serves me right, was a moment I shall always treasure. I suppose because I was very young and the whole thing about travelling abroad and having the privilege of being entertained by relatives, who live such different lives in a different climate and culture, was still quite wondrous to me.

I'm boring you. At the end of the meal, Theodoraki got his accordion out and, resting it on his lap, displayed a talent I'd never have guessed he had. He was a slight man; in fact he still is, although now very old, with lined features and high cheekbones. His features were almost more native American than Greek. He played traditional Greek folksong after traditional Greek folksong and all the Greeks round the table joined in the singing. Some of those tunes are very familiar to me now, but they were all new to me then. The table grew so full of empty glasses and bottles and aluminium retsina jugs that it couldn't possibly take any more when the evening reluctantly drew to its inevitable close.

Auntie Vassau, Theodoraki's wife, was huge. She was much, much bigger than her diminutive husband. She was also very much in charge as I read their relationship. But she was lovely. I liked her a lot. I'll never forget the sight of her in the back of one of those three-wheeled trucks that rural Greeks always used to ride around in. They were very compact and had a motorbike engine hidden under a sloping bonnet, not dissimilar to the shape of a shrunken Volkswagen Beetle, though without the mudguards, as there was only the one front wheel. You would see a lot of them in France too in decades past. Christina, Effi, Yvonne, Lela, Dave, Vassau and I had walked along the coast northeastward from Kalamos to the next piece of civilisation, which was a small port called Oropos. At Oropos you could get a ferry over to Evia and we had been there to check out the ferry times for a crossing we were planning as a day trip. It was no small walk and, a little further along the coast from the villas in Kalamos, the road ceased to be tarmac and turned into red earth, full of twists and turns and potholes. At Oropos we had taken some refreshments in the form of ice cream and lemonade at a small zaheroplasteion, and, after checking with the ferry office on the time of the ferry, started the walk back. It was several miles to Kalamos along this twisty and uneven dirt road and all were getting a bit tired.

We decided that should any vehicle come along the "road" we'd try hitchhiking. Picture it, six of us, one of which was twenty stone if she was a pound! The state of this dirt road meant that not many vehicles would even attempt to navigate it, but, sure enough, just when we were wilting in a major way, along came this little farm pickup, the three-wheeled type.

The driver cheerfully beckoned us to climb in the back. Lela got in the cab with him, whilst five of us, including of course Auntie Vassau – all twenty-odd stone of her – clambered into the open back of the tiny pick-up. The driver set off with a vigour that took us all by surprise. He'd obviously recently watched a James Bond film as we were soon being bounced around like hailstones on a pavement.

Remember, the road was only a dirt track and full of potholes and boulders. Now and again there would be a hairpin whilst the "road" negotiated a large outcrop of rock and we'd all swing to one side. If it was Vassau's side we had a soft cushion to fall against, but if it was our side we feared for our lives as all the air was pressed out of our lungs and it felt like we were being smothered and devoured by "The Blob" from a classic 50's sci-fi film. Sometimes we'd be bounced so violently that I was certain that Vassau was going to give herself a pair of black eyes. In spite of the discomfort and subsequent bruising, it was a wildly enjoyable experience and I'll always carry in my mind a vision of large areas of Auntie Vassau's flesh leaping up and down under her sundress in a manner that barely permitted the dress to remain in one piece without being ripped asunder. As fast as we had pulled away at the outset of this fairground ride, we came to a skidding halt at the foot of the lane leading up to the villa at Kalamos. We all clambered down in an undignified way and dusted ourselves off. Lela got out of the cab and wondered what all the fuss was about as we all cheerfully and gratefully waved our make-shift taxi off whilst our hands searched our rib cages in a frantic attempt to count the fractures.

We were all so pleased with ourselves at this shared experience that we took turns at taking photographs (still did in those days) in front of a couple of almond trees before making the climb up to the villas.

The seemingly everlasting evening at the Kalamos taverna had come to a close and we were deciding who was going in which vehicle for the short trip back up to the villas. Eventually, after much debate and several changes of mind that involved various members of the party getting into one or the other of the vehicles and then getting out again; or getting into the front only to be dragged out by the collar and rammed into the back (and visa versa), we all were safely (I know - it's not the most appropriate use of the word, considering how much beer, retsina, ouzo and Metaxa had been consumed) ensconced in the cars and on our way along the little coast road.

We hadn't gone more than a few hundred yards when the sound of rabid howling and vicious barking sobered us up in no uncertain terms and raised the hairs on the backs of our necks. As we were passing the uninhabited part of the road, where it was rocky on either side, with nothing but scrub and trees to our left and the small shingly beach on the right, about six or seven canine creatures resembling a troupe of the "Hounds of the Baskervilles" emerged from the undergrowth to our left and set about pursuing the cars with great enthusiasm. They really did look fierce. They gave one the impression that, had we been on foot, we would have been torn limb from limb like the poor fox at the conclusion of a "successful" hunt. Christina, who was driving our jeep, put her foot down and, with a fair bit of squealing of tyres and weaving about, finally put some road between ourselves and these creatures from a Hammer film.

When we reached the villas, after the usual heart-in-mouth climb up the dirt track, we all decided we needed a

drink to steady our nerves. Both vehicles discharged their
contents and all made a speedy bound up the steps into the
safety of Christina and Taki's villa balustrade. Once we had
taken a little "medication," all began to recount their
impression of the brush with these dogs of horror and tried to
outdo each other with how much surprise or fear we had
experienced. What made the experiences of those who had
walked down to the village earlier in the evening the most to
be respected, was our emphasis on how we could well have
met these demons on the way there! Had we done so, the
evening would have taken quite a different turn. Certainly we
would have anyway! We felt the need to lay around on the
veranda well into the small hours, the vast sweep of hillside,
sea and the island of Evia below us, so as to restore in us all a
sense of calm sufficient for us to be able to sleep.

Next morning there were not a few empty bottles, not to
mention a few zonked out bodies, still on the veranda.

I decided that these were not mountain-climbing wild
dogs. Just as well as it turned out for those who never made it
from the veranda to their beds.

22 - *Agistri*

Yvonne's brother, Paul, had taken the summer off in 1980 and was spending the time on the Greek island of Agistri. Paul met us when we arrived in Athens to spend a few days with the relatives before getting the boat to the island.

He was full of how wonderful Agistri was. There was no direct way of reaching it from Athens, you took the ferry to Aegina (pronounced, incidentally: *egg'innah* and not agee'na as most Brits call it) and from there a smaller boat across to Agistri. Aegina is, of course, on the route of many an island ferry out of Piraeus. So it was easy to get there and hence on to Agistri. Sadly, to me at any rate, Agistri is now well and truly on the tourist trail and is to be found in quite a lot of holiday brochures. When we visited the island on several occasions all those years ago, it was a paradise of calm. There were no motor vehicles. The jetty at which the small boats from Aegina tied up was just a pile of stones with a bit of concrete poured on top of them jutting our from an impossibly beautiful sandy beach. The beach stretched for just a few hundred yards out on a small spit and it backed on to some low sand dunes. Right in the middle of these sand dunes, and only yards from this idyllic beach, the Greeks have now built a great big white church. It seemed to me that the populace of the island was nowhere near adequate for such a large religious structure, but then, the Greek Orthodox Church is nothing if not ostentatious.

A score of small fishing boats bobbing in the clear waters were tied up at the end of the beach where the little boat from Aegina landed. The beach itself was totally clean of sunbeds and parasols. Everyone who went on to it took whatever he or she needed along with them. Those roll-up rush beach mats with the little bit of green sown round the edges were the order of the day and perfectly adequate. As a result the beach itself retained a sort of untouched and natural look. To my dismay, consulting holiday brochures nowadays, I see the ubiquitous white plastic sunloungers and their partners-in-crime, the parasol, all along this once wild paradise of calm.

But in 1978 it was still wonderfully remote. Agistri is a very small island with a mountain in the middle of it. Laying on the beach for more than an hour gave me an irresistible urge to go and explore. Following the dusty track off behind the beach brought me to a small village of one and two-storey houses, all set in little gardens behind low walls and chain-link fences. Huge geraniums were everywhere, and dotted around the gardens were lemon and almond trees and some olive trees. Quite a few of the houses had luscious vines heavy with deep red grapes sprawling over their bamboo canopies and going up their walls. September is a wonderful time to be in Greece. As I walked further up the concreted road through the village the houses thinned out and the concrete came to an end. At this point the road turned instantly into a mass of potholes and boulders and dust. Just as well no one had a motor vehicle here, you couldn't drive it more than a couple of hundred yards.

The track began to rise a little more steeply and, looking up the hill, I could see a very old village perched on its own little hillock, with the island's mountain towering above and behind it. As I entered this village it was like stepping back a couple of thousand years. Large fig trees shaded the narrow streets, most of which weren't flat, but sloped either one way or the other by a good ten degrees or so, possibly more. There wasn't a human soul to be seen. Chickens and donkeys had the place to themselves, apart from me that is. Quite a number of the houses had evidently been renovated, although with old-fashioned methods - to keep them in character. Some had evidently been continually lived in for decades, possibly longer, with little or no changes being made to them, their doors and shutters bearing evidence of still frequent use, though not very recent maintenance.

All the walls appeared to be of rough stone. Whether they were garden walls or house walls, they all had a similar appearance. The whitewash was still there, but struggling to hold on. As I penetrated the village further it became a maze of tiny alleyways, each of which granted a fascinating vista as I turned its corner. Evidently, the entire small populace of this village was asleep to a man, it being around three in the afternoon. I enjoyed furiously the feeling of tranquillity and release that being in such a place can give one. Cats lay sleepily on doorsteps. Swallows and martins darted about catching their lunches on the wing. The odd goat let out a whinny, but I could hear nothing else. Except, perhaps for the slight breeze rustling olive, almond and fig leaves. There were gourd plants too, their almost perfectly formed "bottles" hanging quietly, waiting to be harvested.

I know it's an old cliché, but I wanted time to stand still. In fact, for a half an hour or so it appeared to. I came upon an ancient taverna, with a concrete terrace granting me a view right across the sea to Aegina. It only had about two tables, which at present were also asleep with their equally ancient chairs turned upside-down and placed on their tops. In the wall at the end of the terrace was a really old bread oven, with its arched aperture blackened by years of wood burning and bread making. It was totally out in the open a good twenty yards from the old building that served as the taverna. I couldn't imagine how this place made a living, unless the whole village ate there most nights. Most odd was that the only thing I had seen for half an hour or so which was in any way modern was adjacent to the doorway of this building. It was a five or six feet high stack of Coca-Cola crates, their empty bottles all glistening in the scorching sun. I never drink the stuff, but could happily have downed several when I saw this. These were all empty though, so I would have to wait a little longer to quench my considerable thirst.

I sat for quite a while on the edge of the taverna's terrace, just looking at the glorious view. The "road" here was so rough that it was difficult to believe it was the road at all. It was edged by a two-foot-high rough stone wall, the one on the far side being quite a bit lower than the near side, where I sat. The surface was so rough that it was difficult to walk along, leave alone attempt to navigate with a vehicle of any description. There were large bare patches of stone which were worn to a shine and they gleamed in the sunlight as they showed through the dust.

Reluctantly, I began to make my way back to the track that led down to the more "modern" village and the beach beyond. On reaching the beach I found Yvonne fast asleep and cooking nicely in the sun (she has the enviable asset of skin that never seems to burn. I have to be very careful and often, when misjudging it, turn into a lobster before you can say malignant melanoma, but she covers herself in factor 4 and lays in the sun all day, no problem), so I grabbed a small sketch pad and went to sit on the old jetty, where I passed another hour or so sketching the little bobbing boats.

Another walk on Agistri, which I this time made with Yvonne, was along the level track that joined the village behind the beach to another, about a mile or so along the coast to the west. We did this walk the following year and, having at first decided that the island hadn't changed appreciably, were somewhat dismayed to be passed midway between the two villages by a four-wheel drive jeep type thing, crewed out with blond haired beach boys and girls, evidently enjoying in their own way this formerly tranquil island of peace amid an all-too-noisy world.

The last time we visited the island of Agistri was in 1980. We haven't been back since ...for reasons I described in chapter twenty. C'est, unfortunately ...la vie.

The taverna in the village on Agistri, circa 1978

23 - A Bit of Bread and Cheese

Following a stay on Poros in 1982, the year that Yvonne's mum Lela died, we didn't return to Greece for reasons partly financial and partly pressure from friends who wanted to save us from an eternity of being "sad people" or "Greece-anoraks," until September of 1986. This time we went somewhere we hadn't been before, to Kefallonia.

Betweentimes we had been to France (twice) and Majorca. It was the visit to Majorca that really decided us to return to Greece for our next trip abroad. It just didn't "do it" for us. The friends we went with, at their invitation, were lovely and we enjoyed their company, but Santa Ponsa is just nowhere when you compare it to a Greek island.

So we arrived for the first time at Kefallonia airport. This is turning into a book of laments really. When I think of the airport at Kefallonia as it was in 1986 it starts the old twinges of sadness again. We landed with me sitting on the side of the plane which afforded a view of the terminal building as we touched down. I rather expected it to be a little grander than it was, but was pleased that it was somewhat smaller and more modest than expected. In fact, to many people we have met who visited Kefallonia in the 1980's, it became affectionately known as the "Cow Shed."

The plane came to a halt a few hundred yards from this small building and we enjoyed that wonderful feeling you always get, and never tire of, when the plane door opens and you get your first sniff of the Greek air. We walked down the stairway on to the hot tarmac and across it to the ramp leading up into the "Arrivals" lounge. Looking back at the plane I distinctly remember remarking that several of its tyres were showing a large amount of canvas through their rubber.

"Look at those wheels!" I exclaimed. In response to which everyone within twenty yards obeyed instantly. "Do they always wear aeroplane tyres so far out before replacing them? I'm surprised that one of them didn't blow out when we landed." Quite a few agreed and, since we had now reached the terminal "building" our thoughts were soon diverted to the task at hand – reclaiming our baggage. The late 1980's were the last days of the gone and not much lamented Dan Air charter airline. In fact, in 1986 it was by the trusty "Dan Dare," as they were affectionately known, that we were ably transported. This is significant, as will be seen later (talk about building suspense, eh?).

The "Arrivals" lounge was more like a railway platform under a corrugated iron roof with fresh air on three of the four sides. There were six-foot screens placed in formation across the exit side, so that you would pass through some kind of chicane which enabled the authorities to check your passport before you were let loose on the Greek public. But, whilst you waited for your baggage you stood on this three-sides-open platform, the right hand edge of which was where the open truck carrying the baggage would pull up alongside and you would all help yourselves to your own cases. Of course, this meant that if yours was on the bottom you had a bit of a wait while everyone else rummaged for theirs first.

Once you had rescued your cases you filtered through between the screens and, as you emerged again into the sunshine, a lovely Greek girl in uniform would hand you a single rose and say "Welcome to Kefallonia." To which I replied with not a little excitement: "*Efharisto poli!*"

The first thing we noticed on subsequent visits was that the construction of a more modern terminal building had begun. Now, no doubt the residents of the island were going to be proud of this as it was going to create a more sophisticated impression to those arriving on the island by aeroplane; but all I could think of was that it would inevitably lead to a higher volume of visitors and therefore to a more commercialised atmosphere on the island.

You see I have to confess to being a travel snob. I can't help it. Everywhere we go (Yvonne is the same) we think of ourselves as entitled to be there. But everyone else, apart from the locals, is an infernal nuisance. It's totally hypocritical I know, but we just can't help it. I like to be able to get a flight to whichever island I wish to visit, but I don't want anyone else to be going there. Once there, we try to immerse ourselves into the community and get to know locals by practising our Greek, and get really annoyed if we visit a taverna that's full of Brits or other foreign tourists. The fact that were it not for other tourists going to these places in some numbers there wouldn't be any cheapish flights is neither here nor there.

Mind you, I think we have a bit of a point in some ways. One thing we have never wished to do is go abroad to be housed in some hotel with a whole bunch of people from our own country; being fed English food in the hotel restaurant every night whilst sat among all the rest of the Brits busily bemoaning how the food's not up to the standard of the local chippie back home. Then there's the laid-on entertainment, when some locals (and some not so local, as described in a previous chapter) disdainfully prance around in national costume to the whirring of video cameras (and flashing of the cameras of those less fortunate who can't afford a video camera) and then dutifully grab a few sleeves and get the Brits up on the floor shouting "Ooplah!" in a vain attempt to emulate the Greek shout of *"Oh'pah!"* Then there's the welcome meeting, where the reps have to try and get you to sign up for the "island tour and beach barbecue", which, once again will be enjoyed among a bunch of gradually inebriating Brits and just the one or two Greeks who are earning their living suffering these prize twits whilst steering the boat or organising the barbie and all the time passing round the complimentary ouzo and watching while these pathetic grockles try and show how much they can drink and still dive into the sea off the side of the boat after several large souvlakis before throwing up at the end of the beach, where they're hoping no one will see them.

Soapbox bit over. But I do feel better for it.

Anyway, to return to my hypocritical comments about the airport. I remember arriving there a year or so after the project of the new terminal building was begun, to see it sitting part-built in metaphorical mothballs, all surrounded by sturdy metal fences and with not much going on. Makis, the dancer we had come to know pretty well (the story of how will follow sooner or later) by this time, told us that the Kefallonian authorities had run out of money and had to freeze the project. I had to admit to being pleased. But the last time we went was in 1988 and I'm told that it is finished now. Still, the "cow shed" is fondly remembered by many I'm sure. Certainly by the many who, like us, wanted to keep the place to themselves.

We were staying in Poros, a village at the far southeastern tip of the island. The coach trip from the airport to Poros took the best part of an hour, thus imprinting in the mind how large this island is. Leaving the airport we climbed through several small villages, all of fairly modern buildings, but with very pretty gardens of bougainvillaea, orange and lemon trees and geraniums in abundance. Then we joined the main Argostoli road, which was almost civilised, having two lanes and not too many potholes and undulations. The road then swept along the western slope of Mount Aenos, the highest peak on the island, the western side of which slopes away for a couple of miles right down to the sea. The road to Poros, Skala and Katelios hugs the side of this incline and climbs gradually until it passes round the southern side of the mountain through a small pass, in the middle of which is a village, and dropping down towards the aforementioned resorts.

The last couple of miles before Poros are very beautiful. After crossing a small plain of lemon and orange plantations, the road drops through a smaller version of Cheddar Gorge as it cuts through a small range of mountains that provide the backdrop for Poros. The town is petite, with a smattering of tavernas and shops leading to a long shingly beach to the north, and a small harbour to the south. Into this harbour come ferryboats from the mainland Pelopponese (that's if my memory serves me correctly, and there is room for doubt!).

Our studio was just a hundred yards from the shingle beach. The location was certainly good for anyone requiring a good session of de-stressing. Poros is sleepy and, at this particular time, "sleepy" was what I needed. There was no bank. You had to go to the Post Office to change money. This consisted of a room with a desk in it. But, what the hell, it did the job. Nearby was a small traditional bakery where you could indulge in freshly baked hot *tiropita* (feta cheese and pastry pie), yum. There were several really laid-back tavernas, with small two-person tables covered in bright check oilcloths along the roadside immediately behind the beach and under small trees. Further along the beach to the north there were one or two more tavernas at varying distances one from the next. You could hardly have called the place a hub of excitement. It was perfect. The shingly beach was probably a mile long and, right at the far end was the "spotty tree" taverna. The tables here were all spread out among trees the trunks of which were painted up to about six feet high in white with loads of blue and red spots all over them. We would spend some days right at the far end of this beach, even another couple of hundred yards along from the spotty tree, where the beach was brought to an end by rocks. Here you could quite happily laze around totally naked without a soul coming anywhere near you all day. Not that we did of course, well…

One day we decided to walk along the track that led further up the coast from this end of the shingly beach. It led along the side of the hill, here and there benefitting from the shade of the odd olive tree. It was edged by a few rough stones which, now and again tried to emulate a wall, but without much success. Further up the hillside you could see the Kefallonia pines, which only grow here and one other place in the world, but goodness knows how they tell. They all look like slender pines the like of which you see all over the

Mediterranean to me. Mind you, I'm no dendrologist, or whatever a tree expert is called.

As was often our habit, we made no preparation for this walk. It just took our fancy while we were sitting on the beach. We just donned shorts, daps and rucksacks and off we trotted, rolled up beach mats shoved into the tops of the rucksacks. After an hour or so we had had enough and decided to turn back. The way back reminded us how far we had come and our mouths were quite certain they hadn't tasted water for far too long.

Where he came from I've no idea, but he was exactly what we needed. I imagine he was a goatherd or something, but as we turned a corner and both exclaimed that, come the next sufficiently high part of the "wall" that skirted the road, we would sit down and rest and dream of drops of water dripping onto our tongues ...there he was. An old Greek peasant, dressed in faded blue trousers and a check shirt that had evidently celebrated a lot of anniversaries with him, was sat on the next sufficiently high bit of wall under a large old olive tree. He greeted us and asked us to sit with him, which we did. He had a large bottle of wine and some bread and feta cheese. Yvonne struck up a conversation with him, later telling me she couldn't understand a word he said owing to his dialect, but it appeared to me at the time that they were getting along swimmingly. Without hesitation he spread out the greaseproof paper his banquet was wrapped in, wiped the mouth of his wine bottle and gesticulated to us to share his bounteous feast. It was another one of those "tingle-factor" moments. I remember very quickly feeling light-headed and surveying the scene with great satisfaction. Here we were sat under an olive tree with a genial old Greek we had never met before. The slope beneath us flowed gently down to the blue sea, across which on the horizon you could just make out the Greek mainland. A few sails dotted the ocean, cicadas chirped and the odd lizard basked on the stones further along the road. How much time passed I've really no idea. All I remember is that he took his leave after we had exhausted the food and drink with a vigorous and evidently benevolent handshake, accompanied by a broad grin from his weathered face which revealed not a few gold teeth. Then he was gone round the side of the hill in the direction we had returned from. I couldn't remember having seen any building which remotely resembled a house or farm within easy walking distance right up to the place where we had decided to turn back. But that way he went and we never saw him again.

The sustenance he had shared with us was just perfect to give us the energy and will to make it back to the spotty tree taverna, where several cold beers, a huge bottle of water and a Greek salad were consumed without much delay.

Later that evening we walked in the other direction from our apartment, around the small rocky promontory to the harbour. Here there were several cheerful tavernas, lights beginning to glow in the fast approaching gloom of the evening. We chose a table and were soon enjoying something of which we never tire: a meal al-fresco on a Greek island. Toward the end of the evening we ended up talking to an English bloke we had seen around once or twice before. It was his last night he told us. Tomorrow he was going home, courtesy of "Dan Dare."

We commiserated in that smug way you do when you're not going home for ages yet and eventually said "bon voyage, we'll be thinking of you when we're on the beach tomorrow" and all that stuff and went home to bed.

The next night we were eating in another taverna when,

who should come past but this same chap. "I thought you were going home this morning!" I said, no small element of surprise in my voice.

"I was, but the plane had a problem and we've all been sent to some accommodation for another night."

"What sort of problem?"

"Apparently, one of its tyres is blown and they're having to fly one over from Athens for tomorrow morning so they can fit it and we can go home."

24 - A Frenchman's Dive

Kefallonia has a great deal to offer. It has some of the loveliest beaches you'll find anywhere in the Mediterranean. It has some stunning scenery. It also has enough space for the discerning visitor to get off the beaten track and enjoy the essence of the place without the company of a bunch of other tourists and its people are warm and friendly.

When we were there it had its fair share of "characters" too. I would hope they're all still there, but – who knows? One such was Yiorgo Goulimis, the flamboyant and ever-so-slightly "affected" director of "Goulimis Tours" who organised the Greek Nights for a number of tour operators. He was about sixty, a bit portly and fancied himself as a bit of a singer. His hair was swept back rather dramatically and still had bits of black among the copious streaks of grey. His eyes were very deep under eyebrows which hadn't greyed at all and which overhung his eyes in a prominent fashion, which accentuated the eyes' deepness. His face was quite rounded down as far as mid-cheek, but from there down shrank away to an unusually small and pointy chin. He always wore a short-sleeved shirt outside his cream trousers and at some stage during any of the Greek evenings he hosted would take the microphone in hand and serenade the bemused revellers with a few old Greek traditional songs. I don't think Simon Cowell would have wasted much time trying to ring him – let's put it that way. But when it came to "how big a heart do you have?" – his was enormous. We visited the island several times and, once he had come to know us, he always insisted that we attend any Greek night we fancied as his guests. When we did so, it never cost us lepta and it was always a good night. There is much more about Goulimis to come, much more.

Then there was Dennis (Yes, Dennis!), a gentle man who usually was to be seen sitting behind the electronic keyboard at any of Yiorgo Goulimis' Greek Nights. Dennis was also about 60 and owned of one or two small apartment blocks. He would always take every opportunity to dish out his card to anyone likely to be returning to Kefallonia "under their own steam," as it were.

Then there were the dancers. Now these were the real McCoy. Goulimis had assembled a troupe that danced for all his soirees and they were the business. There were four guys we particularly got to know: Makis, Makis, Nikos and Babys. We first met them at the Greek night Goulimis was running in the village of Poros at the Hercules Hotel, which sported a lovely open terrace, perched fifty feet or so above the water between the village and its small harbour.

The dancers came on and did a few of the usual – *Hasapiko*, *Kalamatiano*, a couple of others I couldn't name if I tried, then the Hasaposerviko, when they try and get all the semi drunken Brits up to make complete idiots of themselves. Of course, we're happy to oblige. It soon, though, became apparent to the four professionals that Yvonne knew all the steps and this led to a series of dances in which she was the only one to join in with them. They all fancied her I'm sure, but were far too gentlemanly to try anything. You may think I'm only saying that because she's my wife. But on many occasions over the years Greek men have directly propositioned her whilst smiling across a table (and an Amstel or two) at me, assuming I can't understand what they're saying. To give an instance: We were sat one evening at a taverna not more than a few minutes walk from our room on Poros island. The waiter, Petros, had a brother whom he had introduced to us and had invited himself to join us for dinner. At one point in the evening Yvonne decided she was a little chilly and needed her cardigan. I volunteered to pop back to the room to get it.

During the five to ten minutes I was gone the conversation went something like this, in Greek obviously!

"Are you happy in your marriage?"

"Yes, of course."

"No 'of course,' many people are not."

"Well, you need have no worries on that score. We're fine, really."

"Even those whose marriages are 'fine' still like a bit of a change now and then. I have a wife and two children in Corinth. But I also have a small apartment in Athens I need for business. I'm going there tomorrow, why don't you join me?"

"Because I'm here with my husband."

"He won't mind. He'll still be here when you get back. It'll only be a day or two. I'll look after you..."

At which point I returned, all smiles, with Yvonne's cardigan. This man looked up at me as though butter wouldn't melt in his mouth and said-

"You have a very beautiful wife. You're a lucky man."

"That's what I'd say; but then, I'm biased." I replied, my suspicions aroused, mainly because I was getting to know Greek men. He remained charming until we had finished the meal and then made his excuses and left.

This has not been an unusual experience. My wife is very attractive. I'm not just saying that; after all, that's one of the reasons I went out with her in the first place.

Anyway, I think we were at a Greek evening meeting the dance troupe.

When the dancers had finished their displays they all drew up chairs and sat with Yvonne and I. The usual high-spirited mega-quick Greek banter ensued, during which I ordered more Amstels and enjoyed the view out across the bay in the starlight. Much laughter and excited planning were evidently going on and I was informed that we were invited to go somewhere with these chaps the next night. I'll have to come back to this because this chapter is meant to be about something completely different. I think I had been introducing some of the Greek "characters" we had encountered on Kefallonia in the late 1980's and I really wanted to get to Andreas Benetatos. ...and now, finally, I have.

Yvonne encountered Andreas one day as she walked along the water's edge on Makris Yialos. This was the beach immediately next to Platis Yialos, which was the one we preferred. Both beaches are gorgeous yellow sand and face west from Lassi, a small gathering of apartments and tavernas on the road over the hill from Argostoli, where we were staying. You could walk to Makris Yialos in about half an hour from Argostoli, which accounts for the plethora of taxis whizzing up and down that particular stretch of road. We were "pitched" on Platis Yialos for the day. "We" being Alain Choupeault, our mad French friend (who lived in Cardiff), his wife Kiersten (her mum's Danish) and their daughter Pascale, who at the time of this vacation was about ten years old, Yvonne and I. Alain and I had decided to go for a marathon snorkelling session, which took us out around the small peninsula immediately to the South of Platis Yialos beach to the small caves and cliffs beyond. A photograph of this peninsula finds its way into many a tour operator's brochure nowadays. The reason is obvious. It has a narrow stretch of golden sandy beach, with sea either side, leading a couple of hundred metres out to a rocky outcrop at its far end. When sparingly scattered with parasols and sunbeds, it's very photogenic.

Alain and I swam out and around this peninsula, investigating starfish, hunting for octopus and chasing fishes. We rounded the far tip of the peninsula and found the wind made the sea here a little choppier. Not much really, but enough to make swimming more of a task. Keeping the southern side of the peninsula's beach about a hundred yards or so to our left, we eventually came to a small cave in the cliff and mooched about there a while. If you've ever gone snorkelling you'll know what usually happens at times like this. You're enjoying yourself immensely when, suddenly without warning, you discover you're very tired, hungry and possibly getting a bit cold. Not that it always is very cold, but because you're tired and hungry and perhaps in a small cave and, out of the sun, you feel cold. Quite often you've stopped swimming and are just bobbing on the surface and this too means you aren't creating any body heat by the movement of your limbs. All this comes upon you when you're half a mile or more away from your nice hot sandy beach.

Whatever; we were experiencing all the above. There was nothing for it but to start swimming back. We reached the south side of the peninsula beach and stopped for a rest in shallow water, sand beneath our feet. We were both bemoaning the fact that we were too hungry to swim when a very small fishing boat chugged around the corner and approached us. It was not much bigger than a dinghy, but with one of those little "cabins" on top with two circular portholes, one either side, and two in the front. The man onboard seemed to be simply whiling away some time and an idea began to hatch. Alain said: "I ask heem for a leeft back to our beach!"

"No harm asking," I replied, "He can only say no."

Before Alain could get close enough to make the request, a voice boomed from the beach in fluent Greek. I didn't catch much of it, but it must have meant something like: "Hey Dimitri! Those two men in the water are my friends! Do us a favour, get 'em aboard and bring them back round to Platis Yialos!" The voice was that of Andreas. But we were quite mystified when Dimitri, or whatever his name was, chugged over to us and, extending his hand, scooped the two of us up onto his boat. All smiles and extravagant gestures, he made it clear we were to sit on top of his little cabin while he ferried us back to the beach. Boy, did we feel important! There were all these tourists on the peninsula beach watching this. We looked as if we weren't like the rest of the grockles. We were "in with the natives."

It was even better when we chugged up to within thirty feet or so of our beach, Platis Yialos. There were quite a lot of faces here we knew. You know - ones you see regularly on the same spot of beach and begin nodding good morning to. A little crowd gathered both in and out of the water to watch our approach. It was time to show off a bit. Not!

I was wearing my mask on top of my head, as was Alain, so I decided to jump in rather than dive. Besides, this close to the beach I wasn't sure how deep it was, I didn't want to hit the bottom and break my neck and become one of those holiday tragedy stories in the paper the next week. I shoved my snorkel through my trunks and jumped in. I just had time to see Alain out of the corner of my eye. He had donned his diving mask and decided that the audience was too good to waste, so he dived. I came up and waved farewell to Dimitri, who returned the wave and chugged away, his good deed for the day accomplished. Alain came up looking straight at me and I immediately noticed two things. One: His glass was missing and water was cascading out from his mask. Two: There was a fairly large and growing patch of deep red on his forehead and spreading down over his eyebrows and nose.

"You're bleeding!" I shouted! Pointing at his face.

"What?" he replied, touching his finger to the bridge of his nose and reacting as if this is what he would have expected. "Uh huh." Was all that came out. He was obviously now having an attack of the "I know. It's no problem, I'm cool." syndrome.

"What happened?" I cried, already fully aware of what must have occurred.

"Eet must 'ave been shallower than I thought. No big deal, my 'ead touched the sand zat's all."

By this time his face was a long streak of red dissecting two flesh-coloured halves. Blood was about to drip from his chin. Among our spectators a few feet away on the sand some were spurting off to the sandwich bar at one end of the beach to get some first aid. As we came right up on to the beach someone handed Alain a paper napkin which he promptly slapped over the wound.

Now Alain Choupeault has a fairly large "widow's peak" coming down on his forehead. He had struck bottom with quite a bit of force with the part of his head about an inch above the hairline. The effect he had achieved, by virtue of the fact that an area of scalp about and inch long by three-quarters of an inch wide had been removed by the sea bottom, was very much in appearance like a cat's bum. Over by the sandwich bar we were hastily offered white plastic chairs and someone administered copious quantities of iodine to the wound. After the bleeding stopped a band-aid was duly stuck on. This didn't adhere too well because of all the surrounding hair, but whilst it was in place drew lots of guffaws of laughter because it looked ...well just plain funny. There were lots of jokes about a fish now swimming round happily sporting its new toupee and I went back in to try and retrieve Alain's glass out of his mask, but with no success. I am still the proud possessor of a photograph showing Alain, cold beer in hand, sitting in the chair by the sandwich bar proudly sporting his Elastoplast. Sitting next to him is Andreas.

Ah, Andreas. How did we come to meet him? As mentioned earlier, Yvonne had met him whilst strolling along the water's edge. This was whilst Alain and I were off snorkelling. It was when she wanted to introduce Andreas to us that they had discovered where we were and Andreas had wandered out on the small peninsula to try and spot us. Having been assured by Yvonne that the two heads bobbing up and down were in fact ours, it was he who had enlisted the help of Dimitri on the small boat to ferry us back to our beach for the introductions. It was also he who had supervised the medical attention which had been given Alain after his dramatic dive and subsequent exodus from the water.

After the audience had dissipated, satisfied that the fun was over for the time being, we sat on the terrace by the sandwich bar and were duly introduced to our newly found philanthropic friend.

Andreas sits and commiserates with an injured Frenchman!
Platis Gialos Beach, 1988

25 - Dinner

Andreas Benetatos was about fifty. He would spend a number of hours on the beach most days each week wearing nothing but a smallish pair of blue trunks and carrying his wallet. He would sit by the sandwich bar with a cool beer, or walk along the water's edge trying to meet people to get to know. We got to know him.

He had a rugged smiling face and longish wavy brown hair, which was quite fair for a Greek. He was very genial and was comfortable in our company from the word go. He laughed a lot and evidently warmed to us, not only because he rather fancied my wife, but, unlike many Greek men, he was the perfect gentleman and enjoyed a good animated conversation more than just about anything else. He never made her feel threatened or embarrassed. Quite often Yvonne would sit under the sunshades over the tables by the small sandwich bar on the beach and enjoy a chat with Andreas over an iced coffee. Meanwhile I would be reading my book or sleeping a few feet away under a shade on the beach. Hard life isn't it?

A lot of locals on Kefallonia, like many islands, did not

own cars. If they had any vehicle at all it was a Japanese moped or Italian Vespa scooter. Andreas, however, had a Renault Five. A bit tired it may have been, but he was always totally insistent that, when we were ready to leave the beach at the end of a long hard day, he take us back to our accommodation in the car. So quite often of an evening there were six bodies and a wheelchair, plus various beach bags and mats in this gallant little car. The wheelchair was necessary because Alain's wife Kiersten had multiple sclerosis and could no longer walk. That didn't stop us making sure she had a thoroughly active holiday. But, in deference to her, we won't dwell on her disability; it's of no consequence.

Driving back to Argostoli Andreas would always manage to wheedle out of us which taverna we were probably going to be eating in that evening. Sure enough, halfway through our meal he would often turn up and join us. He was always welcome to do so. He told us his story in the course of evenings like this.

He had been married. His wife was German and, following their divorce, now lived in Germany. Andreas had been at sea (as have the vast majority of the Greek male population) and knew quite a few British ports. He had settled in Germany and run a business for a while before his marriage had gone wrong, but subsequently decided to return to his home on Kefallonia. He now lived with his ageing parents in the little village of Farsa, which was visible halfway up a mountainside across the bay from Argostoli. At night as you strolled along the Argostoli harbour front, you could clearly see the lights of Farsa twinkling on the mountainside.

Andreas made it evident that he was getting quite attached to us. Unlike quite a few Greeks whom I've always remained suspicious of when it comes to their intentions with regard to

Yvonne, Andreas very obviously enjoyed our company as a group. He would pluck flowers and give them to Kiersten. He would revel in a bit of mickey-taking with Alain and I and would play around on the beach with Pascale and Alain for ages. He would become part of the family during the evenings we spent at various tavernas with him and we would miss him if a day went by without encountering him somewhere.

One day, when we were all enjoying a good chin wag around a table at the beach bar, he invited us to his parents' house in the village for an evening of home cooking and a bit of an impromptu dance. Needless to say, we were delighted and couldn't wait for eight thirty. We had hired a small open top jeep for a few days and so would be able to drive up to the village ourselves. Following his instructions, we arrived without a hitch. The village of Farsa was simply a series of houses spread out along the one road, which ran right through it. To the right the houses were higher than the road and to the left they were somewhat lower. The Benetatos residence was on the left and had a concrete drive running steeply down from the gate in the wall. We parked up alongside the wall and walked down the drive to see a large table set outside the front door and off to the right under a pergola with a substantial vine draped over it. Walking down the drive you could see the lights of Argostoli, the island's capital, reflecting in the water of the bay. Andreas' Renault was parked at the bottom of the drive, to the left of the house, with the front right hand door open wide. From the car was booming the sound of Stratos Dionysiou, Andreas' favourite singer. He's also one of mine now, although sadly he died a few years ago. Andreas ended up giving us the tape as a present, the first Dionysiou album we ever owned. As we arrived at the front door various members of the family emerged to greet us and, with the exception of

Yvonne, who found her way without delay to the kitchen and was immediately immersed both in Greek conversation and food preparation, we all began the usual round of large smiles, back-slaps, double cheek kisses and feeble attempts at conversation through sign language and, where that failed, more large smiles.

Andreas could speak a few words of English, so he mediated and managed to make us understand who the various dinner guests were. There was Cousin Martina, a young vamp who immediately took an obvious shine to Alain – a romantic Frenchman after all. She was studying something somewhere and was home for a visit. There were an uncle and aunt from Illinois, USA. They had lived over there for thirty years, running a small restaurant and sending as much money home as they could to enable them to retire to the island when they ended their working lives. By British standards they looked as if they should have ended their working lives a good decade ago, but they were still working, gold teeth and all. The old uncle spent the entire evening sporting a baseball cap, as if to make the point that he lived in the USA. At first I thought- "good, they'll be able to converse with me," but no such luck. Thirty years among the Americans hadn't made a jot of difference to their linguistic abilities. They hadn't gone to the USA to be like the Americans, oh no! Get immersed in American way of life? No way Spiros! They were there to earn enough money to retire to the first floor apartment, which by then would have been completed above the ground floor home of Andreas' parents and not to become assimilated into the American way of life. They only mixed with fellow ex-pat Greeks; just to be sure their resolve wasn't weakened.

This was an interesting thing we learned whilst we were guests of Andreas and his parents. The houses didn't only sport those ugly metal spikes on the roof in order to fool the taxman. No, they were also very often the foundations of the next floor that was being built on money sent home from those who'd gone abroad and who were eventually going to return and live there. It seemed quite sad to us that so many Kefallonians, and no doubt residents of other islands as well, had to spend all their best years thousands of miles away from home, so they could afford to pass their dotage in the village they were born in. The lack of welfare state and government pensions (at the time) drove home to us how fortunate us British had been all these years.

There were, to sum up the guests around the table when we all eventually sat down to eat, Yvonne and I, Alain, Kiersten and Pascale, Andreas and his parents, cousin Martina, the Illinois Aunt and uncle, plus two little old ladies about whom I never found out a thing.

After we had all been kissed to death a couple of times, Andreas stood around attempting to converse with Alain and I whilst various members of the party dashed or shuffled in and out of the front door carrying saucepans, tureens, plates, plastic bottles full of home-made retsina, cutlery, ladles and glasses. The table gradually filled with all manner of foodstuffs and the utensils to aid their being digested, then the entire party gathered outside to begin filing round it to their respective places.

Everyone immediately assaulted the table's contents from all directions. Hands and arms all fought to avoid colliding whilst each dived for his or her salad, octopus, retsina, taramasalata, dolmades - in fact, you name a Greek dish and I'd bet a penny to a pound (only I don't gamble!) it was on that table. This must have been a specially imported table designed to take all the weight. It's hard to see how any normal table would have stood it. Mind you, it wasn't that heavily laden for long. The steady ingestion and re-loading of plates saw to that. Perhaps someone had sat down and calculated the weight-to-time ratio to see if the stresses would reduce sufficiently before the table gave in and collapsed. There were several things on that table I didn't recognise. All manner of cooked or boiled potfuls of colourful stuff that I would swear were still moving taunted my macho-ness. It was as if they were saying- "Go on then, if you're so brave eat me and see if you can keep me down once you find out what I'm made of!"

Mind you, it's surprising how much nicer and less intimidating these dishes get after a glass or five of homemade retsina from a well-preserved plastic water bottle. I think there were maybe just one or two of the countless pots and pans of stewed whatever that I didn't get round to trying. This was more from the fact that I was several belt-sizes bigger by the time I was getting round to them.

What was really amusing during this meal was the fact that, since we were sitting in full view of the road above, it became quite apparent that many of the locals were going out for a walk on the pretext that they wanted a bit of air, when all they really wanted to do was have a nose at these weird foreigners that the Benetatos family were entertaining on their front terrace. The entire meal was punctuated by neighbours walking halfway down the drive, hailing the hosts and exchanging evening pleasantries from several yards away and, their curiosity satisfied, walking back up and out of the gate and into the night. I wouldn't be at all surprised if the whole village hadn't turned out to see us by the time the meal was finished and we were all sitting round regretting that last helping of something unnameable. It was just like being human exhibits in some open zoological gardens.

The meal finished and, the table looking respectably decimated, I was enjoying that feeling you get when, following a major blow-out, you're supping at a cold beer and totally unable to move. The trousers were completely undone in desperation. It was either that or bust the zip. And they're all plastic these days so you can't be too careful. The entire village had passed in and out of the garden gate and it was about midnight or thereabouts.

"TIME TO DANCE!" Exclaimed Andreas with great gusto. "DANCE?!" I thought. "DANCE?!" I can't stand up leave alone dance.

Now if you, like me (prior to the evening being described here), thought all Greek men were born to dance, I'm here to tell you I got a shock that night. Yvonne, ever able to dance - whatever the state of her stomach - was up in a flash and Andreas opened his car door as far as it would go in her honour, turned up his car stereo to a nice comfy "distort" level and took his stance to share a *Sirtaki* with her. One or two of the old women lined up too, plus Martina. They started to dance and it became immediately apparent to me that Andreas could no more dance than I could speak fluent Chinese. He had absolutely no sense of rhythm whatsoever. A fact which, once it became apparent (and that took a millisecond or two), made those of us unable to rise from our seats fall about in tears of laughter. The little old ladies very genteelly made their steps, in total concert with each other, Yvonne and Martina gelled nicely, but in the middle of it all, Andreas leapt and pranced like a man just released after twenty years solitary. Not only could he not follow the beat, but he was also wrenching at the shoulders of the person either side of him so that they had to perform contortions to keep in time. It was wonderful!! Yvonne was casting "fed up" glances at me because he was ruining her rhythm, which made me fall about even more. Soon Alain, deciding that if Greeks were that bad at their own dances he could do nothing but improve the synchronisation of the group, leapt up and managed to insert himself between Martina and Andreas.

Several dances ensued. Most of which ended up in a mass of stumbling and laughter, with those involved standing round hands on their knees and tears dripping from their noses.

Andreas laughed a lot. He had made for us an evening that fairly bristled with the "tingle factor." But he always seemed to exude an air of apprehension that suggested he thought we'd all go off him if we discovered his dark secret. We eventually did. But we didn't go off him.

26 - In the Dark

One hot afternoon during siesta time the Choupeaults, Yvonne and I had taken a siesta, but got up before the island awoke. We were staying in modest rooms just a few hundred yards along the seafront from the centre of Argostoli; just where the town ended and the road became a lane shaded by pines and olive trees.

We all decided it would be nice to walk along the front into Argostoli whilst everything was quiet. It would be nice to see the place when not much was happening. It was about four o'clock in the afternoon as we neared the port area, where ferryboats came in and you would often see those men all in white uniforms who always seemed to be in charge whenever a boat was offloading or the opposite.

We were walking at a leisurely pace along the right hand side of the road, the opposite side to the wide expanse of concrete, which terminated at the water's edge. Coming towards us on the other side of the road were two Greek men, both very dusty and sweaty from hard grind. One was pushing one of those rubbish carts you often see in big cities. You know the sort of thing; it holds two dustbins and has wheels like you'd find on a bicycle. They wore dirty jeans and singlet tops that had long given up any attempt to suggest a colour of any kind. They'd given in and let the grime take over. The other man was carrying a couple of heavy-duty brooms and looked a bit familiar from a distance.

As we grew closer it became evident that the man with the brushes was our friend Andreas. It also became very evident that he was acutely embarrassed to be spotted at his "place" of work by us, his supposedly affluent tourist friends from Britain. He exuded an air of "shall I pretend not to see them, or shall I come clean and brazen it out?" We all, without hesitation, made the same estimation of his mood and collectively decided to make sure he knew he was still our friend. As far as we were concerned, any man's work is dignified and it made no difference to us what he did for a living. We charged across the road, insisted he introduce us to his associate and made a big fuss of them both. His air of pure relief was palpable. You could see him almost filling up as he realised that it made no difference to us that he swept roads for a job.

His dark secret was out. As we continued along the road, having assured him he'd be welcome to join us at the taverna that coming evening, we discussed how sad he must have been during all the time prior to this moment, ever worrying about what we'd do if we knew he was a road sweeper. When you consider that in the past he had run a business in another country and travelled the world at sea, it wasn't difficult to see why he would not want us to know what he was "reduced" to. But to us he was still Andreas, the cheery and genuinely affectionate man who'd taken us all to his heart and home. And anyway, to sweep roads on the island of Kefallonia wasn't a bad gig when you thought about it. He could spend any afternoon he wanted to on the beach, which he usually did, he had a bit of money in his pocket and he drove a modest little car. He had paradise. Well, relatively anyway.

Just along the road from our rooms and in the opposite direction from the town, there was a small beach right next to the road. All you had to do was scramble down six feet of gently sloping bank and a small shingle beach invited you to get in and cool off. On more than one occasion we did this after midnight. This was the only place I have ever (thus far) ventured out for a midnight swim, but boy was it worth it! We would quietly slip out of our rooms, just carrying towels and wearing our jellies, and make the five minute walk along to this small beach, where we would slide into the cool water and be amazed at the phosphorous flashing in the water around our bodies as we made ripples. I had never experienced this phenomenon before. It is quite wonderful and almost unbelievable.

I remember an old "B" side by Donovan, I think it was on the other side of "There is a Mountain" in the late sixties. It was a song called "Sand & Foam" and I think it's still my favourite Donovan song. But it came back to mind when we slipped into the inky waters near Argostoli after midnight and the little lights glowed all around me in the water. I had never understood his reference in the song, which went ...

"...The simple act of an oar stroke
Put diamonds in the sea
And all because of the phosphorous
There in quantity.
And I dug your digging me in Mexico"

It was all "digging" in the late sixties wasn't it? Well, anyway, I have never forgotten those few lines and never truly appreciated what he was getting at. Not, that is, until a warm September night on Kefallonia in 1988.

While we're on the subject of darkness. There was a time when I thought I'd cost myself a lot of money one dark night in a small apartment near the airport. I mentioned in chapter eighteen how we met Yiorgo Goulimis and his dancers (Makis, Makis, Nikos and Babys) one night in Poros village, Kefallonia. Well, over the time we spent on the island during the years 1986-88, we became a pair of magnets to one of them in particular.

Makis Pantazatos looked like a younger and slightly thinner faced Harry H. Corbett. Not Sooty's original owner and very "close" friend, but the bloke who played Harold Steptoe in "Steptoe and Son." When I say we became a pair of magnets to him, rather it was that Yvonne did. He evidently fancied his chances with her and would join us whenever and wherever we were if he happened to come across us. He had a wife and very young family in some very new link houses on the hill above Argostoli. In fact one night when his wife was at work (she was a nurse in the island's very modest hospital) he entertained us at his place, where we spent an evening almost tearing our hair out in frustration at how he would run round like a fool after his two and three year old children. The Greeks are all like this with their kids. There's no discipline at all. They are their children's' abject slaves from the moment of birth. I've seen it so many times. Greeks worship children, perhaps partly for reasons outlined earlier in this tome, but this worship amounts to the sweet little things running circles round mum and dad as soon as they can sit up in their cots.

Makis was anxious to show us his kids. They were very beautiful, no question about it. Big dark eyes and almost black wavy hair with a ribbon or two just managing to hang on for grim life after having been tugged at with little hands for several hours in the case of his daughter. But to spend an evening in pleasant conversation over a meal whilst they were in the house was as unlikely as a picnic on Gatwick Airport's main runway.

Actually, getting to the house in the first place was an almost unbelievably difficult job. We had a Vespa 125 automatic scooter and had whizzed all over the island on it. We had even taken it down to Myrtos Beach – a totally lunatic thing to attempt if you'd seen the track leading the several miles off the main road down to Myrtos in 1987. But to get to Makis' house just outside Argostoli was worse. As we drove up the lane, which at last left the outer-most houses of the town below us, heading up the steep hill, we could see the several rows of brand new white and ochre coloured houses where Makis lived. But between these houses and us was an army assault course. Well, it looked like one. It looked suspiciously like the Greek army's entire compliment of tanks and armoured vehicles used this terrain for manoeuvres. The potholes in the track, which the road almost immediately became, were so big it was hard to see out of them. Makis had a small red Japanese car in which he regularly drove this way home. Goodness knows how it managed to make the trip. Mind you, it was a bit battered.

In the UK, when a new housing estate is built there's usually a bit of mud about for a while, sure. But pretty soon the roads are surfaced and everyone's happy. Not so in Kefallonia. Makis' day-job was as a Civil Servant in the town hall. He, if anyone, knew the council's plans for roads and housing all over the island, but when quizzed over when there would be a level access to his estate, his response was incredulity. As if we would even expect the council to waste time and money on getting the access road done, it was fine as it was. FINE AS IT WAS! If it had been in the UK it would have been a part of Salisbury Plain, the roughest part and no mistake. To arrive at the small housing estate, which in itself was odd for a Greek island in the first place, was a strange experience. There were several rows of link houses, with small terraces front and back, about twenty to a link (from memory), all of which reminded us very much of the kind of rabbit hutches that are getting thrown up all over the UK nowadays. The only appreciable differences were the shutters and marble floors. Otherwise, they were very familiar. The gaps that one might laughingly have called roads between them were just dust. I can't imagine how these people managed in winter when it most certainly rains on Kefallonia.

Fortunately for us, it was September and they hadn't seen rain for several months. Makis' kids spent a few hours wrecking any attempts we made at conversing, pulling things out of cupboards, hanging from the stairs by their hands, grabbing at Makis' cigarette and running off with it. That's another thing. The Greeks all smoke too much. Stupid expression that. I mean, to smoke is pretty stupid any way. To smoke too much is to smoke at all when you think about it. But the Greeks – they smoke with a vengeance, You'd almost think they had smoking lessons at school. Imagine...

"Right children. As adults you'll all need to practise the correct habits to be accepted by society. Beside each desk you'll find a plastic bowl, that's for you to throw up in after your first couple of drags on these cigarettes I'm passing out to you all now."

In spite of the extreme difficulty we had in enjoying the evening - due to the fact that in my mind's eye I was secretly strangling, shooting and whipping these kids - Makis did manage to enlighten us on how expensive everything was for a young Greek family. To have been able to purchase a home at all was a minor miracle. The cost of this tiny two-up-two-down was relatively many times what it would have cost in Cardiff at the time. Clothes were much more expensive as were all electrical items. Makis was doing pretty well to have a small car. But then, his wife worked nights in the hospital and, on top of his day-job, he worked evenings as a dancer entertaining the tourists at Goulimis' Greek nights.

One particular Greek night was taking place way out on the airport road at an isolated taverna that we would have had great difficulty finding. As we were enjoying a Campari and lemonade in the square prior to finding a taverna to eat at, Makis appeared at the street tobacco booth to buy his usual wheelbarrow-load of ciggies when he spotted us. He had just finished work and it was about 8.00pm. His hours were something like 8.00am 'til 12.00pm, then 5pm 'til 8.00pm. He would often appear in the square about 8 o'clock because he knew we'd be sitting at the same bar enjoying an aperitif before eating. He never failed to show when there was a Greek night on and this particular night he said the dancers would pick us up at nine and they would be our hosts at the Greek night. Whenever this happened I was delighted – after all, it meant not having to pay for our meal or drinks all evening!

Some time after nine, a black VW Beetle with fat wheels screeched into the square and stopped with a squeal of rubber near our table at the cafeneon, the door opened and Nikos, another one of the dancers, leaned out and beckoned us to hop in. We hopped in. Well – in the manner that one does when attempting to enter the Guinness book of records for how many adults you can jam into a VW Beetle we "hopped in." All the dancers were already in there, and it seemed to me a couple of other surly Greeks too for good measure. I'd have had no way of telling if any of them were fondling my wife's body en route and she would have thought it was me. She was after all, the only female in the vehicle. At least (mercifully) no one fondled mine.

We arrived at this taverna in the middle of nowhere to see a vast collection of blond heads. It was a Tjaerborg Greek Night. That means all the revellers were from Scandinavia. It was very odd. Still, the food was on the house and they had a guest fiddler to accompany Dennis with his electronic keyboard so it promised to be a bit of fun. The fiddler looked as old as the island and as thin as a broom handle, but he could play all right. Which means he was entirely out of tune most of the time. If you've ever listened to Greek folk music from the islands you'll know what I mean. But at least it was authentic.

The dancers did their party piece and the evening passed much as many others. Yiorgo Goulimis regaled the bemused Vikings with a few traditional Greek songs in his own inimitable style and eventually the coach arrived and took the tourists away at around midnight; at which time the locals, children and all, emerged from the woodwork to pass a further couple of hours without leaving the dance floor. Yvonne was perpetually among them, often dancing at the head of the procession and joined to Makis and the rest by a white handkerchief.

When things finally wound up, Nikos said he'd give us a lift back. The problem was, we were staying in the wrong direction for the rest of the car party. One of them came up with the perfect idea, they'd take us to a friend's vacant holiday apartment and they'd be back to pick us up in the morning. Of course, as per usual, all this went on and was agreed without my cognisant knowledge, since it was all gabbled in super-fast Greek and signed and sealed before Yvonne could explain anything to me. I can't say I was all that happy with this arrangement. We drove along various single-track lanes until we came to a halt outside a large whitewashed wall with an arch in it, filled by a wrought iron gate. We all fell out of the car, someone arrived at the gate from inside, a bit of spirited discussion went on and the car tore off into the blackness in a cloud of dust leaving Yvonne and I at the mercy of this total stranger. I can't even remember anything about this person. We only remained in their company for around thirty seconds. Just enough for them to lead us across a courtyard containing large terracotta pots with exotic plants bursting out of them, up an open-air stairway a couple levels to the front door of a cosy studio/apartment where we were evidently going to sleep. We had absolutely no idea where on the island we were. We didn't know which direction we were looking. Apart from a few subdued courtyard lights downstairs, all around was total darkness. The only light was from stars twinkling way above, but there was no moon that night.

The individual pointed to a key which was stuck in the door and bade us "kalenichta" and was gone down the stairway in a trice.

Greek accommodation always has a little electrical "box" in the wall somewhere. Often these boxes have glass fronts, through which you can see various fuses and switches, some of which glow red and some don't. Frequently the owner will show you when you arrive which switch operates which circuit. If, for example, they don't have solar heating for the hot water system, you have to throw one of these switches to get hot water, always remembering to switch it off once you've showered or whatever. These switches are not like the ones in the UK, which tend to be fairly substantial and feel as thought they carry a lot of current. The Greek ones always feel like toy ones and often the whole switch panel will move as you attempt to throw one of the switches. I have never enjoyed having to mess with these boxes.

We let ourselves into the studio and were pleasantly surprised to see in the gloom that it looked fairly new and well arranged. We could just make out a comfy-looking double bed and bedside lamps on its little bedside tables. So far so good. The problem was, none of the lights responded to the switches.

After a bit of gingerly playing with the electricity box, I appeared to have thrown the right switch to get the bedside lamps to work. We undressed and decided that a visit to the bathroom was in order before turning in. The bathroom was in such total darkness that it was impossible to enter it without getting the light to work. This meant another visit to the "box." I dreaded it but there was nothing else for it. Once again I stared for an age at the little paper labels above each switch. But in the available light it was no easy task. The nearest working light was the one on the bedside table and that was still some distance away. The labels were written in very small "English" evidently by a Greek who thought they knew how we spoke and spelled. They were wrong.

Finally I decided I'd have to throw one of them and elected for the one I thought would do the job. I threw the switch.

Oops. That wasn't precisely the word that went through my mind, but it will suffice. Total darkness descended like a blanket, as all the little red lights in the box went out. The bedside lamps went out. The lamps in the courtyard outside and two floors below went out. There wasn't anything to be seen. We were left in absolute darkness. Yvonne cursed me for being a ham fisted something-or-other and I yelled in a really loud whisper that it wasn't my fault! There was nothing for it but to grapple for the bed and get in, waiting for the twilight of the dawn to make our escape before being discovered and charged for the repairs.

I didn't sleep much that night. It must have been about 2.00am before we were getting into the bed anyway and I wanted to be up and away at the crack of dawn to avoid the consequences of fusing the entire block's electrics. All night I dreamt of mechanical diggers digging up the road outside to find the fault. It never occurred to me that all their power was in overhead cables.

As light began to seep through the blinds the next morning we were both wide-awake and dashing for the bathroom to reduce the bladder pressure before exploding. Then we hurriedly donned our clothes, crept out onto the balcony and I left the key back in the door where it had been when we'd arrived a few hours before.

We managed to creep down the stairway and out through the wrought iron door into the road outside. Now what?

It was some unearthly hour and we were standing in a small lane miles from anywhere. Across the lane the land fell away dramatically and we could see the runway of Kefallinia airport (They spell the name of the airport's location that way) and the sea just beyond.

It was now that I began to complain that we should never have allowed the dancers to bring us here. "How do we know they plan to come and get us? They might forget, or simply not be bothered!"

"They said they'd come first thing."

"Well, there aren't many 'things' more first than this! Anyway, what is 'first thing' to a Greek dancer who's danced half the previous night away?" I was also not a little worried that the owner of the apartment would come out and arrest us or something for causing criminal damage.

As if by a miracle, Nikos came up the lane in his Beetle, this time on his own (thankfully) and we got in as quickly as was humanly possible. Fifteen minutes later we were back in Argostoli and no one walking the earth was more relieved than I.

We went for a shower and got changed and then headed off to a taverna for breakfast. We got chatting to the waiter and I risked relating the story of how I'd fused all the lights at this little apartment complex.

"What time you say you switch switch?" Asked Costas (or whatever his name was, but Costas is a pretty safe bet in Greece).

"It must have been about 2 o'clock."

Costas emitted a large belly laugh and it took us a few minutes to get him to explain himself. Apparently, due to the Greek economy being in such a dire state, they now had an electricity curfew.

All the domestic power on the island went off automatically at 2.00am.

27 - *Don't do it*

So far I have tried to write chronologically. But I confess I'm impatient. It was after a visit to Leros; two visits in fact, in the summer of 1996, that I decided to commit all our experiences in Greece to writing. We had such a clutch of experiences there that it just seemed such a good idea to start recording them.

I sat down to compile a list of all the places we'd been in Greece and soon had a list of locations and events to which they were related, which I arranged chronologically and began to write. The fact is that at the end of chapter 25 I'd only reached the late 80's and still had a long way to go to reach 1996.

So, who cares? Let's go to Leros now anyway.

The first thing about Leros is that if you're not well-heeled enough to fly there directly on a small plane from Athens, you'll be slumming it like we did and have to get there by sea from Kos, or elsewhere in the Dodecanese. We flew to Kos with a certain well-known travel company. Now the TV campaign for this particular Tour Operator several years ago always featured the line: "If T_____ don't do it – don't do it!" This was to give you the impression that only with T_____ could you be sure of being well looked after by professionals. Only with T_____ would you be sure that all the arrangements would be taken care of professionally. Only with T_____ would the entire experience be enjoyable, with nothing of any consequence to complain about. We hadn't been in Greece for more than an hour when I began wondering how they could possibly proudly boast such a promise. In the brochure it says the transfer from Kos to Leros would be several hours by ferryboat, stopping off at Kalymnos en-route. This brought to mind enjoyable trips to Poros out of Piraeus, sunbathing on the top deck of the inter-island ferries that ply those waters continually, stopping off at Aegina, Methana, Poros, Hydra and others. We had always enjoyed those trips. The ferry crossing had been a great start and an almost indispensable part of the holiday. You could always get a cold beer or frappe and something to eat on-board. A quick change into the swimming cozzie, more often than not already worn under the travelling clothes, and extracting the current novel from the handbaggage made the experience several hours of bliss.

All this went through our minds as we merrily confirmed our booking with T_____, the company who tell you confidently- "If T_____ don't do it - don't do it!"

The day arrived and so did we. We landed at Kos airport, which, like all Greek arrival lounges (with the exception of the old one at Kefallonia - now sadly gone), should carry a health warning owing to the thick atmosphere of cigarette smoke you have to endure during the tedious wait for your luggage. Towing my wheeled suitcase out into the sunshine and gasping for some oxygen, I found Yvonne, who had already found the T_____ rep and we were directed on to coach number whatever for the short trip to the harbour to board the ferry, which, four hours later would deposit us at Leros. I was looking forward to this.

We arrived at a little quay on a very quiet part of the island in a small coastal resort that seemed to have been annexed by Germany. If there were any British here, they were probably interned somewhere behind a wire fence dotted with watchtowers. In fact, one would have been mistaken for thinking the outcome of the last great conflagration had been quite the other way round. Not that we haven't encountered some very charming German tourists over the years mind you. It was just, well, we get a bit conditioned by all those gung-ho war films we watched as kids I suppose.

The coach mercifully drove out onto the jetty and we all clambered off to catch our first glimpse of the water transport laid on for us. It wasn't quite what we had expected. Handling our baggage for ourselves we struggled aboard whilst the few Greek crew of this rather modest little boat (I wouldn't call it either a ferry or a ship really) watched us in a bemused manner. There was one guy standing right where we boarded, which was rather tight for space on the boat side of the three or four foot gap we had to leap, the males among us also sporting various sizes of suitcase as well as our video cameras, handbaggage et al. The small gap in the boat's parapet (or whatever you're supposed to call it) was such that you had to almost pop your pecs to lift your cases over as you passed through. Then there was a very narrow bit of deck between that and the wall of the boat's superstructure.

This deeply tanned Greek with his little well-worn flat sailor's cap watched expressionless as all the fellas just managed to avoid falling the eight feet or so to the water between boat and quay, but each time a well proportioned female attempted to board he very attentively extended both hands to aid the grateful (?) girl in her transition from shore to vessel.

Once aboard we were ushered into a cramped little cabin to deposit our cases, a task which - once accomplished - reduced the available space in this room by a good 40%. Yvonne had already climbed up to the top deck intent on enjoying the breeze and the view as we made the voyage first to Kalymnos, then on to Leros. I made the ascent and instantly began to appreciate how all those poor souls who tried to escape Vietnam by sea must have felt back in the seventies.

This vessel would have been OK for half as many passengers to travel a quarter the distance. But four hours or so on this with so many bodies, one could tell was going to be sheer torture. This boat was no bigger than the one used to ferry pedestrians back and forth the short 30 minutes or so it takes from Aegina to Agistri in the Saronic Gulf. It was no inter-island ferry. Our resourceful tour operator (you remember, the ones who said: "If [we] don't do it ...don't do it!) had evidently chartered this aging iron bath exclusively for our comfort during the crossing. Their idea of passenger comfort was evidently quite different from that of most of the passengers on this boat.

The crossing to Kalymnos wasn't too bad. It was helped by the fact that the island was clearly visible right from the quay at this little place on the north coast of Kos, plus it was only about three quarters of an hour, still mid afternoon and we were all glad to be in the fresh air after nearly four hours on a plane and another hour getting used to passively smoking in the arrivals lounge at "baggage reclaim." But once we chugged out of the quite picturesque harbour at Kalymnos and round the headland to the western side of the island, things took a turn for the worse. The Dodecanese islands are much nearer to Turkey than they are to the Greek mainland. They are in the south-eastern Aegean. An area that is prone to the Meltemi, a wind that blows most of the year down from the Bosphorus in the north. This wind isn't altogether unpleasant when you're strolling along the harbour front on an island in the region, although it can reach gale force at times! But when you're perched on the top of a boat that really isn't meant to carry quite so much luggage and so many passengers at once and certainly not this distance – well, the Meltemi can be a bit of a nuisance. You see, the Western side of Kalymnos, and indeed most of the Dodecanese, receive much more of this wind than the eastern side. So, in their infinite wisdom, the boat's crew took us up the western coast and we were sailing into a pretty big swell. Not that a regular-sized ferry would have had much trouble, but this little thing was regularly enduring spectacular crunches as its bows broke through waves that gleefully crashed all across the deck and even across the windows of the very cramped indoor lounge below us.

Stabilisers were probably only an idea in some ship-designer's head when this little baby slid down the ramp, as we were also swaying from side to side a bit like a giant slow-motion metronome as we sat on the hard benches on the "sun deck." It wasn't long before various shapes, sizes and genders of passenger were hanging over the side depositing their temporarily ingested airline food into the Med for the fishes to re-digest.

By the time we gracefully crawled into Lakki harbour at Leros, we were all remarking on the aptness(!!!) of the tour operator's TV campaign: : "If T_____ don't do it – don't do it!" Most of us vowed that, whether we liked Leros or not, this wasn't the way to do it.

It wasn't as though it was merely the transfer to Leros that had us doubting the wisdom of this particular tour operator's using the slogan "If [we] don't do it – don't do it!" Whilst there we decided to hire a car for a couple of days. There isn't much point having one for any longer on Leros anyway, there isn't enough island to make it worth while.

Ever the cautious ones where road and vehicle safety is concerned, we thought it best to ask the company's rep, who was a very nice young slip of a girl who lived in the apartment below us at Thassos II apartments, Aghia Marina. That way we'd presumably get a fairly new, if nonetheless compact (and therefore cheap to hire!) car.

"When do you want it and for how long?" Asked Lisa (for reasons of security, names have been changed).

"Thursday morning; say, from 9 0'clock, for two days would be fine."

"OK, I'll have Nikos bring it to the apartment."

By the way. If you're a seasoned Greek island visitor you'll know that, no matter which island you go to, there'll only be one principle bloke's name and just about everyone except for those who've moved there from elsewhere will be called by that name. Kind of reminds me of the old Monty Python sketch, set in the Australian outback, in which everyone is called Bruce and when a man is introduced to the group who isn't, they say, "Mind if we call you 'Bruce' to avoid any confusion?"

Well, on Leros every second fellah you meet is called Nikos.

So Nikos arrived on the Thursday morning at a Greek 9.00 am. That is to say, a quarter to ten. The look on his face expressed the opinion, without the need to express it verbally: "Well, what's the rush, you don't have a train to catch do you?"

Hearing the sound of a car engine and with all our "stuff" packed into our rucksack for a day's sightseeing we eagerly trotted out into the street expecting to see a nice little recent Daihatsu or Daiwoo or something, probably still with that "new car" smell when you get inside.

"No, that's not for us. Can't be. ...can it?" I opined, with more than a little concern.

"Well he's looking at you and smiling, so it must be," returned Yvonne, with that "if you'd listened to me and got it from that little office down the road, things would have turned out much better!" tone to her voice.

We stood and gazed at a ten year old (possibly more), very small, formerly red but now all sorts of faded shades of pink, Yugo 3-door hatchback. Oh, and it was dusty beyond belief. Now as I said before, we thought that to arrange the car hire through the rep would be the safest thing to do. Well, you would normally wouldn't you? Especially when their promotional slogan for that particular year was: well, I reckon you know by now. Well, Nikos eagerly approached extending a hand and saying, "All yours. There is a little benzini (petrol) in the tank, so you have enough to find nearest service station (me thinks: you mean there's more than one on the island?!). I come back here day after tomorrow." Then proffering me the key he made as if to walk off towards Aghia Marina.

"Hold on! What about the forms, you know, insurance and all that?" I asked.

"We no need to worry for now. We do when you bring car back. It's OK." He replied cheerily, with a dismissive wave of the hand, and continued to beat his retreat. We stood there and took in what would be our stately mode of transport for the next 48 hours.

"Oh well," I began, "might as well make the best of it. It wasn't expensive after all. Let's chuck the "stuff" in the back and get going."

"If you'd listened to me and got it from that little office down the road, things would have turned out much better!" came the rather unnecessarily critical reply, or so I thought anyway. "At least their cars all look like hire cars. Whereas this looks like an old Greek farmer's had it and never either washed it or serviced it in ten years!"

So we piled in and I started her up and began wiggling the gear stick (as you do) to get the feel of the gears. "Well," I thought, "there must be some gears in here somewhere, I just need to keep wiggling it around, foot hard down on the clutch pedal, and I'll find them eventually." If there ever had been a "gate," - you know, that position in the middle to which the gear stick on most normal cars will revert if left to its own devices, so you know where it is and can navigate from there to whichever gear you want to select – it gave no indication of it now. So I kept swishing it around and more by luck than judgment came across what was probably "first" and attempted to ease ourselves out into the road.

Dammit. Must be third. More stirring, rather after the manner that you'd stir a sweet cup of tea, and I finally found "first" and we were away. First junction we came to was at the top of the gentle rise from the apartment, where the road met the one from Lakki, which, if any road could on this island, probably laid claim to being the "main" road round the back of the "town" of Aghia Marina.

I applied the brakes. Well, pushing down on the pedal in

the middle is what I'd usually call "applying the brakes." Not much difference in speed. Pushing so hard as to drain all the blood from my right leg eventually resulted in our slowing a little. Fortunately no road in Leros is all that busy. In the middle of the "main" road we finally halted. I thought I'd try the handbrake since we hadn't met any other cars and there were none evidently within "crashing" distance. So I confidently pulled said lever up and released the footbrake, left foot firmly on the clutch pedal.

Gently rolling backwards is not all that unpleasant a feeling. That is, unless you're attempting to assume control of a half a ton of metal on a road where other large lumps of metal are liable to come into view, the drivers of which will assume you are in control of your half a ton. I decided the best course of action was to fish for a gear and attempt to resume forward motion, which, mercifully I was able to do just before a taxi appeared around the corner from the direction of Lakki at a not inconsiderable speed!

"Everything all right?" enquired Yvonne, I felt with a considerable degree of irony and sarcasm mixed in equal measure in there somewhere.

"Fine. You know how it is, takes a few minutes to get used to a strange vehicle. Fine now."

"Strange would describe this vehicle all right!" she retorted. I decided on a course of not risking further antagonism and stared cheerfully out the windows with an air of "what a lovely day for a leisurely trip out" about me.

Two days later we heard a knock on the apartment door (at a Greek 9.00am, that is to say, in this instance, 10.00am!) as Nikos returned to collect the pride of his hire fleet, along, presumably, with his fee and the papers for us to sign. How we'd got through those two days without killing ourselves or getting air-lifted to another island for medical treatment I'll never know. I opened the apartment door.

"*Yiassou!* Everything OK? *Neh?*" enquired Nikos, with I felt not a little apprehension in his voice.

"Fine. Apart from the fact that the car was near impossible to drive, had no brakes of any note and we couldn't lock any of the doors." Actually, not being able to lock doors on a small Greek island is of no consequence at all, but I wanted to add to the weight of my argument.

"Bravo. You have thee keys, *se parakelo?*" he quipped, noticeably relieved.

I tossed them, along with the required fee, into his outstretched palm and was about to say: "so do I sign the forms now?" when he turned and with an "*efharesto poli!*" was gone down the stairway in a trice.

At this point we came to realise that, to be fair to our trusty tour operator (whose slogan for this season was… oh alright, I know you know …this deal never was with a car hire company. It was pretty evident now that our friendly young rep had a bit of a "deal" with this particular "Nikos" to put a few readies in both of their back pockets.

Which, come to think of it, is I suppose why we love Greece so much. When it comes to abiding by such trivialities as the correct forms, paying your taxes, giving receipts where a flash of the readies does equally as well, even wearing helmets on motorbikes and such like; well, the Greeks simply very often …don't do it.

28 - A Missed Appointment

I don't know what it is about Leros, but something just grabs you about the place. I suppose it helps that for the confirmed Grecophile it is refreshingly devoid of the hordes of holidaymakers that have effectively ruined so much of the Med as a holiday destination for the more discerning tourist. Oh, all right then – the elitist snob.

But the moment we chugged into the deep natural harbour of Lakki we knew we'd found somewhere just a bit special. Everyone was just glad at the prospect of getting off this awful boat we had just spent what seemed like days aboard, since it was woefully inadequate for the task to which it had been assigned. Still, it had got us here; a little nauseated maybe, but we were here nevertheless. We arrived in the early evening, when there seemed not a breath of wind, which was quite a relief after the Meltemi we had braved for the past several hours.

The boat sidled up to a concrete jetty where several grey Mercedes taxis waited to whisk us off to our various accommodations. The usual officials in their immaculate white uniforms did their bit and we stepped onto dry land with not a little relief, I can tell you. Lakki is a bit stately, but virtually deserted. It's got a grandness about the size of its roads and several tavernas and bars, one of them Italian, strung along its lacklustre harbourfront, but it gives the impression of a ghost town. On our arrival I put this down to the time of day. "They're still coming round from their siesta," I thought to myself. We were soon assigned our taxi and the wiry Greek in his early thirties who drove it was soon immersed in conversation with Yvonne, who sat in front alongside him. It gave him evident pleasure to find that one of these "grockles" was Greek-speaking. Every time he passed us on the road from then on throughout the two weeks we were there in June, and even when we returned in September, he would acknowledge us with a toot of his horn and a wave. This despite the fact that we never availed ourselves of his services again after this, apart from when he turned up to drive us back to the ferry at the end of our holiday.

We were staying at a brand new modestly sized apartment block in Agia Marina, just across the narrow isthmus at the centre of the island from Lakki and north a bit. Lakki was on the west, Agia Marina on the east, at the southern end of the bay, the other end of which was Alinda, the only faintly touristy place on the whole island, which isn't very big anyway. It's about 53 square kilometres in land area. What that is in old money I'd have no idea. Due to the fact that the island sports many deep indentations in its coastline, the distance around the island to and from the same point is about 71 kilometres.

Although Agia Marina is in a bay, it is nevertheless quite windy. This is because it is at the southern end of the bay and faces due north, thus copping its fair share of the Meltemi for a large part of the season. A half-hour walk up through the old town of Platanos and down the hill on the other side brings you to south-facing Pandeli beach, a small shingly beach with a couple of tavernas and no wind at all. Absolutely idyllic (oh, sorry, that word again). I'll come back to Pandeli later. In fact, as I write this I'm making a mental resolve to go back to Pandeli one day, especially as I'm writing this in the UK in August and it's raining cats and dogs outside.

One evening, to escape the ever present wind at Agia Marina, we sought out a little taverna in a street just back from the front and only five minutes walk from our apartment. I can't remember the name of the taverna, but I'm fairly sure it had "Captain" in it somewhere. For the sake of this tale, I'll call it "Captain's Ouzeri." It was set in a tiny back alley, with three or four small tables outside and a few more within. The staff were all family and about three in number. We enjoyed an excellent fish meal there and were nicely fed and watered and sipping our complementary Metaxas when I noticed a smallish man, probably in his early sixties, sitting alone at the table next to ours. He began to chat with us.

As per usual, I picked up only snippets of the conversation. No doubt he was promising my wife a very good time if she could shake me off for a while. But then, some of these older Greek chaps were quite gentlemanly and he seemed to be this sort. His name might have been Dimitri. It'll do anyway. He was very unremarkable in appearance. I would have said he was probably a fisherman from Agia Marina harbour, which supported a clutch of brightly coloured boats, which at the crack of dawn could be seen sorting their catch on the harbour side each morning; something I delighted in getting up early and going to watch. I was quite happy to sip at my Metaxa and smile occasionally at the Taverna's staff as they stood, hands behind backs, at the establishment's threshold ever on the lookout for either potential customers or the opportunity to visit someone's table.

After a conversation of about twenty minutes, Yvonne informed me that Dimitri was leaving, so we bade him *"kalinikta"* and shook his hand and the slightly drab yet affable chap quietly faded away along the darkening alley into the warm Lerian night.

"He wants to meet us on Friday." Said Yvonne.

"Where and what time and what for?" I replied cautiously.

"He says one o'clock at Taverna Artemis, Blepouti bay. He says he has a big house up there and runs a fish farm and would like to take us out on his boat."

"Do you want to go?"

"Not really. It'll probably be boring. He probably won't show anyway. We'll probably end up sitting in front of an old dilapidated hovel on a small porch sipping some homemade retsina and making small talk with his wife or something. Anyway, I don't like to be regimented. So I don't know about you but I can't be bothered."

"OK. Suits me. Might be worth taking a trip to Blepouti some time to check it out though. I think I caught the bit where he said how beautiful the bay was."

"Well, we could spend a day up there. He reckons you take the central road up through the island and when you come to Partheni, you go right and Blepouti's just along the coast. He said it's very remote and there's just the one taverna there, Taverna Artemis."

This would have been about a Tuesday. We had a couple of days before Friday, when, apparently, although my dear wife had said she didn't want to bother, she had in fact told him we'd show up. She doesn't like to upset people you see. Can't say no. She doesn't mind upsetting them from a distance by not showing up, but face to face ...can't do it.

There arose a bit of an argument now over the fact that she'd promised him we'd come and yet told me she didn't want to bother.

"You shouldn't have said we'd come. We can't let him down now. He might be sitting there for ages wondering where we are. That's not very nice. And what if we bump into him again?"

"Oh we can tell him we forgot or something. They don't mind. He probably didn't mean it anyway. He was probably just being polite."

So it went on, with the problem not really being resolved. Save for the fact that we decided to rent a Vespa and trot up there anyway on Wednesday or Thursday for a look at the place.

Thursday morning was hot (as usual) and it found us charging up the rather uneven solitary road to the north of the island on our Vespa. As is our habit, we were loaded down with all kinds of stuff. I remember a rather perceptive American comic once doing a routine about humans and their "Stuff." I don't recall his name but it creased me up. He was saying how it was that humans always need to be surrounded by their "stuff." In our homes we have stuff everywhere. And the larger our homes – the more stuff we acquire in order to fill them. Then, when we travel, we have to make sure we have stuff with us so that when we get to our accommodation we can get some of it out and arrange it around the place. We place some stuff on the bedside table, we fill up the bathroom with all kinds of small stuff and make sure we pack drawers and wardrobes with our stuff. But we always hold a bit in reserve for keeping with us. This was so that wherever we spent the day we would be able to arrange some of our stuff around us in order to feel comfortable. You never see a human without some of their stuff.

So here we were bombing along at a mindblowing forty to fortyfive kilometres an hour, on a road that threw our bodies around with much more efficiency than a fairground ride, on a Vespa with loads of our "stuff." We had those reedy beach mats with the green cotton edges, our sun cream, the camera (with the mandatory spare film), snorkels and masks, towels, inflatable collar for making the head comfy on the pebbles or sand, walkman and various musical choices for placing therein, books, sunblock for the lips (a must for me because I don't wear lipstick), Yvonne's pared down – yet still fairly substantial - make-up emergency pack, jelly sandals for wearing in the sea, caps to keep sun off face, little leather purse of money, sunglasses plus bread rolls and beef tomatoes for lunch and a big bottle of water. We needed some "stuff" I can tell you. All this was in a rucksack the size of a small haybail on Yvonne's back, since she was riding pillion. The problem whenever we hired a motor scooter was, with all this weight at the back, we had to lean forward most of the time to stop the front wheel coming off the ground! Happy days.

We were enjoying the ride anyway because it was one of the few ways to keep a little cooler, when, quite unexpectedly, a large and very forbidding looking fence appeared alongside the road and it became very apparent that this was a military camp. The first picture it brought to my mind was Steve McQueen in The Great Escape. There were actually lines of uniformed men clearly visible in the camp square doing what I would call "square-bashing." For the uninitiated, "square bashing" is not what sixties swingers with a penchant for violence would do to someone unhip. It is, as far as I know (which isn't far – I know), the routine of training that soldiers go through in their camp square on a fairly regular basis.

I called over my shoulder to Yvonne: "You haven't got the camera out have you? They'll shoot us!"

She responded with a squeeze of the knees to my thighs and we slowed to a respectable thirty KPH or so and gingerly drove through the camp. Well, not actually through it, but between it because, as I recall, it had section on both sides of the road. I remember reading somewhere about this camp that it was used between 1967 and 1974 as a detention camp for Democratic leaders during the Military Dictatorship that prevailed at the time. It still looked like it was very much in business.

Mercifully we put the camp behind us without being shot at and arrived at a dusty T-junction at which we were presented with the choice of Partheni to the left or Blepouti to the right. We turned right and followed a small lane which, after another mile or so of twists and turns, descended to Blepouti bay.

The road deposits you at the West end of the bay, which looks due North, but is protected from the Meltemi by the fact that it is a very deep inlet with hills on either side. The water was in fact the calmest I have ever seen. The proverbial mill pond would be a surfer's paradise by comparison. A few yards long the beach, behind which the small lane runs for the length of the bay, was Taverna Artemis. The perfect sight when, apart from one or two villas dotted about at maybe half a kilometre distance from eachother, there is no other sign of human presence. The taverna was cheerful in appearance, with twenty or more tables out front, some of which were under the usual large vine-covered shaded area, with others suffering the full glare of the merciless sun. It was run by a small family whose two children, perhaps in their early teens, were working as waiters.

The beach at Blepouti is barely eight feet wide, but, remembering there is no tide to speak of, that's quite wide enough. It's not sand, but a fine shingle, which suits me because it doesn't get into everything. Dotted at about twelve feet intervals all along the beach by the road side are small trees, giving just enough shade for the likes of me, whilst allowing those who can roast themselves with apparent impunity, like Yvonne, the opportunity to do so without having to set up camp too far away from their more fragile partners.

It had probably taken us about half an hour to get here from Agia Marina and was now mid-morning. So we began unpacking and arranging our "stuff" and settled down for some serious inactivity. An hour or two passed with one or two short expeditions into the water to cool off or have a nose around with the snorkel. The only sounds were goats' bells, birds and the gentle lapping of the two inch waves. Of all the places I have chilled out in Greece, this became (and still is) my favourite. What made it all the more delicious was the fact that, at around midday, a Mercedes bus, one of those that seats about fifteen and was more like a converted van, arrived at the taverna just across the road behind us. Out stepped an assortment of British tourists all sporting cameras and whatever "stuff" they deemed necessary for a round-the-island bus tour. Some made straight for the Taverna and hastily partook of cold beers, others wandered along the bay snapping pictures and peering at lizards, while still others were quick to throw of their clothes and disturb the mirror-like surface of the bay by plunging in for a swim.

Why would I say this made our experience of Blepouti delicious? Because those too fearful to investigate such places apart from the comfort-blanket type security of an organised tour would never truly hear the quiet of the place. Plus, they only had an hour. So, almost as soon as the ones who'd taken to beach had got settled, they had to gather up their "stuff" and beat a hasty retreat to the bus. The ones in the Taverna had to virtually arrest the thirteen-year-old girl who had waited on them in order to pay for their beer before the bus went without them. It seemed that almost as soon as the bus had trundled down to the bay, disturbing the enchanting tranquility of the place, it was gone up the lane in a cloud of dust, leaving us once more to savour the quiet and be glad of our trusty Vespa. I know, I know, I'm a holiday snob. Just can't help it I'm afraid.

In fact, some way up a dusty track behind Taverna Artemis, there was one small two storey block of self-catering apartments. So no doubt those staying there viewed any who turned up in hired cars or on Vespas for the day as intruders. C'est la vie. Actually, Yvonne and I prefer to have our accommodation within walking distance of the nightlife (by which we mean a few tavernas and cafeneions) and to travel a bit in daylight, than to have to negotiate poorly lit and badly surfaced lanes after dark to get a bit of company and chat. Yah-boo sucks and all that.

Anyway, to return to our little friend Dimitri the fish farmer. Did we want to come back again tomorrow at 1.00pm and meet him?

We didn't go. I felt bad about it, but Yvonne assured me that Greeks don't mind that sort of thing, so I had to trust to her greater experience of the Greek people.

Some days later, maybe Tuesday of the next week, we found ourselves again at the Captain's Ouzeri enjoying a wonderful fish meal. We ended up chatting to the owner at midnight after all the other diners had left and the other members of his family were busy clearing up for the night. The conversation eventually came round to Dimitri the "fish farmer." For the sake of brevity, I'll render the conversation as though it were in English. The Taverna owner:

"Dimitri was here last night."

"Dimitri?" Asked Yvonne. "Oh, yes, the little old chap we met here last week."

"He says he was let down by two tourists. Not very nice. Dimitri is very kind man."

"Let down? What did he say?"

"He say he was waiting at Artemis for more than an hour on Friday. They said they would come. He was going to take them out on his boat."

"On his boat? What's that, a little fishing boat then?"

"Oh no! Dimitri has very nice boat. You'd call it 'cabin cruiser' or 'luxury yacht', Dimtri has a very nice boat."

A horrible realisation of a lost opportunity was dawning in the brains of both Yvonne and I. So I said:

"How come he has a very nice boat? He's only a fisherman isn't he?"

"Only fisherman? No! Dimitri owns a fish farm, he is the richest man on Leros! He likes to show people round his big house and give them a nice trip on his big boat. But only if he likes them he does this."

The following Friday, had you been at Taverna Artemis at Blepouti bay, you may have noticed a couple of tourists sitting at a table looking as if they were hoping someone would join them. No one did.

Agia Marina, Leros, 1996

29 - A Family at War

The Tassos II apartments at Agia Marina, Leros, were literally across a small road from the water's edge. The only thing which slightly impeded a beautiful view across a wide bay stretching from the small quay at Aghia Marina (to our right) to right up to beyond Alinda to the left, was the *"Psistaria,"* or grill-house, of Mikalis and his family, virtually right opposite and sitting on it's own tiny bit of rock, flanked on three sides by the sea. The side facing the road had several entrances to the establishment and, looking down at it from the vantage point of our sunny balcony on the 2nd floor (there were no more floors, only those metal spiky things sticking up through the deliberately unfinished-looking roof) to the right there was a small uneven shingle-covered outdoor terrace strewn with a half a dozen or so rickety tables, each spread with a chequered oilcloth and dressed with small cruet set.

The view further out beyond the psistaria and across the bay included the hilly bulge of Kryphos and Panagies, still a part of Leros and reaching from the centre of the view all across to the left where it merged into what one could see in the direction of Alinda. Just a few hundred yards or so along the shore from our balcony was a pleasant shingle beach, backed by a small walkway, some benches, trees and private residences. At the far end of that beach on a small outcrop was an aging windmill, right on the water's edge, all painted white and adding aesthetically to the bright blue scene.

Looking right ahead one could see the open sea and, on the horizon not many miles away, the hills and mountains of southern Turkey. To the right was the hill above Aghia Marina, topped as it was by the *Kastro*, a Byzantine castle founded on the ruins of an ancient acropolis in the seventh century and completed by the Venetians some time later. This hill towers over Aghia Marina and demands to be explored, if only for the breathtaking views it affords those intrepid ones who trek up to the top. If you're a bit wimpish, you can drive or take a taxi up there too. A winding lane, that starts from just below Platanos (the island's capital) on the way down to Pandeli, twists and turns all the way up to the top, passing a string of old windmills on a visually dramatic ridge en route.

The family-run grill house opposite was a constant source of entertainment for us whenever we were relaxing on our balcony, just twenty feet or so across the melting tarmac. There seemed to be so many children it was difficult to be sure just what the actual total was. Mikalis, the father, was a wiry man who looked well into his fifties, with a lined face and more grey than black in his still thick hair. The oldest son was about fifteen, then the others of both sexes ranged down to the youngest, a little girl of perhaps three, named Serafina. It was easy to remember her name because her mother (a homely woman of no more than forty who was just beginning the transition from approximately the right shape for a woman to the typical chubby Greek mama) was perpetually calling her. We would no sooner arrive back from a day on the beach or wherever, strip to swimwear, make a nice cup of Earl Grey, grab a book and some Greek cinnamon biscuits, park ourselves out on the balcony for another couple of hours of safer sunshine when we'd hear:

"SERAFINA!"

The child seemed to be perpetually where the mother wasn't and visa versa. One evening, when the family were evidently occupied with preparing the place for the anticipated influx of diners, a fact made evident by the clanking of pots and pans which could be clearly heard emanating from the kitchen, as the light was fading we were positioned on our balcony enjoying the evening's cool breeze when we spotted the aforementioned Serafina most definitely where she wasn't meant to be. The building opposite was of approximately the same height as our balcony. It was sort of two buildings in one really. The left half of the roof, as we viewed it, was of pitched terracotta tiles, while the right was a flat roof without a parapet, which only occupied half of the width from sea to road, the other half being made up of a fairly substantial balcony, which faced ours and was mostly occupied by stacks of plastic chairs, high enough for any enterprising tot to clamber up and hence on to the flat roof, from which it was very easy to clamber on to the pitched terracotta part too. The flat roof was mainly clear, save for a chimney pot or two and the ubiquitous twisted iron spikes that shoot up from the roof of virtually every flat-roofed house in Greece. The far edge of this flat roof presented one with a sheer drop of two stories straight to a few jagged rocks and the sea itself. On the road-side of the building, a faller would fare no better because the road would break the fall.

To our horror, we looked across to see the lovable little thing ambling about on the flat roof. Then, as we watched, she clambered on to the terracotta tiles and on up to the highest point. She soon became aware of her audience and put on a show accordingly. Just for once there was no shout of "SERAFINA!" as the family, to a man, were busily chopping pork for souvlaki and lettuce and feta for salads.

No amount of gesticulating on our part would get her to climb down. I don't know to this day why we didn't rush down and go across to tell her parents where she was, but we didn't. Maybe we came to the conclusion that she made a habit of this and did it just to alarm the tourists in the apartments opposite. More likely it was sheer horror that made us stay rooted to the spot. Whatever, she finally clambered down again and disappeared into one of the doors on the upstairs balcony, to the evident relief of several pairs of eyes observing from our side of the road.

The oldest boy in the family had a bicycle. It looked fairly smart and he evidently was proud of it and was to be seen racing all over the place on it most days. Although whenever he came home on it he would dismount and let it drop to the floor outside whichever of the three doors into the building through which he chose to enter.

Mikalis, the dad, had a battered old Vespa scooter. Like most continentals, he had mastered the art of carrying anything and everything he wanted on this 125cc wonder machine. He would regularly arrive home from shopping, or the early morning visit to the Aghia Marina quayside, laden with large wooden or cardboard boxes deftly balanced on any remotely usable ledge or surface, with one hand holding something or other for fear it would fall off and the other operating the accelerator grip on the handlebars. Quite often he would charge off down the road in a haze of blue smoke with numerous children hanging from both his body and that of the Vespa. These things are to be seen in just about any southern European country, but then you probably already know that.

It was the Vespa and the eldest son's bicycle, which were to become the focal points in a father-and-son argument that erupted for reasons unclear early one evening.

The first we were aware that there was something going on was when we were hovering in and out of the shower and planning our evening. The sound of excited, nay agitated, voices and loud banging drew us out on to the balcony to view the "show." Father and son had evidently fallen out over something. We never were to find out precisely what. They were both standing in the street with a distance of approximately twenty or thirty feet between them and they were shouting at eachother at the top of their voices. Neither appeared to be all that interested in what the other was saying, but the temperature was rising rapidly. Boiling point was imminent. You know, like when you're waiting for the kettle and the tone of water being heated from within suddenly drops a lot lower and you can see the steam charging out from the spout. The banging sounds were evidently caused by the boy, who was standing right next to his father's Vespa, as he - in his evident frustration at his father's attitude – would turn spasmodically and thump its side panel with his fist.

Now it just so happened that the son's bicycle was leaning against the wall of the building right next to where the father had taken his stance for the fight. He would wave his right hand menacingly at his son, sometimes as a fist and sometimes with the index finger pointing accusingly at his (according to his view, evidently) errant offspring. The other hand, clenched as a fist, was placed authoritatively on his hip. His legs were about a foot apart and planted in such a way as to take his body weight evenly. He was up for a good shouting match. Each time the boy would thump the Vespa, the father grew visibly more angry, yet made no attempt to approach the boy. It appeared as though the boy had just about reached that age and size that rang alarm bells in dad's mind. Thoughts like "Dammit, he's bigger than me now. If I hit him he'll make mincemeat of me!" were no doubt flashing across dad's mind and rooting him to the spot.

Nevertheless, the father Mikalis evidently was looking for some way to retaliate at the sight of his beloved Vespa becoming more and more dented; notwithstanding the fact that the paintwork had long seen better days. The panels had been, up until now, pretty much the same shape as when they first rolled out of the factory many years earlier. But this was changing rapidly. Not only that, but the Vespa was parked precariously right alongside the low wall, maybe only eighteen inches or so high, that separated the road outside the house from the rocks and pebbles and gently lapping sea just a few feet below. Once the son's rage reached the level where his hands were sufficiently sore from thumping dad's scooter that he decided to begin a fresh assault – only this time with his right foot – Mikalis realized he had to wreak some revenge somehow.

Glancing to his left the father caught sight of the boy's bicycle leaning against the house wall almost within his reach. This was the point where I started to feel a bit sick. I have to say that the level of vehemence that this man vented on his son's poor bike made me shiver. He lifted the cycle up with both hands and threw it with all his might to the floor, not once but again and again. The floor in this instance was the sun-baked tarmac of the road outside the house, across the other side of which and just up a storey, were the two observing British vacationers in the shape of Yvonne and I, both standing with towels wrapped around our modesty and open-mouthed at the intense anger and violence of the scene just below us. Little Serafina was standing in one of the doorways and wailing at the top of her lungs to add to the cacophony before her. Eventually her mother's voice was to be heard above the two gladiators and shouting "SERAFINA! *ELLA MESA!*" (Serafina, come inside!) whereupon the little girl disappeared inside the house, assisted vigorously by the hand of someone much older, which had grabbed her by the arm to ensure she obeyed the order.

Father and son continued yelling abuse at eachother, both voices becoming evidently more hoarse by the second. Dad resorted to stamping on the wheels of his son's bicycle until they quickly became quite incapable of revolving any more. The son was possibly about to use all his might to heave his father's Vespa over the wall and into the sea when dad, now at a stage of anger which made him quite forget whether or not his son was now bigger than he was, began a sprint to prevent the act from taking place if at all possible.

This was apparently enough to make the boy decide that perhaps he'd gone far enough and now would be a good time to make good his escape. He released the battered motor scooter and fled off along the road at his maximum running speed and was soon lost in the harbour area of Aghia Marina.

Yvonne and I stood for some moments staring down at the mangled wreck of the bicycle on the road outside the little grillhouse. Mikalis proceeded to make an inspection of the damage to his Vespa whilst muttering many and varied oaths in profane Greek. We then shakily retreated to the inside of our apartment to discuss the events we'd just witnessed and continue preparing for our evening's taverna expedition.

We never did find out quite what had started the battle. What astounded us the most though, was the fact that the following morning both father and son were happily working together to repair the bike, chatting away like a loving parent and child should. We never saw any aftermath of the duel. It was as though both had totally forgotten all about it. As though they had come out one morning to discover that someone else had vandalised their respective modes of transport; except that such an occurrence is still virtually unheard of on a small Greek island.

Perhaps there was something of a lesson on the Greek nature in all of this. Back in the UK it was far more likely that the son would have been away from home long enough for the parents to notify the Police after frantically ringing all the boy's friends and family in a vain attempt to discover his whereabouts after he had fled. Or perhaps a father-and-son feud would have continued for weeks or even months, with mother trying to get them to patch things up. Worse though, one could well have imagined that it would have become a bruising fight between the two right there in the street and goodness only knows what would have been the outcome.

But there they were the following day, acting just as if nothing had happened. I believe it was that particular night that we ate there and, as the evening was drawing to a close, the father and mother got all the kids to demonstrate their prowess (parentally perceived at any rate) on various musical instruments. After each serenade we clapped vigorously and downed another free ouzo. They were almost like the Von Trapps in a way. Perhaps it was good that the bicycle and the Vespa took the full brunt of all the anger. It spared anyone physical injury. No lasting harm was done. The son was soon to be seen again strolling up the road carrying a newly straightened set of forks for his bike and stopping just before the house alongside his dad, who was to be seen carefully hammering the dents out of his Vespa's side panels.

They exchanged a word or two and dad affectionately slapped son on the shoulder as son carried on into the house. Happy days, eh?

30 - Honda 90

In the "centre" of Aghia Marina, Leros, was to be found Taverna O Costas. Not that everyone visiting Leros would agree that Aghia Marina was big enough to have a "centre," but if it could be described as such, this was where Taverna O Costas was located.

Just a few yards from the quay where the Flying Dolphins would tie up, in amongst the local fishermen's' bobbing and brightly-coloured boats, after stepping over the drying fishing nets, you would arrive at some tables and chairs which could be accessed right from the waterside, across the small road from the Taverna itself, which had a further smattering of tables and chairs immediately outside the front and under its awning, from which hung rather precariously a small hand-painted sign reading (as you may have guessed by now) – "Taverna O Costas."

Costas was a stocky man of around forty years of age, with his thick shock of wiry dark hair now turning grey at such a pace as to make it difficult to decide whether it had passed the halfway stage yet. His face was jolly and usually could be seen sporting a smile as he either flashed in and out, hands full with plates of *taramasalata*, *Tsatsiki*, Greek salad or *souvlaki*, or sitting – cigarette in hand - chatting with clientele at one of the tables out front.

One couldn't say the same about his wife. Where Costas was articulate and hailed originally from Athens; his wife was a Lerian and anything but loquacious. Whereas her husband was outgoing and would regularly wave vigorously at passers-by, his wife would sit at a table just outside the door, cigarette in hand, and stare out at the world as if she were an alien who had just landed and couldn't quite make anything out; one who perhaps couldn't see the point in attempting any communication as it would doubtless only be a fruitless exercise anyway.

She was maybe several years his junior, a marital situation not uncommon in Greece. She had, in fact, quite a good figure physically. But from the neck up things deteriorated a bit. Her face was one of those plain visages which defy description owing to the fact that it sported nothing of any note to describe. Her hair was desperately in need of Trevor Sorbie or Nicky Clarke's attention, since it had evidently not been given any TLC by a hairdresser for many a year. When you couple that with the fact that she evidently dyed it to try and achieve a blonde colour, yet only succeeded in creating a sort of dirty ginger, and that it was very thick and created a totally false impression of the size of her head in general, you begin to see that - when I describe her as looking "a bit lacking in the intellect department" – you surely catch my drift.

She may well have been a "Doctor" of some science or other. But, were I a betting man, I'd wager quite a tidy sum that she wasn't. Two more ill-matched people it would be difficult to imagine. During long conversations we had with Costas whilst savouring large Metaxas after a meal at Taverna O Costas, his dislike of his lot in life had become readily apparent. The likes of us would have thought that running a small taverna in a small Greek fishing harbour on a very small and remote Greek island wouldn't be a bad gig. For an educated Athenian however, who had evidently married in haste and done the other bit that comes with that sort of foolish decision, it was nothing short of purgatory.

Costas wintered in Athens and longed for the day when he had saved enough to shut up shop and return there for good. His wife, on the other hand, wanted to remain on Leros and hence close to her family. Thus was created a source of marital strife that was never going to be easily resolved.

It wasn't hard to tell when Mrs Costas was about either. Whenever she was elsewhere he was the "life and soul" type. If she was about (which was usually evident by the fact that she'd be sitting at one of the tables near the entrance to the taverna, ubiquitous cigarette in one hand whilst the other toyed restlessly with a small alcoholic drink) he was much more subdued.

On our first visit to Leros in 1996 we ate at Taverna O Costas several times. Costas would always profess to be mortified if we got up to leave before the level of business had died down suffciently for him to sit at our table and engage Yvonne in long conversations. We always made it a practice in later days not to visit the same taverna every night, as if we owned the place or were frightened to go anywhere else once we'd made friends with the waiter or owner (whatever). I believe that one of the reasons people do this is their fear that they'll hurt the feelings of the proprietor/waiter of the first place they visit if he sees them subsequently going elsewhere. This characteristic is readily seized upon by wily Greek caterers who know the value of tourist loyalty and exploit it to the full - for obvious reasons.

If you've ever had a vacation in Greece it's probably happened to you. Your first night out having been a pleasant affair while you're still excited enough to love the food and take in the atmosphere; a large meal and several jugs of retsina later and the Taverna's owner starts his little routine of protecting his interests. For some reason he's taken to your little party and wants to sit with you and have a drink. A round of free Metaxas arrives to oil the wheels of human relations and, in his broken English, he soon makes you his "special friends." He's probably been to somewhere in Britian when he was in the navy and so would like your address. Who knows, maybe he'll come over again some day and would love to come and see you. By the time you've all staggered back either to your little yacht, hotel room or apartment, you've become firm friends and can't imagine going anywhere else to eat the whole time you're there.

But, next night you all set out for a promenade past all the tavernas along the front and you notice there is a huge choice and, with few exceptions, they all look worth sampling. Plus, of course, each establishment has its "persuader," the man (and even sometimes woman or girl) who obstructs your passage by the front of their particular eatery and regales you with: "Yes please. Come inside, please. Hello. Gooden haben." Or perhaps, "We have fresh fish, very cheap, best food on the island. Sit here please!" and all sorts of other little oft-used phrases. Sometimes they'll thrust a menu at you or steer you with a very persuasive arm to the menu they have mounted on a stand just in front of the first table, which is conveniently still unoccupied and just waiting for your bums on its seats.

The problem is that just along the way is the taverna you ate at last night and you're sure he'll see you. Fear flows through your every sinew. Thoughts like "He'll be really upset. He'll think we don't like his food. Maybe he would have been kind to us and invited us out to his boat or house some day and if he sees us going in here that's all out the window," all course through your brain.

What's worse is that sometimes you have to pass his place before you've completed your pre-meal stroll and he's out there ready to run up to you and give you all a hug and kiss on both cheeks and welcome you to your favourite table (even though you've only ever sat at it once before). Before you've begun to explain that you want to take a walk first he's steering you to the kitchen to see what delights they've prepared (especially with you in mind) for tonight. His brother is over from Athens and will be along later and he's promised him that – since you're all such nice people and have so much in common (You remember! You're from Manchester and he's been to Liverpool once and it's amazing really he didn't bump into you during that 48-hour stop-over in 1977) that he's just got to introduce you.

Well, when we stayed at Aghia Marina on Leros we didn't have to pass Taverna O Costas unless we wanted to anyway, so the problem was sort of alleviated. Walking into the harbour area from our apartment, we came to the right turn leading up the steep hill for half a mile or so into Platanos, the island's "capital," well before passing Costas' place.

We nevertheless chose to eat there on several occasions and Costas was (as one would expect) always pleased to see us. He would usually make a bit of a fuss until he got used to the fact that we weren't going to show up every night, but was always very attentive and always had time for a natter towards the evening's end.

It was Costas who told us where we'd find a *Bouzoukia*, a

live Bouzouki club where there would be dancing. It was at Alinda, at the far end of Aghia Marina bay and a good thirty minutes walk from Aghia Marina harbour itself, following the road as it wound in and out of numerous little bays and coves, backed by the occasional clutch of low-rise tourist apartments and peppered with occasional tavernas. Walking this route at night you took your life in your hands because locals and tourists would tear along the road in various small vehicles and on mopeds and would often squeal on the shiny sun-baked tarmac as they rounded a blind bend and had to swerve to avoid pedestrians such as us, who were too mean to take a taxi to Alinda.

We didn't care much for Alinda. It was the only part of Leros which seemed to have been affected somewhat after the manner of some of the resorts of Corfu's east coast. Not that it was anything like as busy; the sheer effort involved in getting to this island prevented it from becoming a favourite of the "Club 18-30" types. Yet there was a fairly new plaza behind the beach sporting a fast food restaurant, one or two swish bars which resemble those along the front on some island in the Canaries and more of the tacky souvenir shops along the front than one would have expected on such a remote and generally unspoilt island. Even so, there were one or two tavernas here that were set right on the front, with all the tables sitting on a man-bulldozed shelf of shingle at the water's edge, reached by several steps down from the road, across which the waiters would scurry busily all evening.

It was whilst enjoying a meal at one of these establishments that we got into a conversation with an elderly British couple who had made Leros their home in retirement. I had become fascinated by the gentleman doing some fishing with a small plastic frame, small enough to fit into the palm, wound around which was a fishing line, the other end of which dangled in the inky waters of the darkness beyond the small oil lamps of the taverna's tables. The man, who was scarcely more than skin and bone, a description which would have described his wife too, had thrown some pieces of bread into the water and had attracted as many fish as you would have imagined being hauled into their boat by the twelve during one of the miracles of the gospels. The water just adjacent to their table was literally boiling with fish. After watching him for a while we locked eyes and I smiled, he smiled and so a conversation ensued.

"Kalispera…" I began, hoping to impress a wiley old Greek with my grasp if his tongue. ""Ow-do." Came the reply, which instantly informed me that I'd been quite mistaken in thinking this old "sea salt" was, in fact, such.

"First time on Leros is it?" he asked in a very definitely Northern English accent. So the conversation sped up apace once it became clear that both parties shared the same tongue (after a fashion, when you consider I was a Welsh-tinged Bathonian and he a dyed-in-the-wool Yorkshireman) and we got around to their particular situation.

It is no exaggeration to say that both this gentleman and his long-standing wife were very thin. Years of sticking rolled up burning tobacco leaves in their mouths and setting fire to them had taken their toll on the facial features and physique of both. The voice of his very amiable wife was very suggestive of some lung disease which either miners or heavy smokers frequently contract in later life. It transpired that they had been to Leros a couple of years before for a package holiday, liked it and moved lock, stock and couple of suitcases out here to live. They would go back to Britain for a month or so each year, but spend the rest of the time living in a small holiday apartment somewhere between Alinda and Aghia Marina and eating every night in the couple of waterside tavernas where we encountered them. Whilst eating the husband would cast his line into the waters and catch his lunch for the following day. It sort of made the evening's taverna trip even cheaper in real terms. I can't help thinking now, some years on, that it's so unlikely that they'd still be there. Despite their evidently relaxed lifestyle, it was apparent that they wouldn't be around for much longer, but what a way to pass your remaining few years.

Anyway, I digress (as usual). I only really got on to the subject of Alinda because it was where the Bouzouki club was situated. Costas very generously offered to take us there when he'd finished work one night. So it was that at around 1.00am one evening we met Costas outside his taverna and shared a taxi along the five minutes or so of coast road to Alinda. Having disembarked from the taxi we entered a small doorway, were given tickets by a couple of surly Greeks in the small lobby and climbed some stairs to the steadily increasing volume of music that almost blasted your eardrums clean away when we pushed open the internal doors to the Bouzouki club.

Once inside the club one's conversation decidedly resembled that which one would expect to find at a sign-language class. I don't think I've ever left one of these places at some unearthly hour without suffering two very distinct physical effects: one – my ears would ring for 24 to 36 hours afterwards and two – I'd have a hoarse throat for something like the same time period. But it has invariably been worth the suffering. There is usually –and this place was no exception - an excellent band playing with a live bouzouki player taking much of the limelight. Coupled with that there are several professional singers that take the floor seamlessly one after the other, occasionally with one remaining to duet with the next one on. The whole set is punctuated with the occasional dancing exhibition. At the early stages the dancers are usually professionals, and as the night wears on, these are gradually replaced more and more by the enthusiastic crowd, usually aged in their twenties and thirties, all of whom were raised on local dances which they perform almost perfunctorily in some cases, but always with absolute choreographic precision.

The interesting thing about this club was that, since we were in Leros and could almost hear the Turkish shepherds on the hillsides across the water, the music and dancing likewise reflected the Turkish influence on Lerian culture. Every twenty minutes or so a belly dancer would appear on stage and – whilst Yvonne and Costas were busily yelling into each other's ears - I found the time passed much more quickly. I discovered the ticket that had been thrust into my hand when I had entered the establishment had been payed for by Costas. It was about the equivalent of £5 or so, but could be exchanged for one's first drink, a drink I would add that it was very wise to make last as long as you could, because irrespective of whether you were on coke or gin - each drink from thereon in was around £3 regardless. I found out when we had finally bade goodnight to Costas that he'd attempted to kiss my wife across the table during one of my trips to the gents. It didn't surprise me. After almost twenty years of visiting Greece I sort of knew what to expect. The thing is, they don't even mind if you know. They don't expect you to be bothered about it anyway!

So, to the reason this chapter is called Honda 90. The only means of transport Costas possessed on Leros was a battered old Japanese moped of this particular model. You know the ones. They have long been out of production now and you'll very rarely see one in Britain these days. In Greece however, there are still millions of them. They were always either red or blue (and occasionally green, but always faded!) with cream-coloured plastic knee guards and trim. It was our last night on Leros and Yvonne, as per usual, had procrastinated for too long over whether to buy a Greek CD or not. She had already bought several by Parios and Dionyssiou over previous years and wanted something different. What did Costas recommend? Who did he like? Without hesitation Costas said we were mad to consider Karras (too moribund), Parios was past it anyway and Dionyssiou was dead.

We were sitting at one of Costas' tables early in the evening debating this very important subject before walking up to the square at Platanos for a pre-meal drink and Costas insisted we buy the latest by Sfaganiakis. He played us a sample over his stupendously bad Taverna audio system, but it was enough for Yvonne to decide that – yes - she'd like to buy it. The only thing was that time was now against us. There was one solitary music shop just below Platanos on the steep hill going up from Aghia Marina and it was about to close at 8.00pm. It was now 7.45.

"There's no way we can get to the shop before it closes, so you'll have to go without this time." I pronounced confidently.

"Nonsense!" Declared Costas. Take my Honda. You can be there before they close if you go now." This seemed a good solution. I'd driven mopeds and motorbikes for years and so it held no fears.

"OK. Thanks, write down the name of the album and can I have the keys, please?" Costas scribbled down something totally undecipherable to my English eyes and handed me the napkin on which he'd written it. "And the keys?" I repeated.

"No need! It's stuck in the ignition. Has been for years! You'll find it a bit peculiar to drive, but it goes OK. You must hurry, it's nearly time!"

The Honda 90 was propped on its side stand just beside the taverna's clutch of tables and chairs at the edge of the road. I threw a leg over, twiddled the key and kicked it to life. So far so good. It started and I revved it a bit to get the feel of the throttle. The seat was seriously ill though. Not much was left of the original vinyl and not a lot of the hoards of black tape that had been stuck all over it when the vinyl had first begun to crack up and crumble away. Not much of the foam rubber remained either, so the metal frame of the seat's under-structure was apparent to one's bum. I kicked the stand up and twisted the throttle and eased into the road. Funny noise. Looking down I saw that the side stand had decided that its spring wasn't good enough to hold it in the "up" position any more, so I'd have to put up with it sparking off the road surface on a regular basis. I sped along the hundred metres or so to the turning which led up to Platanos. Good job there wasn't much traffic at Aghia Marina that time of the evening. As I turned the corner I just remembered I should be on the right hand side of the road.

It was not more than a half a mile up hill all the way, starting off at a very gentle rise and becoming very steep for the last couple of hundred metres. The warm evening breeze felt wonderful and the evening smells of charcoal and bougainvillea played with my nose. I felt good. I felt like a local Greek. There were always numerous Greeks of all shapes and sizes zipping around on these things. Who needs a car living in a place like this? The shiny sun-baked tarmac made the tyres squeal as I slowed to a halt outside the tiny CD shop on the steep hill just below Platanos square. I made sure the side stand was in the fully "down" position and tilted the machine on to it. Turning it off I swung one leg over behind me and stood satisfied and warmly windswept outside the little establishment. From my top shirt pocket I pulled Costas' napkin and smoothed my sticky up hair down a bit and tried the door.

Fully expecting to have made it in time and that the door would yield to my enthusiastic attempt to open it I almost broke my nose on the glass. The shop was closed. A sign written in poor English said something like "We are closed. Please to be coming tomorrow after ten." The only problem was, tomorrow after ten we would be sitting on a small tub of a boat on our arduous voyage back to Kos for our flight home. Costas' kindness in lending me his Honda was to prove in vain after all. Ah well, there was nothing for it but to go back down to the taverna and break the news to Yvonne.

Even after only having driven the Honda for around 3 minutes, I was already beginning to feel I knew it. Yes the seat was uncomfortable. Yes the throttle took a split second to "kick in" so to speak. Yes the tyres were a peculiar mix of black and beige in the places where the canvas cheerfully showed through. But, swinging my leg over and remounting I told myself "you're a seasoned two wheeled campaigner. You get used to these things in no time. This is fun." After all, the gear-change was automatic. All you had to do was accelerate and brake really.

I kicked it into life, waited for a couple of vehicles to pass in both directions and began my descent. As you've probably realised, since it was up-hill all the way coming, it was now going to be downhill all the way back, starting off really steeply and becoming less steep as one approached Aghia

Marina and the T-junction where I would need to turn right to cover the last 100 metres or so to the waiting Yvonne and Costas. I took the first couple of hundred metres with carefree abandon until the road went through a gentle double bend. A slight right as it passed the schoolyard on one's left, followed by a gentle left. I applied the brakes at this point.

Bit of a mistake not checking that the brakes were in working order before I set out. They weren't only not very good, they'd taken a vacation! Somehow I made it through the double bend and began praying that I wouldn't come up behind a truck or bus or something. Plus the fact that, should any pedestrian try to cross in front of me, they'd be sharing my ambulance. That's always assuming there were ambulances on Leros. How on earth was I going to slow down sufficiently to negotiate the near 90 degree bend at the bottom of the road in Aghia Marina? I kept squeezing the brake lever on the left handlebar whilst pumping gingerly at the footbrake. The tarmac here was so smooth that you couldn't afford to try an emergency stop anyway. There was absolutely no doubt that you'd skid for miles.

I decided that the only recourse open to me was to sacrifice my shoes. So I applied my feet to the road as visions of what it was going to be like to be laying in a small Greek medical centre with drips coming out of my orifices and both legs in plaster flashed through my mind.

Just as I was becoming convinced that the road was about to burn right through my shoes and start eating the soles of my feet I arrived at the corner and somehow (and to this day I don't know how!) I got round it. The 100 metres or so to the taverna was mercifully flat and I was able to reduce velocity sufficiently to effect a complete halt with the aid of a chair and table at the taverna. Both of which thankfully survived the contact.

Yvonne jumped up from her chair and enquired excitedly, "Did they have it in stock?" Meanwhile Costas was approaching from the other side and excitedly enquiring about how I got on with his pride and joy. I must have seemed a little distant because I was mentally still checking myself out of hospital and wondering if I'd be able to afford the plane ticket home after having missed my flight due to being incapacitated.

"I said," repeated Yvonne "did they have it in stock?"

"What? Eh? Oh, no." I whimpered. "They were closed. I missed them after all."

"No problem." Said Costas. "I buy it for you tomorrow and send it in the mail."

Which is precisely what he did. That was good of him, wasn't it?

31 - *Paradisos*

Vromolithos bay, Leros, can be reached from Aghia Marina by a twenty five minute walk up through the old capital of Platanos, and on past the road leading down to Pandeli. It's a fairly pleasant, although not particularly exciting, bay with a narrow strand of shingle beach where it's not especially easy to get into the sea owing to a rocky ridge just a little out from the water's edge which somewhat complicates matters underfoot.

En route out of Platanos there used to be a small bakery, just near the taxi rank, where we would avail ourselves of a hot *tyropita* (feta cheese pastry pie) en route. Almost made the walk worthwhile in itself. We actually made the walk to Vromolithos more often in the evening than during the day. The reasons for this were a) the poor beach and b) the fact that the only inhabitants of the bay area were a couple of Greeks who ran the taverna & shops behind the beach and quite a lot of British tourists who were staying in the several two-storey apartment blocks that circled the bay. The place had little character to speak of. A little way up from the beach and higher on the gentle hillside was Taverna Paradisos.

Paradisos was a pleasant and fairly large taverna, set on two levels, the higher of which was covered with an extensive canopy extending out from the building. The lower level was reached by crossing the upper terrace and descending one or two steps down to this more exposed area, which then melted into the undergrowth, through which one would no doubt have found a way down to the small road which threaded its way behind the holiday apartments below. There was more than a hint of the English Georgian house and garden about the place.

Yvonne was not particularly enamoured with the staff at Paradisos. They were among those who persisted in speaking to her in English although she never did so to them. Whenever this happened she would often not want to return to the establishment a second time. Among the reasons we broke the pattern with Paradisos was the fact that there just weren't that many tavernas in this part of Leros to afford one the luxury of only visiting them once during a two week stay. The food was good at Paradisos too, making it worth a return visit and all endeavours to get the waiters to talk to us in Greek. Nevertheless, when we'd get up to leave and utter a farewell in our very best Greek, the words floating back to us from the kitchen doorway would inevitably be: "Thank you. Goodnight!"

Yvonne always views it as a bit of an insult if a waiter doesn't speak to her in Greek. "After all," she'll say, "Most tourists can't speak a word of the language. So when someone obviously can speak Greek you'd think they'd be grateful not to have to struggle to communicate." I'll often add the thought that perhaps they actually think they're being nice to us by speaking in English. To which she'll counter –"But that means the place must be too touristy. I prefer the tavernas where they are more traditionally Greek and don't want to, or can't even speak a foreign language."

The discussion usually becomes more lively and continues for some time. But I'm boring you already, I know. Why did I mention Taverna Paradisos in Vromolithos bay? Oh yes, I remember: we'd already eaten there once and decided, primarily from the sheer lack of choice in this small island, to go there again. At least the food was good, even if the waiters did insist on speaking to us in English. And another thing, they never seemed to stop by our table for a bit of a chat. Definitely not the sort of taverna we'd usually re-visit. But, following the long and slightly sweaty walk from Aghia Marina, we descended the gentle slope of the concrete path leading into the taverna just as the last of the sun's rays were sending red shafts across the western sky. Far across the waters the Turkish coast loomed forebodingly and there were to be seen the occasional flashes of an electric storm over the Turkish mountains. Above us the first stars were becoming distinct in the darkening sky and it felt very good to be a sentient being.

It was immediately obvious on entering the upper terrace that a large party of people had arranged to come to Paradisos that night. Apart from a few individual tables at the outer edge of the terrace, situated half out of the vine-covered canopy and close to the balustrade and steps down to the lower, gravelled terrace; all the other tables on this level had been placed together in a long row, covered in white paper table cloths, the edges of which were punctuated by those little metal clips to secure the paper to the tables against the breeze. Those little metal clips always remind me of when I used to go to art classes. We'd always use them to secure a piece of cartridge paper to the drawing board when we all sat round to draw a model. It was apparent that they were expecting some thirty or more in the party.

"Oh no. Looks like we've come on the wrong night. No doubt a bunch of tourists are having their "Greek Night" here or something. We won't hear much Greek spoken tonight!" That was the slightly caustic response of my dear wife to the scene that greeted us. But already the least Greek-looking waiter (the one with the kind of sixties Beatle-cut fair-ish hair and boring glasses) was suggesting a table at which we might like to place ourselves. We were either going to have an argument in front of the taverna staff, or we were going to sit down and then decide whether to stay or go somewhere else. Somewhere else? That would have meant another considerable walk in this part of Leros. We'd selected one of the few tables still available on the upper terrace, adjacent to the long row of reserved tables set for the shortly-to-arrive party. We decided to stay and hope for the best.

Which is is just what occurred that night – the "best." Contrary to all expectations, our Greek salad was half consumed and we were starting to feel the wine beginning to relax us (even so much as to dissipate Yvonne's annoyance when the waiter still spoke to her in English) when the large party of guests began arriving, slowly drifting down the wide concrete drive from the road above. It only took Yvonne a microsecond to realise that they were all Greeks. Varying in age from early twenties to "on their last legs," they came, the women with cardigans draped around their shoulders (after all, it was only 25 degrees Celsius in the evening. They didn't want to get cold now did they!). the men in smart slacks and La Coste polo shirts. The older ones wearing collar and tie. Plenty of gold teeth about too. It was a family and friends "do" for some reason or other. Yvonne's ear went symbolically to the ground in an instant. This could turn out to be a good evening.

The guests all spent several hours (seemed like it anyway) in a dispute over who was going to sit where. On not a few occasions they were all seated when someone would suggest that someone needed to sit somewhere else for some else's benefit and they'd all get up and change seats again. That accomplished, one or two of the women would then send word down the length of the table that they'd left their handbag at their old position and a cuffuffle would arise as the item was ceremoniously passed along from hand to hand. When finally they had all decided that they were seated appropriately, the din of a Greek family gathering began in earnest.

It's a bit of a tradition among Greeks that they all dispute who'll sit where before actually settling at a taverna table. I've only recently come to realise why it always happens when Yvonne and I go to a restaurant, whether in Greece or anywhere else. It's simply in her blood. The Greek part of her definitely gets the upper hand at times like this. When Greeks arrive at a table (after first having anyway discussed at length the virtues of every available table in the establishment) they circle it, each extending a hand to the back of the nearest chair, before one will decide they want to be the opposite side from where they currently stand, so they can "see better" or perhaps because some part of the surrounding foliage (always present at perimeter tables in tavernas) is brushing their back and carries a "creepy crawly" potential. So they'll then all rotate to new positions and once again take hold of the back of the chair they now stand closest to. This doesn't mean that these positions are the ones finally to be adopted. This can occur several times before the scraping of chair feet begins in earnest and they finally take their seats to eat. In our case, even after the last stage has occurred we frequently all get up and rotate again because – having seen the panorama from a seated position - my wife will decide she can see better (to "people-watch") from the other side after all.

If you've never witnessed a Greek family gathered en masse for a special occasion, you've missed a fascinating, if sometimes alarming event. For example, on the Island of Crete it may well include guns being fired at, say, a wedding reception. Fortunately, this was not the case here on Leros. But one thing this type of occasion always included was much vigorous waving and thrusting of hands and arms and voice levels that would make a British person think fists would soon begin flying. This is just the Greek way. They cannot have a conversation without throwing themselves into it body and soul. If this means relating a story with full Oscar-winning acting methods then so be it. There will also always be a political argument raging somewhere round the table. Greeks don't talk about politics in the manner we do. No, each argues as though threatening to rape the other's wife! But this is their custom. They'll soon slap each other on the back and clink glasses of Metaxa as firm friends as David and Jonathan.

It was a fascinating exercise just to watch as the waiters gamely attempted to take orders. First it was the drinks, with much pointing and shouting on the part of the various male members of the party. They (as – it has to be said – also happens in Britain) would get furious as they made vain attempts to interrupt the women to ascertain what they would like to drink, whilst the women were midway through a tale about someone's dramatic dash to get the doctor when

someone else was just about to deliver a child. Or perhaps it
was merely a horror story about a shopping trip to Rhodes or
something, I couldn't tell anyhow. How the waiters managed
to get any true picture as to who was drinking what I don't
know. It occurred to me that they just brought out tray after
tray with a varied selection of drinks and thwacked them into
the middle of the table whilst guessing (probably quite
accurately) that the guests would merrily pick out what they
wanted and carry on. I have to say that the waiters always
impress me when they can vigorously place a bottle of beer on
the table, whip out their bottle opener and open the bottle
one-handed whilst the other simultaneously holds a tray full of
glasses, jugs and bottles at head height. I know, you're
thinking: 'it doesn't take much to impress him.'

As a result of this large party having arrived and
thoroughly absorbed the entire waiting staff – and one or two
from the kitchen too I shouldn't wonder – in caring for their
every need, the service we were to experience this particular
evening was going to leave a lot to be desired. Under normal
circumstances this would without a doubt have brought out
the Victor Meldrew in me. But as this evening progressed we
ceased caring. After some hours and when the long table was
thoroughly covered in the debris of a particularly sumptuous
Greek family feast. When the kids were still tearing round the
perimeter of the diners and crying at the least little thing due
to being desperately over-tired. When the keen
photographers among them were bemoaning their having
forgotten to bring a spare film and others were still busily
snapping away getting shots of groups of rosy cheeked people
with red-eye at a furious pace. When the older men had
loosened their ties and were fingering large Metaxas and
slapping each other on the backs as they swapped heroic

wartime tales. When some of the women were sitting stony-faced at not being included in any one group's conversation and so they turned to staring at tourists like us. Yes, at this time somewhere between 11.30pm and midnight, one or two of the males in the party produced their musical instruments.

Now I have seen many a Greek band playing *Bouzouki* music. I have seen a lot of old Greek men playing *Nisiotika* music with flat-sounding violins. But these instruments I had never seen the like of before. There was something stringed which resembled a cross between a balalaika and a mandolin. I couldn't tell from my vantage point how many strings it had, but it soon was joined by another of similar appearance, but slightly smaller. Then there appeared a wind instrument resembling the Scottish bagpipes, with the bag almost white in colour and evidently a skin of some animal or other. It was either brand new or its owner was meticulous about keeping it clean. He didn't blow into anything, but tucked the skin bag under his right armpit and appeared to accomplish air pressure for the pipes by squeezing the thing under his arm. There was apparently a small bellows with which he replenished its air supply. They soon joined in producing a sound which instantly evoked Greek island life of centuries gone and a lifestyle still to be found in remoter parts of the Aegean. It was magic to behold and entrancing to listen to.

The older men and women took turns at singing their unique song as the others of the party listened in respectful, attentive silence. At the conclusion of each song the whole clientele of the taverna joined in rapturous applause. Not that the quality of singing necessarily merited it, but the total commitment to the song's sentiment on the part of its singer most certainly did.

Soon various members of the party were on their feet

dancing. Old island dances seldom seen were performed among the tables with taverna staff appreciatively standing at the doorway clapping and whistling. Now and again a dancer, usually one of the more ancient among them, would almost take a tumble as one of the smaller children in the group darted among them when they were in full swing. Still others would rip the flowers from the geranium plants growing all around the perimeter and toss the petals over the dancers' heads in appreciation and approval of their endeavours. When someone couldn't lay their hands on a poor unfortunate geranium, they'd just grab a handful of paper serviettes from the small dispensers scattered about the table-tops and toss these.

It seemed all too soon that the gaiety began subsiding. What time it was I don't remember, but it was certainly in the wee small hours. Toddlers were still running around, or those that were now grossly over-tired were looking for opportunities to ball at the least little thing. The tables groaned under the weight of half-empty plates and innumerable empty bottles and those funny aluminium jugs in which tavernas serve up their draught retsina. The party began to rise and gradually don their cardigans and sweaters. The ladies unhooked their handbags from the backs of the little wooden chairs with raffia-type seats that so many tavernas seem to sport. These look so ethnic and traditional, but cut off the circulation in my legs regularly. Some of the older ones linked arms, some just wandered off into the night with the faintest smile of a good evening well-passed on their faces. Those men who had supplied the evening's musical entertainment carefully replaced their precious instruments in their cases, doubtless wondering when next they would have opportunity to again bring them out into the light of day.

Soon, much too soon, the whole party had departed and so, it seemed, we should do likewise. The joy of the occasion had quite driven away our annoyance at the waiter who always spoke to us in English. That is, until we had settled up our account and began walking towards the exit.

In flawless Greek my wife, Lela's daughter, called a cheerful *"kalinichta, kai s'efarestoume parapoli!"* to the staff in the Taverna's doorway.

"Goodnight and thank you very much!" Came the reply.

32 - *Current Affairs*

I mentioned some chapters ago that we arrived at our new home in Rhodes on August 23rd 2005 to a cheerful expression on the face of Gary our builder as he informed us (with not a little glee I felt) that we still didn't have mains electricity or "revma" as the locals call it (which literally means: "current").

Gary had provided us with a generator for the interim, the constant drone of which was to become our audible backdrop for 3 months almost to the day before the Greek electricity company (DEH) finally and grudgingly connected us to the mains and gave us the joyful prospect of power cuts which were to prove totally unexpected, unpredictable and of unspecified duration.

Before long I was getting to know Manolis, the nice affable young chap in the local filling station, as I was there every two or three days with my two big plastic drums to buy diesel for the "genny." No sooner would I drive onto the forecourt than he would appear from the door of the office and make for the diesel pump, where we'd mutually commiserate owing to the fact that his new house 4 kilometers up the valley in the village of Asklipio was also awaiting its "revma."

To begin with, we'd be driving everywhere in Mitsos, our trusty Mitsubishi L300 van (long wheelbase, remember!) as it was still our only means of transport. It usually elicited enquiries from the locals, whenever we struck up a conversation with them, about how we came here and were we going to want to sell it at all? To which we replied yes and could they find anyone who might be interested. They usually couldn't. Or if they could it would result in some surly Greek bloke turning up at the house with some other younger chappie in tow, whereupon they'd disembark the 4WD pick-up or whatever they'd created the inevitable dust cloud up the kilometer of goat track with and stroll slowly and deliberately around the van making tutting noises and kicking the tyres before taking a long lung cancer-inducing drag on their ubiquitous cigarette before saying something like, "Iss right-hand drive. I want really left-hand. How much you say anyway?"

When I told them, it would elicit further tuts and sharp intakes of breath before they'd offer me a ridiculous and much lower sum, which usually drew the response from me: "I'd rather park it up behind the house and use it as a shed than sell it for that!" Following a bit of half-hearted haggling (after it had become apparent that they weren't going to buy it anyway, but had only come up the track to have a good nose at these new arrivals from *"Anglee-ia,"*) they'd get back into their pick-up and create another kilometer-long dust cloud as they hared back down to the main road and off for their siesta or something.

We eventually did manage to sell it to a nice Greek Cypriot fella who lived about ten kilometers away and wanted it for his mobile mechanic business. Considering what we'd paid for it and what it had accomplished for us in completing the voyage successfully, we considered we'd more than got our money's worth and were not a little sad to see it go when Adonis drove it away one hot November afternoon. But by then we were the proud owners of a little 5 year-old Suzuki Swift and transport costs were inevitably suitably and agreeably reduced.

The Greek sky at night is awesome in summer, as I may have mentioned in earlier chapters. Our house is blessed in that it is situated well away from any light pollution and so, when I'm up in the middle of the night (which I frequently am as I'm not a good sleeper), I often walk outside and stand on the drive out front and get a crick in my neck as I stare up in wonder at the vastness of it all. When you don't have to fight any light pollution the Milky Way is clearly visible as a – well - milky way stretching as a band right across the sky from one horizon to the other. I can always make out the North Star as I still remember from a trip to the London Planetarium many years ago how to locate it using the last two stars in the "Plough" or "Great Bear" constellation and, aside from the fact that we're a little further south than we were in South Wales, UK, it gives me a sense of belonging to see exactly the same patterns in the night sky.

Of course, during the first three months from our arrival we had no electricity at night anyway as we were in the habit of turning the generator off at bedtime for two reasons; 1. to conserve diesel and 2. to get some relief from its constant droning, which would certainly have kept us awake most nights.

The first week or so the noise was much worse as Gary

had left us a fairly old un-sound insulated generator with a woefully inadequate fuel tank, which meant it had to be filled up several times during a day. We tried filing it up without turning it off, but the tank was situated almost directly atop the combustion cylinder and would vibrate so much that you'd get 75% of the smelly liquid all over yourself, the generator and the ground and 25% in the tank. He took great delight though in telling us how much he'd had to fork out for the new generator he brought us after a week or so. In fact he takes great delight in telling us almost every week about some financial disaster or extra expense he's had to incur owing to someone else's having let him down in some way. In this instance it was the Greek electricity company to blame.

"We've given the buggers 20,000 Euros to bring the supply up this valley from the main road, but they'll only actually do the installation when it suits them. Could be next week, could be next year, ...welcome to Greece." ...he'd frequently say, evidently expecting to impress us with his superior knowledge of all things Greek, including how long they take to do things here. The fact that my wife is half-Greek and we're both Greek speaking (well, I'm becoming Greek speaking to be precise!), that Yvonne has been coming over here since she was a young tot when she was bridesmaid at her cousin's wedding in Athens in the late 1950's and the fact that we've been coming here as a couple for thirty years and not just for "holidays" in the usual sense of the word, but to make visits on our relatives in Athens and other parts and have thus a fairly good grasp of the Greek mentality and mode de vie is of no consequence to our Gary. He knows it all and we've only been here five minutes and he's damn well going to impress us with all he knows, having dealt with the Greek system for six or seven years.

Our first 6 months here weren't the easiest of our lives for many and varied reasons, but dealing with Gary and his attitude hasn't made it any easier. Still, he did build us a house and, it has to be said, it's a very nice house. In more recent times our relationship has (thankfully) thawed somewhat, but for the first year or so of our time here, Gary (bless him!) didn't make it very easy for us. Maybe it had something to do with the fact that we weren't the owners of the house. Our Friends John & Wendy were and we were their tenants. Perhaps Gary thought we ought to thrust our hands into our pockets and buy another one that he'd build for us, who knows.

Anyway, the new generator made things a little easier, but only for a short while. It was rolled out of Gary's old Belgian-registered Mercedes van with great fanfare, all gleaming bright yellow in the Greek sunshine and giving promise of less noise and much less frequent re-fuelling sessions to come.

Having explained to us lesser mortals how to start the thing up and switch it off again, Gary and his "boys" were off down the lane in a righteous cloud of dust, leaving us alone with our new power source. That's another thing (while I'm on my "Gary" soapbox): my dad was an electrical engineer before he retired and had taught me a wealth of electrical know-how all through my childhood. But good old Gary is the kind that doesn't wait to find out what you may or may not know. He assumes you're an imbecile by comparison with him and treats you accordingly. The fact that I could strip down an internal combustion engine and re-build it is something he still isn't aware of to this day. I reckon he heard I was a "mouse-pusher" and so assumed I'd know not one thing about anything practical at all. I soon realized it wasn't worth trying to disillusion him. He (in a figurative sense you understand) doesn't have any ears! As I said a little earlier, more recently things have thawed considerably between us, so maybe if he gets a mention in my hoped for sequel to *"Feta Compli!"* he'll fare much better.

It has to be said that for the first week or two it was almost civilized using this new genny. It was markedly quieter and only needed refueling once every morning and would then cheerfully throb away all day without any further attention being needed. So I soon fell into the schedule of wandering in my early morning daze as soon as I got up across the dusty fifty metres or so from the house to the genny and opening the filler cap, whereupon I'd heave one of the plastic drums into position and pour the horrible fluid into the ridiculously impractically-positioned filler pipe, which was situated right slap bang in the middle of the top of the thing. To have attempted to fill it without a funnel would have been totally impossible and even with one the drums still dribbled diesel fuel all over my slippers. Not to mention the top of the generator's shiny new yellow housing.

Sad it may be, but one of our pass-times when we were first here was to stand out the front and gaze down the valley imagining, in fact willing, the electricity poles to appear all up the valley to our home. It could at times be very disheartening to stand there with the genny humming mockingly nearby, whilst looking down a pole-less valley and wondering just how long our wait for the elusive "revma" was going to be. Manolis (at the filling station) would say each time I went there: "Still ochi revma eh? Egho to ithio, ("me the same"). This is 2006 for goodness sake! It will be Christmas soon and it's not good enough! I know other people who waiting like us, we think of getting together to go to Arhangelos to DEH office to all complain together. You want to come if we do?" To which my reply was in the affirmative, of course.

Then one day in late September it happened. A "hole-drilling and post dropping" truck was working its way up the valley. We stood excitedly out front and watched as it torturously slowly drilled a hole with its great big corkscrewy thing, then using its grabber would pick up and drop a tar-blackened post into the freshly made hole. We'd be on-line before the week was out.

Nope. Wrong there. Once they'd dropped the posts into their holes all the way up to our perimeter fence (which you had to imagine as it was nowhere to be seen as yet), they beat a hasty retreat and were gone. A further week passed before anything else happened. Every Greek rural dwelling has to have its electricity meter mounted on a concrete obelisk somewhere in the vicinity of the building. The perameters for these eyesores are very precise. Once again, Gary took delight in explaining that the power couldn't be connected until we had a meter box, with a meter within it and securely mounted on this obelisk, which would be a couple of meters tall, about a foot thick and four or five feet wide. Plus there would need to be a large metal tube, somewhat like a scaffolding pole in the UK, sticking out the top of the concrete to a height of four or five meters.

"So where's our 'concrete bus shelter' (as Gary calls them, with good reason I'll admit) then?" we asked, unable to conceal a slight note of panic.

"Still waiting for the bloke to come and build it. Hopefully he'll be along next week." Said Gary. We soon became accustomed to everything happening "next week." Although the expression "next week" can mean anything up to a month! Well, some time later (it all becomes a blur) some young chap arrived and spent a couple of days constructing the "shuttering" (after a JCB had dug out the foundation) for our monstrosity of a "concrete bus shelter."

Then, a week or so later, a concrete mixer wound its way painfully slowly up the valley and mayhem ensued at the edge of our property whilst various Greek blokes shouted and gesticulated while they finally got themselves into position and "poured" the thing. There followed, of course, another week or so while the concrete "cured" before the chap that had built the "shuttering" out of all kinds of pieces of old wood arrived once more to take it all down to reveal the concrete obelisk in all its glory. After he'd left we spent several enjoyable hours picking up bent nails, hundreds of which were scattered all across our lane, just ready and waiting to drive themselves into our tyres!

One fine day in late October the "cable" team turned up. "Ah," we now thought "we'll really get connected this time. Yippee! No more messing around with all that smelly diesel fuel." Not to mention stinking the car out with it as it inevitably spilled through the caps of the plastic drums and soaked the floor of the car boot as I'd drive back up to the house after a fuel run to the local service station. Still wrong. The cable team, it has to be said, worked very efficiently and quickly and soon there were three gleaming copper cables attached to the cross-bars of the newly installed poles all the way up to the edge of our garden. Right next to the "concrete bus shelter," in fact. They fitted the necessary transformer to the pole and wired the cables from the T-bar to it. Now all that was needed was for the cables to be taken from the transformer, across to the scaffolding pole and down to our meter, which hadn't, as yet materialized.

"When do they fit the meter, this afternoon?" we

hopefully asked one of the cable team, who turned out to be a Greek South African who spoke good English.

"Nah. Gotta wait until they get some more meters and boxes in from Athens. There aren't any on the island at the moment. Been a bit of a run on 'em."

Now I don't know about you, but were we naïve to assume that a national company, responsible for the entire island's (nay country's) electricity supply, wouldn't keep a stock control system going to ensure they didn't completely run out of meters and meter boxes before ordering some more? No good discussing this situation with our builder, Gary. He'd only put the old record on which played: "Welcome to Greece."

To return to the generator for a moment. Notwithstanding the inconvenience of living with one anyway, we were so grateful for the new and much more quiet one after it replaced "old faithful" as Gary's men called the older one, that for at least a short while we were almost happy with things. Should have known that wasn't going to last. The new genny was barely two weeks old when the young man constructing the shuttering for the meter obelisk connected his arc-welder to it in order to weld a metal ring on to the top of the "scaffolding pole" that was to stick out the top, to which one distant day would be attached the incoming cables from the nearby post. Merrily commencing to weld, he blew a diode or something in the generator's charging circuit. The moment he started to "weld," the genny tripped off. Gary was present at the time and blithely said, "It's no problem, we'll just re-start it. It shouldn't have any problem dealing with the current drain of a welder like that."

He was wrong. Not that he's ever admitted that mind you. People who are always right don't need to humble themselves to that extent after all. They re-started the genny, the young fella tried again to weld with the same result. Genny down and everything in the house dead.

"Hmmm.: mused Gary, "might have to use "old faithful" for his arc welder then." So they duly re-started the new genny and set up the old one for the welding operation. Everything was apparently OK for an hour or two, by which time Gary and his team had left for the day, along with the young welder chappie. We were all alone and it was late afternoon when the genny died again. I smelt the usual rodent and went over to try and start it. It was dead as the proverbial dodo. No life in it at all. For the last few hours it had been running without charging and had now exhausted the battery to a state deader than dead. I knew I now had the rather unpleasant task of telephoning Gary, already sure of his response:

"What have you gone and done to my generator? You've knackered it haven't you."

"I'd say that it's not charging and a diode or something is blown in the charging circuit after that arc welding incident today."

"No, that's not it. Probably a dud battery. I suppose I'll have to drive over there and attach the battery from the old genny for now. I'll be up in half an hour."

The long and the short of it was, after trying to run the generator for a week or two with a battery charger permanently attached, since the generator wasn't charging its battery at all, and having burnt out two domestic battery chargers, both of which literally caught fire from constant use for hours and days at a time, the new genny was packed up back to its supplier in distant Rhodes town for repair and we were back with "old faithful," just in time for the weather to break, so I was out in the wind and rain trying to top up diesel and start and stop the thing as and when necessary. Oh joy!

One day two men arrived at the house with a grey metal box. "Oh goody" said Wendy, our good friend and landlady who was in residence next door when they came, "does that mean we'll be connected now?"

Have a guess at the answer to that one then. Can't get anything past you can I? What they said was: "This is fuse box, it go on pole beneath transformer." So they fitted it to the pole, evidently whilst carrying on a huge slanging match which looked like coming to blows, then left, but not before Wendy had asked, "So when do we finally get switched on?"

"Next week."

"When next week?"

"Maybe Thursday."

Next Thursday was still six days away and it came and went with nothing of any significance happening. One day we came home from shopping to see we'd had a meter box fitted on the obelisk. When we eagerly inspected it we were crestfallen to find that it didn't contain anything that remotely resembled a meter.

The following week an inspector from DEH came up the track in a small car and jumped out, clipboard in hand, and started staring at things and ticking boxes. I ran over to him in fear that he may beat a retreat before I could plead our cause.

"So, do we get our meter now?"

"I'm only the inspector. But everything seems to be in order. But we're still waiting for meters to come from Athens."

"Oh great. So when may it possibly be then? We're getting desperate. It's been months and the weather is starting to change now."

"Next week."

Next week was only shortened to a fortnight because the long-suffering Gary eventually slipped a plain brown envelope to someone somewhere with a view to "short-circuiting" the waiting list as it were. "More unnecessary drain on the finances." he quipped. I was tempted to say, "Welcome to Greece," but discretion and valour and all that stuff, eh?

It was some weeks later when I pulled into the local filling station to be met by Manolis who seemed a tad more cheerful than on previous occasions. "You have *revma*?" he asked, smiling broadly.

"We do!" I replied.

"When you get connected?" he asked. We compared notes to discover that several houses had all been connected in our part of the island on the same day, November 21st. So either the connection team made a small fortune in plain brown envelopes that particular day, or Gary wasted his money.

I prefer to believe the latter.

As to the current state of affairs? At this time of writing we have a garden that's starting to look half-respectable and we're even making regular trips to plant nurseries and buying things to put in. We have almost a perimeter fence and most certainly a very nice pair of wrought iron front gates set into posh white walled posts with a bit of wall extending out from either side and topped with terracotta roof tiles. We have a nice paved drive and have even already built ourselves a second patio on our side of the house thus affording us more privacy. There are still a few finishing touches required, so, after having lived here for now ten months and counting, Gary still pulls up on the drive in his battered old blue van from time to time and we wonder which of the outstanding jobs we may just get finished during this visit. We usually ask rather gingerly when the last few bits and pieces will be finished, in the hope of knowing when we can shut the front gates on him for good some time sooner rather than later. The usual reply we get is...

"Next week."

Feta Compli!

Author's Supplementary Note

When we first visited the island of Leros in 1996, we came across a gentleman called (more by the locals than by himself) *"O Ree-ganos,"* which was a nickname given him owing to his preoccupation with things

herbal, especially origano. This was because he would appear most evenings on a little Japanese moped with a basket fashioned from an old fruit crate, on the front of which was hand-written "Botana, herbs, origanos" in Greco-English capital letters which got smaller as they approached the right hand edge of the crate.

He would spend most of his daylight hours in the hills around the island gathering fresh herbs, which he'd then take back to his little room above a fruit store in Platanos, Leros' "capital" (if a small village with a bit of a square and a couple of bars and tavernas could be called that) where he'd diligently begin his various treatment processes to turn them into herbal remedies. He would also dry them and pack them in small paper packages and sell them to the dining tourists in the clutch of tavernas around Aghia Marina and Platanos of an evening.

There is much to tell about George, as that's his actual

name, and most of it will have to wait until I write another tome to follow up this one. The weird thing is, I first got the germ of an idea to write this book after we encountered and became quite good friends with *"O Ree-gannos"* in June 1996 and then again in September of that same year. I hope he's still there, but as the book began to develop and I reached thirty one chapters I realized that I still had so much more to tell that it would have to become two books instead of one. Plus, I haven't even got round to writing about him yet.

So, if you have in any way been entertained by this book, maybe you'll find *"Moussaka to my Ears"* a pleasant diversion if and when it makes it into print.

Now regarding Gary, who built the house we now live in. He doesn't get a very good "press" in this book. The fact is, I told it like it was and, Gary - if you're reading this, I have a message for you: "Don't worry, you get a much better showing in 'Moussaka to My Ears,' the next one! Be honest, you'd be the first to admit too that we didn't get off on the right foot, did we?" The fact is, in more recent times we seem to have established a peace and relations have definitely warmed since the events related in this book took place. In fact I have to say I can nowadays actually say we're friends.

Thank you.
JM. March 31st 2007.

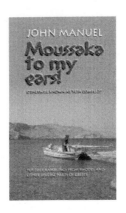

Volume two of John Manuel's witty Grecian Memoir,
"Moussaka to My Ears" takes up where *"Feta Compli!"*
leaves off.

It once again serves up a clutch of anecdotes from all kinds
of places, while also tracing the history of the author's first
three years on Rhodes. Many of its chapters are postscripted
with photographs of the subject matter. The action takes
place in such locations as Corfu, Leros (again), Samos, Symi,
Halkidiki, Athens (again), with the emphasis this time being
much more on events on Rhodes as John and Maria get to
know some local characters, customs and the frustrations of
Greek bureaucracy.

Moussaka to My Ears is available from:

www.lulu.com
www.amazon.co.uk
honorarygreek.blogspot.com

ISBN No. 978-1-4092-6732-4

"Tzatziki For You to Say" is Volume 3 of John Manuel's *"Ramblings from Rhodes."* Some of the comments readers have made about **"Tzatziki"** include:

"I have read many of the 'I moved to Greece and wrote this book' books and reckon yours are up with the best."

"Another fabulous book – I thoroughly enjoyed it from start to finish. The insight and observations are fascinating....
[Tzatziki] is another book which when you start to read it you cannot put it down."

Tzatziki For You to Say is available from:

www.lulu.com
www.amazon.co.uk
honorarygreek.blogspot.com

ISBN No. 978-1-4466-4709-7

Follow the author's regular diary from Rhodes at:
http://honorarygreek.blogspot.com

3598576R00183

Printed in Great Brita
by Amazon.co.uk, Ltc
Marston Gate.